Accession no.
36178059

D1627959

In An Age of Prose

THE SOCIETY OF BIBLICAL LITERATURE
MONOGRAPH SERIES

Adela Yarbro Collins, Editor
P. Kyle McCarter, Jr., Associate Editor

Number 36
IN AN AGE OF PROSE
A Literary Approach to Ezra-Nehemiah

by
Tamara Cohn Eskenazi

Tamara Cohn Eskenazi

IN AN AGE OF PROSE
A Literary Approach to Ezra-Nehemiah

LIS LIBRARY

Date	Fund
29|05|13	r-che

Order No

2402397

University of Chester

Scholars Press
Atlanta, Georgia

IN AN AGE OF PROSE

by
Tamara Cohn Eskenazi

© 1988
The Society of Biblical Literature

Library of Congress Cataloging in Publication Data

Eskenazi, Tamara C.
　　In an age of prose.

　　Bibliography: p.
　　1. Bible. O.T. Ezra--Criticism, interpretation, etc.
2. Bible. O.T. Nehemiah--Criticism, interpretation,
etc. I. Title.
BS1355.2.E85　　1988　　　222'.7066　　　88-30608
ISBN　1-55540-260-7
ISBN　1-55540-261-5 (pbk.)

Printed in the United States of America
on acid-free paper

TABLE OF CONTENTS

LIST OF ABBREVIATIONS

AB	Anchor Bible
BASOR	*Bulletin of the American Schools of Oriental Research*
b. B. Bat.	*Babylonian Talmud, Baba Batra*
b. B. Meṣ.	*Babylonian Talmud, Baba Meṣi'a*
BETL	Bibliotheca ephemeridum theologicarum lovaniensium
Bib	*Biblica*
BibS(F)	Biblische Studien (Freiburg)
BJRL	*Bulletin of the John Rylands University Library of Manchester*
BTB	*Biblical Theology Bulletin*
BWANT	Beiträge zur Wissenschaft vom Alten und Neuen Testament
BZAW	Beihefte zur ZAW
CBQ	*Catholic Biblical Quarterly*
Chronicles, ICC	*A Critical and Exegetical Commentary on the Books of Chronicles,* ICC
CTM	*Concordia Theological Monthly*
DH	The Deuteronomistic History
FOTL	Forms of the Old Testament Literature
FRLANT	Forschungen zur Religion und Literatur des Alten und Neuen Testaments
HAT	Handbuch zum Alten Testament
HSM	Harvard Semitic Monographs
HTR	*Harvard Theological Review*
HUCA	*Hebrew Union College Annual*
ICC	International Critical Commentary
IDBSup	*The Interpreter's Dictionary of the Bible, Supplementary Volume*
JAOS	*Journal of the American Oriental Society*
JBL	*Journal of Biblical Literature*
JPS	Jewish Publication Society
JSOT	*Journal for the Study of the Old Testament*
JSOTSup	*JSOT* Supplement Series
JSS	*Journal of Semitic Studies*
JTS	*Journal of Theological Studies*

KB	Köhler, L., and Baumgartner, W. *Lexicon in Veteris Testamenti Libros.* Leiden: Brill, 1967.
LXX	Septuagint
MSU	Mitteilungen des Septuaginta-Unternehmens
MT	Masoretic Text
NCB	New Century Bible
Nehemia	*Nehemia: Quellen, Überlieferung und Geschichte*
NICOT	New International Commentary on the Old Testament
Or	*Orientalia*
OTL	Old Testament Library
RSV	Revised Standard Version
SBL	Society of Biblical Literature
SBLDS	SBL Dissertation Series
SBLMS	SBL Monograph Series
TLZ	*Theologische Literaturzeitung*
VT	*Vetus Testamentum*
VTSup	Vetus Testamentum, Supplement
ZAW	*Zeitschrift für die alttestamentliche Wissenschaft*

ACKNOWLEDGMENTS

This book is dedicated with love and thanks to David Eskenazi, who, throughout the years, has been true עזרה and נחמה, true help and comfort. Gratitude is extended also to our children, Willa, Kay, Joanne, Michael, and David, who have contributed as much to my education as I may have to theirs and who, as the insightful and generous adults they have become, enrich my life in every way.

The book began as a dissertation and was shaped by the finest committee. My thanks to each one of its members. I thank, most of all, the dissertation adviser, Kent H. Richards, who guided me deftly through the tangled vines of appealing possibilities and kept me firmly rooted in a structure. His probing questions stimulated my own research; his ideas and insights enriched this book in every way. I owe more than I can ever say to his skill and imagination. Thanks go also to Frederick E. Greenspahn whose delight in philology made wrestling with Aramaic seem more like dancing, and who generously shared his multifaceted knowledge; to David L. Petersen whose own impressive accomplishments both inspired and spurred me to work, and whose astute and spirited criticism helped sharpen my vision; to J. William Whedbee who tirelessly responded to the manuscript in its various versions, and whose own work demonstrates that scholarship at the hands of a genuine poet is both profound and precise. The joint efforts of these scholars made the writing of the dissertation an unmitigated joy.

Thanks are extended also to Abbey Poze Kapelovitz whose editorial recommendations enhanced this manuscript, to Maurya P. Horgan and Paul J. Kobelski for their help and teachings, to Joanne D. Cohn for tracking down manuscripts in Chicago's libraries, and to Ira Sandperl who introduced me to Heller's *In the Age of Prose* and to many other books and ideas that shaped my understanding.

1
INTRODUCTION

> Freedom. It isn't once, to walk out
> under the Milky Way, feeling the rivers
> of light, the fields of dark—
> freedom is daily, prose-bound, routine
> remembering. Putting together, inch by inch
> the starry worlds. From all the lost collections.
> Adrienne Rich, "For Memory"[1]

Hegel distinguishes between poetry and prose not merely as styles of writing but rather as ways of being. The great epic eras of antiquity reflected, for Hegel, a fundamentally poetic state of the world, or, as Erich Heller puts it, "a world in which poetry is not merely written, but, as it were, lived."[2] Hegel considered his own epoch to be an age of prose, one from which the gods had absconded, where, lamentably, the prosaic mode prevailed.

Ezra-Nehemiah is a book written in and for an age of prose. It is a book where the words of Yahweh from the mouth of the prophet have come to a kind of closure (Ezra 1:1: לכלות דבר יהוה), where poetic utterances are suspect (Neh 6:12–13), where even prayers of the heart flow in prose (Ezra 9). It is a book where God does not speak directly and where life is lived in the dailiness of placing stone upon stone. It is also a book, however, that does not long bemoan the loss of poetry and the loss of grandeur. Instead, it sanctifies the prosaic, the concrete, and the common hallowing of a life that gathers together "inch by inch, all the starry worlds. From all the lost collections."

Ezra-Nehemiah affirms the prosaic in the very manner with which it depicts the return and restoration. The narrative deflects attention from the heroism of great leaders to the community. It represents the movement from the one to the many. It also shows a shift from the veneration of ecstatic and inspired spoken word to the dogged and persistent execution of the written. Authority is transferred from leaders to text. Ezra-Nehemiah construes history and life as graduated progress punctuated by regress; as cycles

---

[1] *A Wild Patience Has Taken Me This Far* (New York: W. W. Norton & Co., 1981) 22.
[2] *In the Age of Prose* (Cambridge: University Press, 1984) 3.

1

through time, not as dramatic movements toward a sweeping climax. Life is lived in the present with no glorification of either past or future. Indeed, Ezra-Nehemiah rejects a "theology of glory."

In what follows, I argue that three dominant themes combine in Ezra-Nehemiah to deemphasize the heroic and affirm the prosaic. First, Ezra-Nehemiah shifts the focus from leaders to participating community. Ezra-Nehemiah places the people as a whole, not merely famous individual leaders, at the center of its narrative as the significant actors in the book. Second, Ezra-Nehemiah expands the concept of the house of God from temple to city. Such expansion broadens the arena of special sanctity to include all who dwell in the holy city (Neh 12:30). Third, Ezra-Nehemiah emphasizes the primacy of the written text over the oral as a source of authority. In so doing, Ezra-Nehemiah wrests power from charismatic figures and provides a more publicly accessible, and publicly negotiable, source of authority.

These themes work together to depict the return and reconstruction as an era in which the important accomplishments are not the achievement of a few illustrious and inspired men trailed by an anonymous mass of followers. Instead, these accomplishments are the product of broad ranging communal involvement, over time, inch by inch. Leaders do emerge. Their importance and individuality are affirmed. But they are finally subsidiary to the main concern: the people of God who build the house of God in accordance with authoritative documents.

I will illustrate Ezra-Nehemiah's distinctive emphases by examining the literary markings and the book's internal dynamics and by delineating how the book conveys its three basic themes. A comparison with 1 Esdras, a book depicting the return and reconstruction as a heroic age, will highlight Ezra-Nehemiah's own emphases.

Ezra-Nehemiah and 1 Esdras are our primary sources for an era which remains as obscure as it is important. Both books have either been treated primarily as a means to an (historical) end or dismissed as too unhistorical to merit serious consideration. They have been analyzed as if they were darkened windows through which we might try to reconstruct what truly happened and then discredited whenever they failed to produce satisfactory "history."

The present study, however, is less concerned with what truly happened and more concerned with how Ezra-Nehemiah portrays the era. Historical questions are placed in the background and used occasionally to help assess the special orientation of the book. The focus remains on the intention of the text as it has been preserved in the Masoretic tradition.[3]

---

[3] The reader is referred to the following excellent summaries of the scholarly issues in Ezra-Nehemiah studies: P. R. Ackroyd, "The Historical Literature," *The Hebrew Bible and Its Modern Interpreters* (ed. D. A. Knight and G. M. Tucker; Philadelphia: Fortress; Chico, CA: Scholars

Method

Ezra-Nehemiah's distinctive perspective comes to the fore when one explores the book by means of a literary approach, i.e., utilizing primarily literary methods rather than historical tools. The term "literary approach" is currently attached to related, but by no means identical, methods of biblical analysis that share certain presuppositions, chief among them is a focus on what Meir Sternberg calls "discourse-oriented analysis."[4] The literary approach is associated in recent years most notably with Robert Alter, S. Bar-Efrat, Adele Berlin, J. P. Fokkelman, and David M. Gunn.[5] Sternberg is a special case. To some extent Sternberg appears to have spawned, or at least given fresh impetus to, much that goes by the name of literary approach. On the other hand, he disassociates himself from this label, preferring instead to speak of the poetics of biblical narrative. Sternberg's magisterial work, *The Poetics of Biblical Narrative: Ideological Literature and the Drama of Reading*, provides the theoretical underpinnings for the literary approach by offering a poetics that is systematically applied to the Bible and articulates both the universal, literary aspects of the Bible and its particular characteristics.[6]

Poetics, which takes its name from Aristotle, is associated in its modern garb most prominently (but not exclusively) with names such as Jonathan Culler, Tzvetan Todorov, and Boris Uspensky.[7] Poetics is:

Press, 1985) 297–324, esp. pp. 305–311; B. S. Childs, *Introduction to the Old Testament as Scripture* (Philadelphia: Fortress, 1979) 624–638; R. W. Klein "Ezra and Nehemiah in Recent Studies," *Magnalia Dei: The Mighty Acts of God* (ed. F. M. Cross, W. E. Lemke, and P. D. Miller; Garden City, NY: Doubleday, 1976) 361–376.

[4] Meir Sternberg, *The Poetics of Biblical Narrative: Ideological Literature and the Drama of Reading* (Bloomington: Indiana University Press, 1985) 15. Sternberg makes the following illuminating distinction between two types of inquiry: "Source-oriented inquiry addresses itself to the biblical world as it really was, usually to some specific dimension thereof.... Discourse-oriented analysis, on the other hand, sets out to understand not the realities behind the text but the text itself as a pattern of meaning and effect. What does this piece of language—metaphor, epigram, dialogue, tale, cycle, book—signify in context? What are the rules governing the transaction between storyteller or poet and reader? Are the operative rules, for instance, those of prose or verse, parable or chronicle, omniscience or realistic limitation, historical or fictional writing? What image of a world does the narrative project? Why does it unfold the action in this particular order and from this particular viewpoint? What is the part played by the omissions, redundancies, ambiguities, alternations between scene and summary or elevated and colloquial language? How does the work hang together? And, in general, in what relationship does part stand to whole and form to function?" (ibid., 15).

[5] Alter, *The Art of Biblical Narrative* (New York: Basic Books, 1981); Bar-Efrat, *The Art of Narration in the Bible* (Tel Aviv: Sifriat Hapoalim, 1984) [Hebrew]; Berlin, *Poetics and Interpretation of Biblical Narrative* (Sheffield: Almond, 1983); Fokkelman, *Narrative Art in Genesis* (Assen: Van Gorcum, 1975); Gunn, *The Fate of King Saul*, JSOTSup 14 (Sheffield: JSOT, 1980).

[6] Sternberg considers the term "literary approach" as "ambiguous" and much of the practice of the method as suffering "from the deficiencies of the underlying theoretical framework" (*The Poetics of Biblical Narrative*, 3). His *Poetics of Biblical Narrative* rectifies the situation.

[7] See Culler, *Structural Poetics* (Ithaca, NY: Cornell University Press, 1975); Todorov, *The*

the systematic study of literature as literature. It deals with the question
'What is literature?' and with all possible questions developed from it. . . .
How is a story made? What are the specific aspects of works of literature?
How are they constituted? How do literary texts embody 'non-literary'
phenomena? etc.[8]

Todorov takes his methodological stance from a remark by Valery that
"Literature is, and cannot be anything but, a kind of extension and applica-
tion of certain properties of language."[9] Berlin helps draw the implications of
such insight for poetics. She explains that poetics

aims to find the building blocks of literature and the rules by which they
are assembled. In order to explain poetics as a discipline, a linguistic model
is frequently offered: poetics is to literature as linguistics is to language.
That is, poetics describes the basic components of literature and the rules
governing their use.[10]

The following list, taken from Sternberg, specifies the features of narrative which occupy a central place in poetics and bear on the present study:

1. Temporal ordering, especially where the actual sequence diverges
    from the chronological.
2. Analogical design: parallelism, contrast, variation, recurrence,
    symmetry, chiasm.
3. Point of view, e.g., the teller's powers and manipulations, shifts in
    perspective from external to internal rendering or from narration
    to monologue and dialogue. . . .
4. Representational proportions: scene, summary, repetition.
5. Informational gapping and ambiguity.
6. Strategies of characterization and judgment.
7. Modes of coherence, in units ranging from a verse to a book.
8. The interplay of verbal and compositional pattern.[11]

These categories form the backbone of any discourse. Attention to their
interplay in a text allows us to perceive the intention of a text.

Poetics of Prose (Ithaca, NY: Cornell University Press, 1977); Uspensky, *A Poetics of Composition*
(Berkeley: University of California Press, 1973).

   [8] B. Hrushovski,"Poetics, criticism, science: remarks on the fields and responsibilities of the
study of literature," *Poetics and Theory of Literature*, I (1976) xv (cited in S. Rimmon-Kenan,
Narrative Fiction: Contemporary Poetics [London: Methuen, 1983] 2).

   [9] Todorov, *The Poetics of Prose*, 19.

   [10] *Poetics and Interpretation*, 15.

   [11] Sternberg, *The Poetics of Biblical Narrative*, 39.

Although all of these elements play a role in Ezra-Nehemiah (and most of them will be utilized in my analysis), this study concentrates on those that are most prominent in the book. It is generally recognized that the "seams" in Ezra-Nehemiah are, to put it mildly, abrupt. There are dramatic shifts between first and third person narrative, repetition of long lists, certain innovative genres (notably the so-called "memoirs") — all of which bespeak a compilation whose main guiding principles have eluded interpreters. This seeming confusion has all too often been attributed to the contingencies of the process of transmission which determined the ways these documents have been combined. The literary approach postulates, instead, that these distinguishing characteristics of Ezra-Nehemiah are literary devices that carry the meaning of the text. I intend to use these striking particularities as clues pointing to Ezra-Nehemiah's intention. Intention, as Sternberg defines it, "is a shorthand for the structure of meaning and effect supported by the conventions that the text appeals to or devises: for the sense that the language makes in terms of the communicative context as a whole."[12]

Three reasons make a literary study of Ezra-Nehemiah necessary and fruitful at this time. First, Ezra-Nehemiah is exceptionally literary in that it displays a remarkable reverence for the written word. This reverence manifests itself in the many ways the written text is authoritative and paradigmatic for the life of the community. It is from a written text that the messages of God are conveyed in Ezra-Nehemiah, as the public reading of the book of the Torah clearly illustrates (Nehemiah 8). It is also from the written text that other effective powers are exercised, as the interplay of authorizing correspondence (Ezra 4–5) and the written oath of the people of Israel (Neh 10:1) indicate. Ezra-Nehemiah thus demonstrates a self-consciousness about the power and significance of the written word. Such sensitivity to and concern with the literary mode — the coalescing of significance and meaning in the written text — are taken here as an invitation to an analysis of the book that attends to its literary dimensions.

The history of the interpretation of Ezra-Nehemiah provides a second reason why a fresh assessment of the book from a literary perspective is necessary. Most of the work on Ezra-Nehemiah thus far has tended to be what Robert Alter terms "excavative,"[13] or what Sternberg calls "source-oriented." The dearth of "discourse-oriented" studies is indicated in Childs' summary:

> ... the discovery of a larger number of difficult literary and historical problems associated with the writings of Ezra and Nehemiah has caused

---

[12] Ibid., 9.

[13] Speaking of biblical studies in general, Alter argues that "Virtually all this activity has been what we might call 'excavative'—either literally, with the archeologist's spade and reference to its findings, or with a variety of analytic tools intended to uncover the original meanings of biblical words, the life situations in which specific texts were used, the sundry sources from which longer texts were assembled" (*The Art of Biblical Narrative*, 13).

many scholars to regard the present canonical shape of these books as confused and distorted. They have usually concluded that a proper understanding of these writings entails an extensive reconstruction of the present form of this collection. . . .[14]

Childs' own canonical approach is a corrective to the general trend in Ezra-Nehemiah studies. The inevitable brevity of his discussion, however, necessitates further studies of Ezra-Nehemiah that address the text in its entirety, though not necessarily from a canonical perspective.

The emphasis on a source-oriented rather than a discourse-oriented approach to Ezra-Nehemiah has been primarily influenced by the designation of Ezra-Nehemiah as "historiography,"[15] and the concomitant presumption that historiography is somehow exempt from literary conventions. The new awareness of the role of literary techniques and imagination in historiography provides a third reason for a literary analysis of Ezra-Nehemiah. As the prominent historian Hayden White points out, history is not an independent reality "out there," nor is historiography the objective recording of such reality. On the contrary, putative objectivity—so often associated with historiography in contrast to literature—can be more easily granted to annals or chronicles (though, as White demonstrates, not even there). But history writing is distinct from those genres precisely by the fullness of its narrativity.[16] After all, events in real life do not present themselves in the coherent manner which history grants them, with a beginning and an end. The ordering of experience as history "arises out of a desire to have real events display the coherence, integrity, fullness, and closure of an image of life that is and can only be imaginary. . . ."[17] And it is this shaping of events and the fullness of contextual interpretation of details, i.e., narrativity, which separate historiography from annals or chronicles. Hence, historiography is a literary construct rather than a mirror of reality. The literary shaping of the material, therefore, requires literary sensitivities from the reader.

---

[14] Childs, *Introduction to the Old Testament*, 626–627.

[15] See, for example, S. Japhet, "Sheshbazzar and Zerubbabel—Against the Background of the Historical and Religious Tendencies of Ezra-Nehemiah," *ZAW* 94 (1982) 68.

[16] White writes: ". . . it is the modern historiographical community which has distinguished between annals, chronicle, and history forms of discourse on the basis of their attainment of narrative fullness or failure to attain it. And this same scholarly establishment has yet to account for the fact that just when, by its own account, historiography was transformed into a so-called objective discipline, it was the narrativity of the historical discourse that was celebrated as one of the signs of historiography's maturation as a science—a science of a special sort, but a science nonetheless. It is the historians themselves who have transformed narrativity from a manner of speaking into a paradigm of the form which reality itself displays to a 'realistic' consciousness. It is they who have made narrativity into a value, the presence of which in a discourse having to do with real events signals at once its objectivity, its seriousness, and its realism" ("The Value of Narrativity in the Representation of Reality," *On Narrative*, ed. W. J. T. Mitchell [Chicago: University of Chicago Press, 1981] 23).

[17] Ibid., 23.

The works of John Van Seters and Meir Sternberg, with their specifically biblical orientation, confirm the significance of narrativity in ancient historiography and the necessity of applying literary tools in order to interpret biblical historiography. Van Seters, who brings biblical scholarship into conversation with recent classical studies, shows how the nature of ancient historiography has been reassessed in classical studies. Van Seters's discussion of Herodotus, the so-called father of history and presumably a near contemporary of Ezra-Nehemiah, is especially pertinent. In his section on Greek historiography, Van Seters cogently argues two main points: First, that Greek historiography, rather than Mesopotamian historiography or Greek epic, offers the most important comparative material for the Hebrew Bible.[18] Second, that Greek historiography has come to be recognized as highly fictional, i.e., that Herodotus as "author" has a significant role in the creation or invention of his material, including the creation of his supposed sources.[19]

Ezra-Nehemiah, by Van Seters's own definition of the genre, unquestionably qualifies as history writing.[20] But Van Seters's observations teach us that the primary definition of this genre (primary in the literal sense, in terms of historical development, and in the etymological sense) already exemplifies fictive activities. Material in historiography is shaped for the sake of coherence and meaning by the historians and not simply by the given properties of reality. The paradigm of historiography thus ceases to be that of a work that reproduces events as they actually happened but becomes suffused with the spirited invention of the writer(s). For this reason, without necessarily obliterating the decisive difference between fiction and history, one must grant historiography a measure of freedom from the constraints of sources and facts and realize that it invests its account with its own interpretive stance. This is particularly clear in the case of Ezra-Nehemiah and 1 Esdras. The persons or circles responsible for these variant traditions did not slavishly reproduce the documents in their possession but composed their work in order to communicate their perception of reality. The fact that we have two such venerated books, both going back to antiquity, reflects the freedom that the early writers permitted themselves in handling sacred traditions.[21] The time has come to grasp Ezra-Nehemiah's particular rendering of events. This is the task of this study.

For Sternberg, historiographical concerns in the Bible always stand within threefold coordinates which exert pressure on biblical narrative: historiography, ideology, and aesthetics.

---

[18] *In Search of History* (New Haven: Yale University Press, 1983), 18–40 and 51–54.
[19] Ibid., 40–54.
[20] Ibid., 2–3. See also B. O. Long, *1 Kings with an Introduction to the Historical Literature* (FOTL IX; Grand Rapids: Eerdmans, 1984), esp. pp. 6–7 and 18–22 for descriptions of the genres of history and historical story.
[21] The inclusion of Ezra-Nehemiah in the MT and the LXX attests to the antiquity of and

> Functionally speaking, it [the Bible] is regulated by a set of three prin-
> ciples: ideological, historiographic, and aesthetic. How they *cooperate* is a
> tricky question, to which we shall soon come back. But that they do
> operate is beyond question. For at some points—or from some viewpoints
> —we find each laid bare, as it were, asserting its claims and exerting its
> peculiar influence on narrative selection and arrangement.[22]

None of the coordinates of the Bible's controlling trinity is at the blind mercy of the others.[23] All are together and individually part of the Bible's literary nature, and therefore lie within the arena of poetics. Hence poetics is not a competing system to historiography but a mode of assessing how historiography is expressed. Interpretation of historiography requires the tools that poetics has refined. The literary focus, therefore, does not totally eclipse historical questions. Such an act is neither desirable nor possible, especially for a book such as Ezra-Nehemiah. Instead, the literary approach sets literary conventions rather than historicity as the criteria for judgment. One looks at how the story is told in order to understand what is being conveyed.

Alter, Bar-Efrat, Berlin, and Sternberg have amply demonstrated the fruitfulness of the literary analysis of the Bible. Their expositions, as a rule, have been limited to segments of books, selected presumably for their congeniality. Such selectivity permits very detailed analysis of often unrelated texts. The scope of the present study is an entire book. This entails certain additional freedoms and constraints. Minute analysis of many sections is impossible. Much of the complexity of the text will inevitably remain unraveled. Certain questions will be ignored, especially when they have been treated adequately elsewhere.[24] Topics that have occupied the center of the discussion on Ezra-Nehemiah elsewhere remain here in the shadow. I have little to add, for example, to the question of the Levites or mixed marriages.

---

reverence for this book. The inclusion of 1 Esdras as well in the LXX and Josephus's use of 1 Esdras attest the same for that book.

[22] *The Poetics of Biblical Narrative*, 41.

[23] At a later point Sternberg describes their coordination in terms of "tense complementarity" (ibid., 44). Sternberg adds, "Some tension remains, of course, explaining the occasional surfacing of an interest that for a moment appears to have taken charge of the discourse and making for a precarious equilibrium throughout. On the whole, however, the rivals are manipulated into operating as a system, a three-in-one, a unity in variety" (ibid., 44).

[24] The reader is referred to the major commentaries on Ezra-Nehemiah for detailed analysis of the historical, literary, and textual issues that have occupied Ezra-Nehemiah studies. In addition to classical commentaries such as W. Rudolph's, *Esra und Nehemia* (HAT 20; Tübingen: Mohr-Siebeck, 1949), recent ones by D. J. A. Clines, *Ezra, Nehemiah, Esther* (NCB; Grand Rapids: Eerdmans, 1984), F. C. Fensham, *The Books of Ezra and Nehemiah* (NICOT; Grand Rapids: Eerdmans, 1982), and H. G. M. Williamson, *Ezra, Nehemiah* (Word Biblical Commentary 16; Waco, TX: Word Books, 1985), for example, helpfully address such matters with care. I build upon these works even when I do not explicitly cite them.

My goal is not an exhaustive study of Ezra-Nehemiah but an analysis that takes seriously the literary dimensions of the book and observes certain controlling dynamics in the book on that basis.[25] I focus, therefore, on the three themes that the literary analysis of the book identifies as most significant.

The structure of this study is as follows: Chapter Two sets the text before us by establishing its perimeters, especially vis-à-vis Chronicles. Chapter Three is the analysis of Ezra-Nehemiah's structure and themes. Chapter Four gives special attention to the characters in Ezra-Nehemiah. Chapter Five brings Ezra-Nehemiah into relation with 1 Esdras. Chapter Six draws the conclusions together.

---

[25] For technical definitions I use Rimmon-Kenan's *Narrative Fiction: Contemporary Poetics*. Its lucid, fair-minded, and concise articulation of the dominant schools of poetics makes it a genial and responsible source. It is particularly valuable for those terms, presuppositions, and theoretical underpinnings that remain implicit in the works of Alter, Berlin, and even Sternberg. Rimmon-Kenan's book is a distillation of several current methodologies and theories of poetics. It draws largely on areas of consensus in the works of Todorov, Propp, Hrushovsky, Culler, Greimas, Kermode, Gennette, Levi-Strauss, and Sternberg, while also specifying differences and affinities. She writes, "My presentation draws upon Anglo-American New Criticism, Russian Formalism, French Structuralism, the Tel-Aviv School of Poetics and the Phenomenology of Reading" (ibid., 5).

2
THE PERIMETERS OF EZRA-NEHEMIAH

The perimeters of Ezra-Nehemiah have been challenged in two different ways. On the one hand, the diversity within the book has called into question its unity, with the result that it is frequently treated and described as two distinct books.[1] On the other hand, Ezra-Nehemiah's similarities to Chronicles and the parallels with 1 Esdras have called into question the distinctiveness of Ezra-Nehemiah as a book, with the result that Ezra-Nehemiah is often construed as but a portion of a larger work attributed to the Chronicler.

I will examine Ezra-Nehemiah as it has been preserved in the MT.[2] The fact that the MT transmits Ezra-Nehemiah as a single, unified book decisively establishes the perimeters of the book for the present study.[3] Nevertheless, even though the unity of Ezra-Nehemiah is taken here as a presupposition and not as a position to be defended, a review of the scholarly debates on the book's perimeters is relevant because it sheds light on the central themes of the book. The following review examines first, the unity of Ezra-Nehemiah and second, the book's distinctiveness from Chronicles.

I. The Unity of Ezra-Nehemiah

The unity of Ezra-Nehemiah is attested in all the ancient manuscripts available and in the early rabbinic and patristic traditions. In the LXX Ezra-Nehemiah, as Εσδρας β, is one book.[4] The rabbis consider it one book, Ezra's

---

[1] Note, for example, Fensham, *Books of Ezra and Nehemiah*. Note also the separation of the two in English translations of the Bible.

[2] The basic edition used in this study is *Biblia Hebraica Stuttgartensia*, ed. K. Elliger and W. Rudolph (Stuttgart: Deutsche Bibelstiftung, 1967/1977). The choice of this edition in no way implies assumptions about its priority to or superiority over others; it serves merely to define and limit the scope of the study. English quotations follow the RSV unless stated otherwise.

[3] The most obvious indication of this unity are the Masoretic notations. They clearly sum up the verses of both Ezra 1–10 and Nehemiah 1–13 together. In addition, they locate the center of the book at Neh 3:32, which necessarily includes Ezra 1–10. In this manner the Masoretes announce that "Ezra" and "Nehemiah" are one book. They also show that Ezra-Nehemiah is separate from Chronicles which follows it.

[4] See, e.g., *Codex Alexandrinus* (Royal Ms. 1 D v–viii in reduced photographic facsimile. London: British Museum, 1930–1957).

book, completed by Nehemiah.[5] Ezra-Nehemiah forms a single book in the oldest extant Hebrew manuscripts, i.e., the Aleppo Codex (930 C.E.) and Leningrad Codex (1008 C.E.).[6] It also appears as a single book in the earliest church fathers (such as Melito of Sardis).[7] Origen (who acknowledged the unity of Ezra-Nehemiah, saying that they appear "in one") was the first to divide the book into two,[8] and this division was adopted for the Vulgate.[9]

In spite of the unanimity of the most ancient traditions, the separation of the book continues to dominate both scholarly and non-scholarly circles (as the tables of contents of most modern Bibles show). The pervasive doubts about the unity of Ezra-Nehemiah have been nourished by factors external to the book itself and by factors internal to the book.

The major external factor has been the separate treatments of the figures of Ezra and Nehemiah in all other extant ancient literature. Sirach (Sir 49:12b–13) and 2 Maccabees (2 Macc 1:18, 20–36) mention Nehemiah but not Ezra. 1 Esdras accounts only for the activities of Ezra and replicates in a continuous story material which is dispersed in Ezra-Nehemiah. Josephus alone mentions both men, but even he keeps their activities and careers separate. Nehemiah (*Ant.* XI. 159–183) appears only after the report about the death and burial of Ezra (*Ant.* XI. 120–58). This phenomenon has been the backbone of the assertion that Ezra-Nehemiah was not a unified book prior to the first century C.E.[10] Challenges to this assertion come from scholars, such as H. G. M. Williamson, who can account for the silence concerning one or the other figure on the basis of the overall tendencies of Josephus, 1 Esdras, Sirach, or 2 Maccabees.[11]

Factors internal to the book appear to play the more influential role in separating Ezra-Nehemiah into two. Ezra-Nehemiah is a book with diverse and clearly separable sources. The book contains the words of both Ezra and Nehemiah and thus announces multiple authors. In addition, the book includes documents within documents, preserving thereby additional "authors" such as King Artaxerxes, whose letter is purportedly reproduced (Ezra 7:12–26).

---

[5] *b. B. Bat.* 15a; cf. *b. B. Bat.* 14b and *b. Sanh.* 93b, which also indicate the unity of the book.

[6] See, e.g., *Aleppo Codex* (Hebrew University Project; ed. M. H. Goshen-Gottstein. Jerusalem: Magnes Press, 1976).

[7] See Eusebius *Historia ecclesiastica* 4.26.14.

[8] Ibid. 6.25.2.

[9] See Fensham, *Books of Ezra and Nehemiah*, 1, for a convenient summary of the manuscript evidence, and Williamson, *Ezra, Nehemiah*, xxi, for additional support for initial unity. See, also, E. Würthwein, *The Text of the Old Testament: An Introduction to the Biblia Hebraica* (Grand Rapids: Eerdmans, 1979), esp. pp. 12–41 and 49–57.

[10] See, for example, K.-F. Pohlmann, *Studien zum dritten Esra* (FRLANT 104; Göttingen: Vandenhoeck & Ruprecht, 1970), esp. pp. 74–126, and C. C. Torrey, *Ezra Studies* (Chicago: University of Chicago Press, 1910), esp. pp. 30–36.

[11] See, for example, H. G. M. Williamson, *Israel in the Books of Chronicles* (New York: Cambridge University Press, 1977) 21–29.

Modern scholars usually sort Ezra-Nehemiah into the following distinct sources:

1. Nehemiah memoirs (encompassing most of Neh 1:1–7:5, 13:4–31).[12]
2. Ezra memoirs (encompassing at least Ezra 7:27–9:15).[13]
3. Aramaic documents (Ezra 4:7–24a; 4:24b–6:18; 7:12–26).[14]
4. Lists and genealogies (Ezra 2//Nehemiah 7; Ezra 8:1–14; 10:18–43; Neh 3:1–32; 10:2–28; 11:3–36; 12:1–26).
5. Other Hebrew sources and material.

Scholarly debates revolve around determining the boundaries, authenticity, and chronology of these units.[15] The most widely held rationale for dividing the book is the presence of two memoirs and the repetition of the list of returnees. Shemaryahu Talmon provides an example of the logic behind such partition:

> If indeed Ezra and Nehemiah at one time were two separate works written by different authors, this could help in explaining the duplication of some events and literary units in both, such as the list of returning exiles (Ezra 2 = Neh. 7), and the intermingling of constituent components when the two entities were combined, e.g. the placing of Ezra material in Neh. 8–9.[16]

I consider Ezra-Nehemiah to be a single work. To interpret the text in the wholeness of its present canonical shape is not to ignore the fissures within the book. It is, however, to insist that the transmitted unity take precedence in the interpretation. From a literary perspective, the divisions and fissures cease to be occasions to sever limbs but become, instead, clues to the book's overall intention. The very tension among the parts in Ezra-Nehemiah, the diversity of sources, the jagged edges, the rough seams, the so-called memoirs which allow persons to "speak" in their own voice—all these convey something about Ezra-Nehemiah's own concept of unity. They tell us, for example, that "unity" for Ezra-Nehemiah does not annul tension and differences. The book does not advocate homogeneity. Lack of homogeneity within the book exemplifies a unity which strives to encompass diverse entities—persons, documents, ideologies—without obliterating

---

[12] For a discussion of the genre, see U. Kellermann, *Nehemia, Quellen Überlieferung und Geschichte* (BZAW 102; Berlin: Töpelmann, 1967) 4–56, with summary on pp. 55–56.

[13] See Kellermann, *Nehemia*, 56–69; A. S. Kapelrud, *The Question of Authorship in the Ezra-Narrative* (Oslo: I Kommisjon Hos Jacob Dybwaad, 1944).

[14] See L. V. Hensley, "The Official Persian Documents in the Book of Ezra" (Ph.D. Dissertation, University of Liverpool, 1977).

[15] For a good summary of the discussions, see Williamson, *Ezra, Nehemiah*, xxiii–xxxiii.

[16] "Ezra and Nehemiah (Books and Men)," *IDBSup* (Nashville: Abingdon, 1976) 318.

distinctions among them. Not the "melting-pot" model of unity, to borrow a modern expression, but tapestry or symphony more accurately express Ezra-Nehemiah's unity—in form and, as we shall see, in content.

II. Ezra-Nehemiah and Chronicles

More controversial than Ezra-Nehemiah's internal unity is the question of the book's external boundaries. Here the relationship between Ezra-Nehemiah and Chronicles is of paramount importance, even as it remains an unsettled issue. The oldest extant manuscripts show Chronicles and Ezra-Nehemiah as separate books. In Codex Vaticanus, Ezra-Nehemiah (as Εσδρας β) is separated from Chronicles by 1 Esdras. Codex Sinaiticus has a large lacuna between these books but appears to follow the same order as Vaticanus at this point. In Codex Alexandrinus, Ezra-Nehemiah is separated from Chronicles by most of the prophets and by several "historical books."[17] In the Vulgate, Ezra-Nehemiah precedes Chronicles. In the Aleppo Codex, Ezra-Nehemiah closes the collection and is separated from Chronicles by the Psalms, Job, Proverbs, Ruth, Ecclesiastes, Lamentations, Esther, and Daniel. There is no indication in the early lists of biblical books that early collections counted these books as one. The church fathers kept them distinct,[18] and so did the rabbis.[19]

In the nineteenth century, however, L. Zunz[20] suggested that many of the puzzling peculiarities of Ezra-Nehemiah and Chronicles could be resolved as soon as one recognized that Chronicles and Ezra-Nehemiah—in that order—constitute a single, continuous work, composed by a single author, i.e., the Chronicler. This single work, Zunz maintained, was later

[17] See *Codex Vaticanus 1209* (*Cod. B*; Milan: Vatican Library, 1904–1907); *Codex Alexandrinus; Aleppo Codex; Codex Sinaiticus* (Petropolitanus and Fredrico-Augustanus; photos by Helen & Kirsopp Lake; Oxford: Clarendon, 1922).

[18] See H. B. Swete, *An Introduction to the Old Testament in Greek,* rev. R. R. Ottley (New York: Ktav, 1968) 199–215 for lists of biblical books in antiquity.

[19] Some critics cite the rabbis as proof of the antiquity of the tradition about common authorship. E. L. Curtis thus writes: "The Books of Chronicles are usually assigned to the same author as that of Ezra and Nehemiah. . . . This is not only the general opinion of modern scholarship but also was that of the Talmud, which ascribes them to Ezra (*Baba bath* f 15 I)" (*A Critical and Exegetical Commentary on the Books of Chronicles* [ICC; New York: Charles Scribner's Sons, 1910] 3). A similar statement surprisingly comes from Talmon, who writes: "Early Jewish tradition considered Ezra and Nehemiah as one work written, together with (most of) Chronicles, by Ezra but completed by Nehemiah (T.B. B.B. 15a; cf. Sanh 93b)" ("Ezra and Nehemiah [Books and Men]," 317). Such citations, however, are erroneous. The rabbis do not claim such unity of author. Baba Batra 15A, to which Curtis and Talmon refer, states: ‫עזרא כתב ספרו ויחס של‬ ‫ . . . דברי הימים עד לו,‬" "Ezra wrote his book [the book that bears his name] and the *genealogies* of the Book of Chronicles up to his own time" (emphasis added). This implies a relationship between the genealogies of Chronicles and Ezra-Nehemiah, but it is a far cry from implying that Ezra wrote the book of Chronicles.

[20] "Dibre hajamim oder die Bücher der Chronik," *Die gottesdienstlichen Vorträge der Juden* (Berlin: Louis Lamm, 1919. Orig. publ. 1832) 21–32.

separated into two distinct books. Zunz's view was quickly adopted by most scholars and established itself as the norm for all subsequent interpretations of both Ezra-Nehemiah and Chronicles.[21]

Zunz's influential article remains the most definitive and concise presentation of the case for common authorship. His arguments claim and rely on the following four basic points:

A. Parallels between the beginning of Ezra and the conclusion of 2 Chronicles
B. Linguistic similarities between Ezra-Nehemiah and Chronicles
C. Theological and ideological similarities between Ezra-Nehemiah and Chronicles
D. The evidence of 1 Esdras

Linguistic studies by S. R. Driver[22] as well as Curtis and Madsen[23] have since supplemented those of Zunz, illustrating similarities between Ezra-Nehemiah and Chronicles. Yet none offers a systematic and comprehensive examination of these issues. Consequently, we do not possess for this theory of authorship the kind of carefully argued position that we have for the Deuteronomistic History or the Documentary Hypothesis. Zunz's hypothesis won favor rapidly and without the challenges that invariably elicit forceful argumentation in favor of a new position. So complete was its dominance that Martin Noth could write in 1943:

> Es ist jedoch sicher und allgemein anerkannt, dass wir in 1/2 Chr. + Esr./Neh. ein Werk vor uns haben. Es braucht also in diesem Falle nicht erst wie bei Dtr. der Nachweis der literarischen Zusammengehörigkeit geführt zu werden.[24]

---

[21] As Williamson states, "For the past 150 years, the view has reigned almost unchallenged that the books of Chronicles, Ezra and Nehemiah were originally all part of a single work. Although there had been some who earlier hinted at this idea, it was in 1832 that L. Zunz set out the evidence which, with later additions and refinements, convinced the overwhelming majority of scholars. Confirmation of this statement may be found by reference to virtually any modern commentary or introduction written from that time down to the present day" (*Israel in the Books of Chronicles*, 5).

[22] *An Introduction to the Literature of the Old Testament* (New York: Scribner's Sons, 1899) 516–554.

[23] See *Chronicles*, 27–36.

[24] *Überlieferungsgeschichtliche Studien* (Tübingen: Max Niemeyer, 1943) 110. It is not clear how or why this position won such an overwhelming acceptance. But by 1913 L. W. Batten could write: "It is indisputable that Ch. and Ezr.-Neh. come from the same hand. There is no book in the O.T. which has more marked peculiarities than Ch. These cover both literary features, favourite words and expressions, peculiar style, etc. (For a list of which see Curt. [Curtis] 7), and also historical features, for the Chr. had his own way of looking at history, and his theory colours his work so markedly that it is often quite valueless to the student of history. There is scarcely one of these peculiarities that is not found also in Ezr.-Ne." (*A Critical and Exegetical Commentary on The Books of Ezra and Nehemiah* [ICC; New York: Charles Scribner's Sons, 1913]

Even C. C. Torrey does not question this literary relation between Ezra-Nehemiah and Chronicles, arguing only that Chronicles-1 Esdras represents the original sequence of that unity.[25]

The general consensus that the Chronicler was the author of both Ezra-Nehemiah and Chronicles and that the books form a single, continuous work has come apart in recent decades. Scholars such as M. Z. Segal,[26] Sara Japhet, H. G. M. Williamson, Roddy L. Braun and James D. Newsome, Jr., to mention only a few,[27] have challenged the unity in two basic ways. On the one hand, these scholars have brought to the fore evidence which undermines the very foundations of the theory of common authorship, showing thereby that its bases cannot sustain the edifice that had been erected. On the other hand, some of them have marshalled an impressive array of differences, forcing a reconsideration of the very plausibility of a common author for both books. In addition, occasionally in response to this challenge, the concept of the Chronicler has changed. The initial theory has been rephrased and modified. One finds references to several authors, associated according to Frank M. Cross, for example, with different editions of Chronicles.[28] One finds also a redefinition of the Chronicler not as an author but as an "exegete."[29] Perhaps most influential is Kapelrud's and Ackroyd's broadening of the term "Chronicler" from an individual to a circle or a school.[30] Ralph W. Klein's summary illustrates some of the dominant positions among those who hold to a measure of unity between Chronicles and Ezra-Nehemiah:

> While Martin Noth and Ulrich Kellermann have ascribed the arrangement
> of the Ezra-Nehemiah materials to the Chronicler himself, and Wilhelm

---

2). The atmosphere of *fait accompli* is evident also in Pfeiffer: "The literary analysis of the Books of Ezra and Nehemiah has shown beyond the shadow of a doubt that their author is the Chronicler and that he utilized written sources" (R. H. Pfeiffer, *Introduction to the Old Testament* [New York: Harper & Row, 1941] 830). Pfeiffer himself does not present such a literary analysis, nor does he specify who does.

[25] *Ezra Studies*, 32–33.

[26] "The Books of Ezra and Nehemiah," *Tarbiz* 14 (1943) 81–103 [Hebrew]. Since Segal's work is in modern Hebrew, it informs the discussion more indirectly.

[27] Japhet, *The Ideology of the Book of Chronicles and Its Place in Biblical Thought* (Jerusalem: Mosad Bialik, 1977) [Hebrew]; "The Supposed Common Authorship of Chronicles and Ezra-Nehemiah Investigated Anew," *VT* 18 (1968) 330–371; Williamson, *Israel in the Books of Chronicles*, esp. pp. 1–70; Braun, "Chronicles, Ezra, and Nehemiah: Theology and Literary History," VTSup 30 (1979) 42–64; Newsome, "Toward a New Understanding of the Chronicler and His Purpose," *JBL* 94 (1975) 201–217.

[28] "A Reconstruction of the Judean Restoration," *JBL* 94 (1975) 4–18.

[29] See P. R. Ackroyd, "The Chronicler as Exegete," *JSOT* 2 (1977) 2–32; also T. Willi, *Die Chronik als Auslegung* (FRLANT 106; Göttingen: Vandenhoeck & Ruprecht, 1972).

[30] Kapelrud, *Question of Authorship in the Ezra-Narrative*, 95–97; Ackroyd, "History and Theology in the Writings of the Chronicler," *CTM* 38 (1967) 503.

Rudolph contends that the original order of the Chronicler can be reconstructed from the present disarray, G. Hölscher and Sigmund Mowinckel have ascribed the present arrangement (and amount) of materials to post-Chronistic redaction. This last hypothesis is supported by the arrangement of the materials in III Ezra (I and II Chronicles, Ezra 1–10, Nehemiah 8), an arrangment for which Karl-Friedrich Pohlmann has recently offered support as the original shape of the Chronicler. Pohlmann believes that III Ezra, which shows no trace of the Nehemiah tradition, is a fragment of a translation of an original recension although the interpolation of the story of the three pages in III Ezra caused some disarrangement.[31]

The following is a review and evaluation of the four basic arguments for common authorship, taken individually.

A. Parallels between the Beginning of Ezra-Nehemiah and the End of Second Chronicles

The close parallel between the beginning of Ezra-Nehemiah and the end of Chronicles has been taken as an indication of an original continuity between the two works. Indeed, for several scholars this constitutes the most decisive evidence for the unity of Ezra-Nehemiah and Chronicles.[32] Some scholars explain the repetition as deliberate markings, an overlap, intended to signal continuity, employed when Ezra-Nehemiah was separated from Chronicles and incorporated into the canon.[33] Batten, on the other hand, postulates a scribal error which lingered after the documents had already been separated. A copyist, working from an older version in which there was still continuity between Ezra-Nehemiah and Chronicles, forgot to stop at the proper place.[34]

The opponents of the theory of common authorship have attacked all of these suppositions. Segal points out that such "scribal markings" do not occur in the Hebrew Bible even though other books, such as Samuel and Kings, have been divided.[35] Others point out that there is no indication that Ezra-Nehemiah was canonized before Chronicles, thereby requiring separation. In fact, the evidence that we have for Chronicles' existence precedes the evidence for Ezra-Nehemiah's.[36] Furthermore, as Williamson points out, such arguments which speculate on the process of canonization are based on

---

[31] "Ezra and Nehemiah in Recent Studies," 368.

[32] E.g., Wilhelm Rudolph, *Esra und Nehemia* xxii. See Williamson, *Israel in the Books of Chronicles*, 7, for additional examples.

[33] This explanation assumes that Ezra-Nehemiah was canonized earlier than Chronicles. See Curtis and Madsen, *Chronicles*, 3.

[34] Batten, *Ezra and Nehemiah*, 1–2.

[35] Segal, "The Books of Ezra and Nehemiah," 84.

[36] As S. Jellicoe points out, ". . . an account of the history of David and Solomon by the Hellenistic-Jewish historian Eupolemos, itself based on the Greek version of Chronicles, affords additional testimony that the latter was in existence before the middle of the second century B.C." (*The Septuagint and Modern Study* [Oxford: Clarendon, 1968] 294).

a misunderstanding of the process and therefore remain implausible.[37]

In addition, the kind of monumental error by a scribe, which Batten envisions, and the perpetuation of such an error are difficult to accept. It is of course quite credible that scribal errors have crept into the received texts. But the very obviousness of this one makes it seem unlikely that it would have gone undetected and uncorrected.

All this suggests that the parallels between the end of Chronicles and the beginning of Ezra-Nehemiah do not indicate a common author. Consequently it seems more plausible to agree with Williamson that the parallels between the two books resulted from a deliberate borrowing of the beginning of Ezra (Ezra 1:1ff.) to form the conclusion of Chronicles.[38]

The purpose of appending Cyrus's decree to Chronicles would be to provide a hopeful conclusion to the book. Deuteronomy would serve as an analogy and a model. Like Chronicles, it retells much that has been stated earlier and, likewise, ends at the brink of the fulfillment, when all the promises lay before the hearers/readers.[39]

B. Linguistic Similarities between Ezra-Nehemiah and Chronicles

The linguistic argument for common authorship hinges on whether or not Ezra-Nehemiah and Chronicles display shared linguistic elements which differentiate them from other books. Zunz was the first to call attention to

---

[37] Williamson, responding to a recent reformulation of the canonical process as reason for separation, has this to say: "Such speculations, however, are highly questionable. Not only do they postulate a quite unparalleled process in the canonisation of this work for which, pace Cazelles [H. Cazelles, VT 29 (1979) 379–380], no compelling explanation has been offered, but they totally misrespresent the process of canonisation itself. . . . In addition to this, we have absolutely no tangible evidence for the canonisation of Chronicles later than Ezra-Nehemiah, while their separate acceptance in the LXX, which cannot be later than the middle of the second century BC (cf. IBC [i.e., Israel in the Books of Chronicles], pp. 14f., and Allen, I, pp. 11f.), provides strong evidence for both their separate treatment and canonisation from comparatively early times" (1 and 2 Chronicles [Grand Rapids: Eerdmans, 1982] 5).

[38] Ibid., 415. Williamson assumes that this addition was not made by the Chronicler himself, the Chronicler's work having ended with 2 Chr 36:21 (ibid., 419; also Israel in the Books of Chronicles, 7–10). However, Japhet supplies evidence which suggests that the Chronicler is responsible for the present form of Chronicles' conclusion. As Japhet points out, Chronicles tends to have theophoric names with a long ending for the theophoric element; Ezra-Nehemiah consistently uses short endings for such theophoric elements ("The Supposed Common Authorship," 338–441). Jeremiah's name in the opening of Ezra-Nehemiah is short, ירמיה; in 2 Chr 36:22 it is long, ירמיהו, as is typical of the Chronicler. This suggests that the Chronicler's hand is responsible for the inclusion of this portion of Cyrus's declaration in the book of Chronicles. There is, therefore, no reason to rule out the Chronicler's own drive to end the history on a positive, forward-looking moment.

[39] See also Willi, Die Chronik als Auslegung, 233ff. for the relation between Chronicles and Deuteronomy.

linguistic similarities between Ezra-Nehemiah and Chronicles. These similarities include syntax, vocabulary, and style. According to Zunz, they indicate that the Chronicler is the author of both Ezra-Nehemiah and Chronicles.[40] S. R. Driver subsequently compiled a more detailed list, as did Curtis, showing more fully the Chronicler's "linguistic peculiarities."[41] The lists by Driver and Curtis are usually invoked as authority whenever literary evidence for common authorship is discussed.[42]

But as Williamson correctly states, these lists cannot and should not be construed as evidence for unity of authorship. They were not intended as such and they are inadequate as such.[43] A quick glance shows some of the problems with these lists. Curtis, for example, lists 136 items which he labels as the Chronicler's "peculiarities of diction."[44] Even according to Curtis's own tabulations, only sixteen of these peculiarities are unique to Ezra-Nehemiah and Chronicles. Thirty-three are unique to Chronicles. All the rest occur elsewhere in the Bible, most frequently in the postexilic period. The ability of such distribution to affirm or prove common authorship is at best dubious, especially when most of the unique terms found only in Ezra-Nehemiah and Chronicles pertain to the kinds of ceremonies which only they describe in detail, i.e., temple celebrations. But then, as Williamson observes, these lists were not intended as proof but rather as illustrations. The unity of Ezra-Nehemiah with Chronicles had already become such a well established dogma when Driver and Curtis compiled their lists that the question of proof did not arise; indeed, it did not arise until recent decades.

The linguistic consensus about Ezra-Nehemiah and Chronicles remained unexamined until Segal and Japhet challenged it. Of the two, it is Japhet's work that is more thorough and has had the greater impact.[45] Japhet demonstrates that most of the linguistic features that have been used to link Ezra-Nehemiah and Chronicles were merely postexilic tendencies found elsewhere in late biblical writings. At the same time, Japhet presents a list

---

[40] "Dibre hajamim oder Bücher der Chronik," 22–23.

[41] *Introduction to the Literature of the Old Testament*, 539–554; Curtis and Madsen, *Chronicles*, 27–36.

[42] Note, for example, Batten, *Ezra and Nehemiah*, 2. It is probably to these lists that Pfeiffer refers when he states (as we noted above) that "literary analysis of the Books of Ezra and Nehemiah has shown beyond the shadow of a doubt that their author is the Chronicler and that he utilized written sources" (*Introduction to the Old Testament*, 830).

[43] Thus Williamson writes that Driver and Curtis "listed various lexical and syntactical features in order to illustrate the characteristics of the Chronicler's style. These lists were not drawn up primarily with a view to determining the precise extent of the Chronicler's work, for which purpose they are quite unsuitable, but rather started with the unity of Chronicles, Ezra and Nehemiah as a presupposition. However, these lists were generally considered by other scholars to have demonstrated the unity of Chronicles, Ezra and Nehemiah as well" (*1 and 2 Chronicles*, 6–7).

[44] *Chronicles*, 27ff.

[45] Note especially "Supposed Common Authorship."

of what she construes as thirty-six important differences between Ezra-Nehemiah and Chronicles in matters of vocabulary, style, and syntax. Japhet points out that even though both Chronicles and Ezra-Nehemiah share the background of late Biblical Hebrew, each one nevertheless displays distinctive traits, some of which exhibit true linguistic opposition. Therefore they could not have been written by the same author.[46] Williamson, who examines the older lists, concludes, like Japhet, that most of the examples either reflect postexilic phenomena or in fact show significant differences between the two books.[47]

Both Japhet's work and Williamson's have been criticized. A. H. J. Gunneweg, for example, dismisses Japhet's findings by saying that the very paucity of her examples of differences speaks for the probability of common authorship.[48] However, Gunneweg's silence over the paucity of genuine examples of unity in Curtis and Madsen's list (about sixteen actual examples of common features contrasted with thirty-six examples of differences by Japhet) weakens the force of his objection.[49]

At this point it is safe to acknowledge that linguistic studies of Ezra-Nehemiah and Chronicles have been fruitful. They have shown specific differences and specific similarities between the two books. The meanings and implications of these results, however, remain equivocal and ambiguous. Different scholars weigh them differently, most often on non-linguistic grounds. The evidence clearly does not speak for itself. It is therefore wise to conclude with Braun that when it comes to the question of the relation between Ezra-Nehemiah and Chronicles, "linguistic studies [are] at something of a standstill."[50] The linguistic evidence available neither proves nor disproves common authorship.

---

[46] Japhet's examples include: a) the absence of lengthened imperfect consecutive in Chronicles (this form is a normative linguistic principle found in all other texts of the period); b) different technical vocabulary for similar things. Chronicles, e.g., prefers הקדשׁ, "sanctify," whereas Ezra-Nehemiah prefers הטהר, "purify" (ibid., 341). See pp. 335–371 for other examples.

[47] Israel in the Books of Chronicles, 37–59. Speaking of Driver's and Curtis' lists, Williamson writes that "in fact most of the evidence published was not relevant; for instance, much was simply characteristic of post-exilic Hebrew as a whole, some of the items listed did not appear in both Chronicles and Ezra-Nehemiah, and so on. Nevertheless, it was suggested that in a number of cases the evidence of the lists could in fact point in the opposite direction since it betrayed significant differences of usage between the two bodies of writings" (1 and 2 Chronicles, 7).

[48] "Zur Interpretation der Bücher Esra-Nehemia," VTSup 32 (1980) 147.

[49] Williamson's findings have been indirectly challenged (though not refuted) by the results of R. Polzin's work on late Biblical Hebrew (Late Biblical Hebrew [HSM 12; Missoula, MT: Scholars Press, 1976] 159). Williamson takes up this challenge in his recent commentary on Chronicles (1 and 2 Chronicles, 8).

[50] "Chronicles, Ezra, and Nehemiah," 53.

C. Ideological Similarities between
Ezra-Nehemiah and Chronicles

Theology and ideology[51] pose the most complicated issues in the discussion of the relationship between Chronicles and Ezra-Nehemiah. Ever since Zunz, it has been widely assumed that the two works indeed share ideology. This assumption both grew from the conviction of the books' common authorship and contributed to this conviction. Zunz himself described this ideology in rather general terms. The rapid acceptance of his views led to the unfortunate outcome that common ideology had become so pervasively presupposed that clear and thorough demonstrations of it had been generally dispensed with.[52]

Consequently, since Zunz, most discussions of the Chronicler's ideology already include Ezra-Nehemiah. Often such descriptions are so vague that they apply equally to many other portions of the Hebrew Bible. Older works did not examine the question of ideology in these books in a comprehensive fashion. The situation persists; hence the need to focus anew on the debate. Those who presuppose common authorship for Chronicles and Ezra-Nehemiah take similarities between the books for granted or else illustrate them with a handful of examples. It is difficult to assess the weight of such examples because a systematically delineated framework is lacking.

We still lack a major work that argues comprehensively the case for common ideology, taking into account the full challenge by Williamson and Japhet. The articulation of this postion has not developed much beyond Zunz's seminal, albeit sketchy, ten-page article. The challengers to common authorship, on the other hand, have been more systematic, ferreting out specific claims about shared ideology only to refute them.

The following discussion reconstructs the positions on both sides in an effort to clarify the issues, review the arguments, and arrive at a conclusion. The discussion focuses on the six major ideological characteristics which have been singled out as evidence for, or as illustrations of, common authorship by those who uphold that view:

---

[51] Theological and ideological concerns appear to be equated in much of the literature on Ezra-Nehemiah and Chronicles. For example, the "Theology of the Chronicler," by Robert North (*JBL* 82 [1963] 369–391) refers to the same issues as Japhet's *Ideology of the Book of Chronicles*. I use the term "ideology" for both types of concerns, defining it in accordance with Rimmon-Kenan (who relies on Uspensky). Speaking of the ideological facet, she writes: "This facet, often referred to as 'the norms of the text', consists of 'a general system of viewing the world conceptually', in accordance with which the events and characters of the story are evaluated" (*Narrative Fiction: Contemporary Poetics*, 81).

[52] Much of the literature and most commentaries treat this as a settled question, the proof of which has been furnished elsewhere, without ever specifying where. See, for example, J. M. Myers, *Ezra, Nehemiah* (AB 14; Garden City, NY: Doubleday, 1965) xix.

1. Emphasis on David and his dynasty
2. Emphasis on the cult
3. Genealogies
4. Retribution
5. Concept of Israel
6. Anti-Samaritan polemic

Each of these characteristics has been challenged or reinterpreted in recent years by opponents of common authorship. In the following sections I briefly examine each feature, show how it has been used to determine the relationship between Ezra-Nehemiah and Chronicles, and evaluate the positions.

1. David

Scholars are almost unanimous in their opinion that the hallmark of the Chronicler is the emphasis on David. As Gerhard von Rad puts it,

> Mit David beginnt nach dem Urteil des Chronisten eine völlig neue Epoche der Geschichte des Gottesvolkes. Hier hören die nur verbindenden genealogien auf und der Chronist kommt zu seinem Hauptthema: David. David und die Lade, David und das Kultuspersonal, David und der Tempel, David und der Kult, David und Israel.[53]

David in Chronicles receives credit for all the important aspects of Israel's life, including the building of the temple (which 1 Kings attributes to Solomon). He is idealized, along with Solomon, appearing without the blemishes that mark his life in 2 Samuel. The fact that other formative events and persons, such as Moses, Exodus, and Sinai, are largely passed over accentuates his centrality. Chronicles keeps the stage uncluttered by these other events and characters, allowing David and his dynasty to be always in the limelight.

Both Japhet and Williamson point out that although David dominates Chronicles, he is relatively unimportant in Ezra-Nehemiah. David, therefore, constitutes a significant difference between Chronicles and Ezra-Nehemiah, indicating different authors.

The peripheral role of David and his dynasty in Ezra-Nehemiah is evident in that the recounting of Israel's history (Nehemiah 9) never mentions him (nor the temple). Solomon, far from being idealized, as he is in Chronicles, appears in Ezra-Nehemiah as a paradigm of sin (Neh 13:26). David is acknowledged primarily as the author of the Psalms (e.g., Ezra 3:10).

---

[53] *Das Geschichtsbild des chronistischen Werkes* (BWANT IV/3; Stuttgart: Kohlhammer, 1930) 134.

The most striking neglect of David's house and his dynasty in Ezra-Nehemiah appears in the treatment of Zerubbabel. Scholars concur that Zerubbabel is a descendant of David.[54] It is therefore astonishing that this Davidic lineage is never mentioned in Ezra-Nehemiah! Nothing in Ezra-Nehemiah links Zerubbabel with David; nothing hints that Zerubbabel continues the Davidic line and is a vestige of the fulfillment of the earlier promises which are so prominent in Chronicles. It is clear, then, as Japhet says, that in sharp contrast to Chronicles, "The House of David, as a vehicle of aspirations to national unity and as a symbol 'par excellence' of salvific hopes, has no place in this world view [of Ezra-Nehemiah] and therefore is conspicuously absent from the book."[55]

Nor is Zerubbabel, apart from his Davidic credentials, singled out as the most outstanding figure in the section of Ezra-Nehemiah where he appears. He is almost always paired with Jeshua the priest. The two seem to carry equal weight on most matters. We remain uncertain about Zerubbabel's specific role in Ezra-Nehemiah. Laying the temple's foundations is clearly attributed to Sheshbazzar (Ezra 5:16). Only indirectly, and in conjunction with others, is it also attributed to Zerubbabel (Ezra 3:8–10). Zerubbabel is never called "governor." Indeed, he has no title. It is Sheshbazzar who is identified as "prince" (Ezra 1:8) and "governor" (Ezra 5:14).

All of this points to a drastic difference between Chronicles and Ezra-Nehemiah on the importance of David and his dynasty. This difference is so pronounced that it constitutes, in my judgment, a decisive contrast between the two books and renders common authorship implausible.

2. Cult

According to Curtis and Madsen, "Both works [Chronicles and Ezra-Nehemiah] show a fondness for the description of celebrations of special religious occasions ... [and] attention paid to priests, the Levites, and especially to the musicians or singers and gate-keepers, which latter classes are not mentioned elsewhere in the OT."[56] These common features, together with the linguistic similarities and the presence of genealogies, lead Curtis and Madsen to assert: "Thus, whatever are the sources of these writings, *exactly the same* interest and motive of compilation or authorship appear in both, hence the conclusion that both are from the same person is irresistible."[57]

---

[54] As Japhet states, "Hardly anyone questions the fact that Zerubbabel the son of Shealtiel was of the House of David, a direct descendant of Jehoiachin king of Judah. This statement rests on three Biblical sources: Haggai, Zechariah and Chronicles" ("Sheshbazzar and Zerubbabel," 71).

[55] Ibid., 76.

[56] *Chronicles*, 4–5.

[57] Ibid., 4–5 (emphasis added).

Opponents of common authorship do not discount the presence of cultic affinities between Ezra-Nehemiah and Chronicles. They primarily disagree that the delineated similarities demonstrate that, as Curtis and Madsen claim, "exactly the same interest and motive of compilation or authorship appear in both."[58] While recognizing that Chronicles and Ezra-Nehemiah both show interest in the temple and the cult, they also maintain that the force of this commonality is curtailed by three factors.

First, extant literature shows much preoccupation with the cult and temple in other postexilic writings. Ezekiel, Haggai, and Zechariah attest to the lively interest in the cult at that time. Cult, festivals, and temple, in themselves, do not therefore constitute sufficient evidence. One must press for more specific similarities. But, as we shall see shortly, a closer examination yields *differences* between Ezra-Nehemiah and Chronicles in their use of cultic terminology.

Second, most scholars concur that the Chronicler depicts practices of his own day, which he then retrojects into the earlier periods. This means that cultic similarities between Ezra-Nehemiah and Chronicles stem not from shared ideology but, more probably, from the fact that, as near contemporaries, they depict a similar phenomenon: the postexilic cult itself with its own terminology at a particular stage. References to *Netinim*, gatekeepers, and singers, therefore, simply reflect the reality of the cult of that era, not the ideology of the author. Contemporary vocabulary also accounts for the shared terminology, which is mostly cultic.

Third, and perhaps most telling, the cultic details in Ezra-Nehemiah and Chronicles do not always agree, even though the terminology is similar. The Levites are important, but the books do not always assign them identical roles.[59] Nor do singers and gatekeepers receive the same classification in these books. Chronicles at times counts gatekeepers and singers with the Levites, while Ezra-Nehemiah counts them separately (cf. 2 Chr 5:12 and Ezra 7:24, for example).[60] We should observe that von Rad, who does assume

---

[58] Ibid., 5.

[59] Williamson writes, "Welch has argued strongly that a difference between the two works may be detected in their attitude to the status of the Levites. Whilst part of this might be due to their association with the Ark, which of course ceased at the time of the exile, it remains true nevertheless that they are more prominent in Chr. as a distinct group than in Ezr.-Neh., and that they are sometimes given teaching (2 Chr. 18:8, 35:3), judicial (2 Chr. 19:8, 11) and even prophetic (2 Chr. 20:14) functions not paralleled in Ezr.-Neh." (*Israel in the Books of Chronicles,* 69).

[60] Here Williamson's "dictum" seems especially apt. He writes in a slightly different context, but with a logic that is equally appropriate for cultic similarities: "This in itself, however, as has been stressed by Segal, does not prove that they are written by the same man. These interests are often those that would doubtless have been shared by most of the Jews living in Jerusalem at the time. For our present purposes, therefore, it has seemed likely that if differences of outlook between the books could be detected, these would be of greater significance" (ibid., 60).

common authorship, points out some of these differences,[61] consigning them to different sources. According to him, Ezra-Nehemiah retains the earlier usage found in its sources, whereas Chronicles occasionally reshapes this material. This explanation, however, undercuts support for common authorship because it suggests that the references to singers, *Netinim*, and gatekeepers are not the Chronicler's own terminology but belong to his sources. Therefore they cannot be used, as they usually are, as linguistic or ideological evidence for common authorship. Von Rad himself does not draw this conclusion, perhaps because doubts about common authorship had not yet been raised when he wrote.

In light of these three factors, it seems reasonable to conclude that the cultic similarities between Chronicles and Ezra-Nehemiah, though real, do not in themselves support common authorship. The cult therefore neither substantiates common authorship for Ezra-Nehemiah and Chronicles nor refutes it.

3. Genealogies

Scholars often summon genealogies and lists as weighty evidence for common authorship of Ezra-Nehemiah and Chronicles, and a trademark of the Chronicler.[62] Opponents of this view recognize the prominence of genealogies and lists in both books but deny that this fact in itself constitutes evidence for common authorship. M. Z. Segal[63] points out that such genres are not unique to Ezra-Nehemiah and Chronicles; they appear in Genesis, for example, and in other books as well. Moreover, it is argued that a close study of these genealogies underscores their differences, not similarities. One notes that the great number of these "genealogies" in Chronicles are called תלדות (1 Chr 1:29, for example)—a term not occurring in Ezra-Nehemiah at all, but frequent in Genesis. In addition, Chronicles' genealogies are typically segmented (e.g., 1 Chr 1:5–16), whereas Ezra-Nehemiah has no segmented genealogies, only linear ones.[64]

Johnson's work on biblical genealogies particularly emphasizes the differences between Ezra-Nehemiah and Chronicles.[65] He notes that genealogies are most frequent in writings that emanate from priestly

---

[61] *Das Geschichtsbild,* esp. pp. 82–85, 102.

[62] Curtis and Madsen are a good example. See *Chronicles,* 4.

[63] "The Books of Ezra and Nehemiah," 86–87.

[64] See R. R. Wilson, *Genealogy and History in the Biblical World* (New Haven: Yale University Press, 1977), esp. pp. 8–10, for the distinction between segmented and linear genealogies.

[65] M. D. Johnson, *The Purpose of Biblical Genealogies With Special Reference to the Setting of the Genealogies of Jesus* (Cambridge: University Press, 1969). Wilson's landmark study of biblical genealogies, *Genealogy and History in the Biblical World,* does not, unfortunately, discuss the genealogies of Ezra-Nehemiah and only lightly touches on those of Chronicles. But its sophisticated discrimination among forms and functions of genealogies indirectly adds more weight to the findings of Johnson's older study.

circles.[66] Johnson goes on to demonstrate that genealogies in Ezra-Nehemiah and Chronicles have distinctive features which set them apart. Chronicles' genealogies have military terminology; Ezra-Nehemiah's do not. Chronicles constantly accounts for the twelve tribes; Ezra-Nehemiah does not.

> The fact that in Ezra-Nehemiah there is no mention of any of the twelve tribes except Judah, Benjamin, and Levi is somewhat curious in the face of the obvious concern of the author of I, II Chronicles for 'all Israel'. This contrast is especially noteworthy in those passages in Chronicles that are derived from Ezra-Nehemiah: cf., for example, the mention of Ephraim and Manasseh in I, 9:3 lacking in Neh. 11:4.[67]

Furthermore, the function of genealogies differs in the two works. Johnson concurs with North[68] that Ezra-Nehemiah is concerned with legitimation, but points out that Chronicles has a different interest in mind.[69]

Johnson also argues that a close study of genealogies indicates the priority of the genealogies of Ezra-Nehemiah; these appear to have been used and modified by Chronicles.[70] He thus accounts for the genealogical similarities between Ezra-Nehemiah and Chronicles, while eliminating the need to posit a common author.[71]

The study of biblical genealogies is still in its infancy. Additional evidence awaits a close, comparative study of the genealogies of Ezra-Nehemiah in light of Wilson's insights. Enough has been said, however, to show why mere "fondness" for genealogies is insufficient ground for claiming common authorship.

4. Retribution

Chronicles is noted for its distinctive doctrine of retribution, recognized since Wellhausen, and conveniently labelled "direct" or "immediate" retribution. Two recurrent elements mark this doctrine and distinguish it from DH. First, in contrast to DH where retribution is not integrated throughout but placed largely in the framework of the narrative,[72] Chronicles weaves its concept of retribution quite thoroughly into all aspects of its account. In Chronicles all history unfolds in terms of retribution, down to the minute details. Second, Chronicles understands the fate of each generation to be determined directly by its *own* obedience or disobedience to God. Not for

---

[66] *Purpose of Biblical Genealogies*, 80.

[67] Ibid., 69 n. 3.

[68] "Theology of the Chronicler," esp. pp. 370–372.

[69] "This theme of 'legitimating' is probably an apt one in interpreting the few lists in Ezra-Nehemiah, but concerning 1 Chro. 1–9 it raises more [problems] . . . than it solves" (Johnson, *Purpose of Biblical Genealogies*, 76).

[70] Ibid., 37 ff.

[71] It has to be mentioned that Johnson himself does not address the question of common authorship, at least not directly.

[72] Noth, *Überlieferungsgeschichtliche Studien*, 172–173.

Chronicles is the possibility that one generation suffers for the sins of its predecessors. God's blessings in each generation inevitably follow that generation's reliance on God; God's wrath follows faithlessness with utmost regularity. This doctrine so fully permeates the book that, as Braun says, referring to immediate retribution, "It is difficult to find an addition which the Chronicler has made to his *Vorlage* which does not function in these terms."[73]

The fate of King Manasseh is a dramatic example of retribution in Chronicles. 2 Kgs 21:1–9 catalogues the unsurpassed sinfulness of Manasseh. Yet it is also clear that Manasseh was blessed with a very long reign. The longevity of this exceedingly wicked king poses a serious problem for the doctrine of retribution. Chronicles rectifies the situation by reporting that Mansasseh repented from his evil ways and turned to God (2 Chr 33:13). By incorporating the report about repentance, Chronicles is able to reconcile the transmitted tradition about Manasseh with its own distinctive doctrine of retribution.

The pattern of reward and punishment in Chronicles is regular but not simply mechanical. Repentance is always available and efficacious, and prophets appear to call for such repentance.[74] The role of the prophets in Chronicles is particularly significant and carefully stressed. Willi[75] shows how the narrative in Chronicles is intricately constructed to make the points that the Chronicler wants to highlight. The role of the prophets turns out to be central in Chronicles' distinctive exegesis and structure. Chronicles has more prophets than do its sources. These prophets play a crucial role as mediators between Israel and God. They are the cornerstone of Chronicles' carefully worked out retribution. The fate of kings and nation in Chronicles depends directly on how they respond to the prophetic message.

The nature of retribution and the role of the prophets in Chronicles are not disputed. What is subject to dispute is the nature of retribution in Ezra-Nehemiah. Opponents of the theory of common authorship point to the absence of Chronicles' retribution from Ezra-Nehemiah. Williamson, having summed up Chronicles' retribution, writes,

> It is noteworthy, therefore, that no trace of this doctrine is to be found in Ezr.-Neh. The piety of the leaders and/or the people is not reflected in sudden up-turns of fortune, but on the contrary may entail an increase of opposition (Ezr. 4, Neh. 4), neither is there any indication that confession of sin leads to restoration (Ezr. 9, Neh. 9). Rather, the problems of mixed marriages, tithing, the Sabbath profanation seem merely to recur regardless (Neh. 13). The characteristic vocabulary of 2 Chr. 7:14 does not

---

[73] "Chronicles, Ezra, and Nehemiah," 55.

[74] See, for example, W. Rudolph, "Problems of the Books of Chronicles," *VT* 4 (1954) 401–409, esp. pp. 405–406.

[75] *Die Chronik als Auslegung*, e.g., 217–222.

hold the programmatic significance that it clearly does in Chr. This contrast is hard to explain if these books are indeed all part of a single work.[76]

Braun, likewise, observes the different terminology and the lack of emphasis on retribution in Ezra-Nehemiah.[77]

Furthermore, the role of the prophets, so decisive in Chronicles, is almost nil in Ezra-Nehemiah, and very different. Haggai and Zechariah, the most prominent prophets in Ezra-Nehemiah, neither warn the people, nor deliver promises; instead, they exhort the people to build. Willi[78] (among others) considers the minimal role of the prophets and the differences in their function to be one of the chief differences between the two books.

One therefore has to conclude that retribution speaks more clearly against common authorship of Chronicles and Ezra-Nehemiah than for it. A direct or immediate retribution is unquestionably embedded in the basic structure of the book of Chronicles. There is no such retribution in Ezra-Nehemiah. Like most biblical books, Ezra-Nehemiah periodically addresses the question of reward and punishment. It does so, however, in a more nebulous fashion and in language and conceptual framework that differ from Chronicles.[79]

5. Israel and Israel's relation to others[80]

In von Rad's and Rudolph's opinion, Israel for the Chronicler comprises only Judah and Benjamin. Von Rad's succinct formulation, that for Chronicles, "Juda und Benjamin sind jetzt das wahre Israel,"[81] has become an oft repeated adage.[82]

Opponents of the theory of common authorship challenge the applicability of this concept of Israel to both Chronicles and Ezra-Nehemiah. They

---

[76] *Israel in the Books of Chronicles,* 67–68.

[77] Braun writes, ". . . the concept of retribution and the terms related to it in Chronicles are almost entirely lacking in Ezra-Nehemiah. Exceptions appear to be words common to many Old Testament traditions . . ." ("Chronicles, Ezra, and Nehemiah," 55).

[78] Willi also notes additional differences between Chronicles and Ezra-Nehemiah. Since he holds that Chronicles and Ezra-Nehemiah come from the same author, he attributes such differences to the different presuppositions and goals of each book (*Die Chronik als Auslegung,* 182). It is not clear how—or why—Willi holds both to a common author and yet to different presuppositions and goals. For a critique of Willi, see Ackroyd, "The Chronicler as Exegete," 30 n. 63.

[79] See Braun, "Chronicles, Ezra, and Nehemiah," 55.

[80] The concept of Israel and the Samaritan issue are often intertwined. They are deliberately separated here in an attempt to disentangle the web of confusion.

[81] *Das Geschichtsbild,* 10.

[82] See Rudolph, "It is quite true that this leading idea of the Chronicler—'the true Israel is only to be found in Judah and Jerusalem'—provides a point of attack on the claims of the Samaritans" ("Problems of the Books of Chronicles," 404).

show, instead, that Chronicles and Ezra-Nehemiah hold different notions of who constitutes the "true Israel." Japhet and Williamson, who are in the forefront of the discussion, agree that "Israel" is a key concept in Chronicles. However, says Japhet, one of the distinctive features of Chronicles, in contrast to its sources, is an *inclusive* definition of Israel: it retains the twelve-tribe framework for Israel even for those periods when, according to Kings, the northern tribes had ceased to exist. Chronicles acknowledges the division of the kingdom after Solomon but continues, as Japhet demonstrates, to emphasize the wholeness of the people throughout its history.

Japhet uses Abijah's speech (2 Chr 13:2–12) as an example to make her case.[83] She argues that this speech has two points. First, it says that God gave the kingdom to David forever. Rejection of David is rejection of God. Second, the speech insists that proper worship can take place only in Jerusalem. Consequently the North is sinful when it rejects David and Jerusalem. The North, nevertheless, continues to be an organic part of the people of God.[84] Those Northerners who repent and rejoin (and in Chronicles they do) are forgiven and embraced by the rest of Israel. There were always righteous individuals who left their home in the North to join Judah (2 Chr 11:16; 15:9; 30:11). Large scale rejoining takes place partially under Hezekiah (2 Chr 30:11), but even more prominently under Josiah (2 Chr 35:18). Indeed, Japhet maintains that the geographical references in Chronicles and the names of the tribes seem to indicate a gradual expansion of Judah from the time of Rehoboam onward, reaching a climax with Josiah, under whom the Judean kingdom seems to have regained its former Davidic glory.[85] Read by itself, Chronicles gives the impression of the reunification of the tribes and a return to the pattern which existed under David and Solomon (see 2 Chr 34:33, for example).[86]

Williamson, who focuses precisely on the concept of Israel, fully concurs with Japhet on this understanding of Israel in Chronicles. Braun also points out that Chronicles reflects a more positive attitude towards the North than earlier generations of scholars supposed:

> After the division of the kingdom the writer [of Chronicles] is constantly concerned to indicate acceptance of and participation in the Jerusalem cult by people from the north. Immediately after the division of the kingdom priests and Levites from the north take their stand with Rehoboam in Jerusalem, joined by representatives from all the tribes

---

[83] Von Rad had used this speech as proof for an increasingly narrowed definition of Israel (*Das Geschichtsbild*, 32–33). Japhet takes up von Rad's arguments and dismantles them point by point (*Ideology of the Book of Chronicles*, 264–277).

[84] *Ideology of the Book of Chronicles*, 272.

[85] See Williamson's criticism of Japhet's interpretation of geographical data. Williamson, however, wholeheartedly agrees with Japhet's assertion that Israel in Chronicles is an inclusive concept.

[86] *Ideology of the Book of Chronicles*, 255.

(2 Chron. xi 16). The participation of Yahwists from the north in the
covenants of Asa and Hezekiah is explicitly noted (2 Chron. xv 9–15,31).
Prophets of Yahweh, such as Elijah and Oded, continue to function here,
and the people of Samaria are said to have responded favorably to their
warning and released their Judean captives, who are twice described as
their kinsmen (2 Chron. xxviii 8,11). Monies collected to defray Josiah's
reformation are ascribed to Ephraim, Manasseh, and the remnant of Israel
(2 Chron. xxxiv 9).[87]

Ezra-Nehemiah is markedly different. Von Rad's statement that "Juda
und Benjamin sind jetzt das wahre Israel"[88] aptly describes Ezra-Nehemiah's
perception. It should be observed that von Rad himself notes this contradic-
tion between Chronicles and Ezra-Nehemiah, but his commitment to the
presupposition of unity of Chronicles and Ezra-Nehemiah seems to prevent
him from drawing certain conclusions. Instead, he tries to harmonize the
twelve-tribe portrait in Chronicles with the exclusive legitimacy of Judah in
Ezra-Nehemiah.[89] He explains the contrast by suggesting that the Chronicler
attempted to reconcile historically transmitted "facts" of his sources (i.e.,
twelve-tribe schema) with contemporary dogma (i.e., Judah and Benjamin as
true Israel). Von Rad's explanation fails, however, because it is precisely
where Chronicles embellishes its sources, and not in what is given in DH,
that the twelve-tribe schema is carefully developed. One is therefore inclined
to conclude that von Rad's interpretation at this point is his attempt to reconcile a present day dogma (i.e., common authorship) with recalcitrant texts.

All this suggests that the concept of Israel separates rather than unites
Chronicles and Ezra-Nehemiah: each book has a distinctive view that can
only be extended to the other through numerous contortions. These
differences strengthen the case against common authorship for Chronicles
and Ezra-Nehemiah.

6. Anti-Samaritan polemic

Noth and Rudolph in particular have argued that the Samaritan problem
preoccupied the Chronicler and shaped his whole work, i.e., both Chronicles
and Ezra-Nehemiah. They claim, therefore, that anti-Samaritan polemic
characterizes both books.[90]

---

[87] "Chronicles, Ezra, and Nehemiah," 57.

[88] *Das Geschichtsbild*, 10.

[89] Ibid., 25.

[90] Scholarly understanding of the nature and date of the Samaritan problem has altered since
Noth's and Rudolph's writings. It has become questionable whether we can speak of a Samaritan
schism in this early period. As Ackroyd cautions, "We must not read back what the later Jewish
and Samaritan communities said about one another into an earlier situation . . ." (*I & II
Chronicles, Ezra, Nehemiah* [Torch Bible Paperbacks; London: SCM, 1973] 228). It is nevertheless
possible to retain the terminology of Rudolph and Noth for the purpose of this analysis, as long
as one limits oneself to the depiction within the books and does not slide into historical claims.

The most explicit example of the so-called anti-Samaritan polemic in the books under consideration is Ezra 4. Here we encounter persons who are usually identified as Samaritans. They are people who, by their own admission, are of foreign origin and have been settled in the area at the time of Esarhaddon (Ezra 4:2) and Osnappar (Ezra 4:10). They represent, as most scholars agree, a phenomenon related to 2 Kings 17. Thus Rudolph, commenting on Ezra 4, writes: "Diese samarischen Kolonisten begrunden ihre bitte um Beteiligung um Tempelbau damit, dass sie seit ihrer Ansassigkeit im Lande ebensfalls Jahwe-Verehrer seien. Das ist ihnen nach der Analogie von 2 Reg 17.25–28 ohne weiteres zu glauben."[91]

Ezra-Nehemiah's position vis-à-vis such people is clear. It considers them to be foreigners and adversaries. Ezra-Nehemiah opposes mixing with foreigners. Consequently, the participation and membership of the Samaritans in the community of Israel is rejected. Their overtures and support are adamantly refused (Ezra 4:3) and they are depicted as adversaries (Ezra 4:1 and 4–5). It is this situation in Ezra-Nehemiah which is generally recognized as the heart of the Samaritan conflict and polemic. According to Noth, this Samaritan conflict is the central organizing principle of the Chronicler's work as a whole.[92]

Japhet and Wiliamson, however, dispute the presence of such anti-Samaritanism in Chronicles. They concur with Noth and Rudolph that Ezra-Nehemiah refers to Yahweh worshippers in Ezra-Nehemiah who, like those of 2 Kings 17, have been imported by Assyria. They allow the general label of Samaritans for these people and agree that Ezra-Nehemiah objects to this group. They disagree, however, that such Samaritans play a role in Chronicles or that the Chronicler is engaged in anti-Samaritan polemic.

As Japhet points out, Chronicles surprisingly ignores the exile of the northern tribes; it reports the exile of only the two and a half tribes dwelling east of Jordan (1 Chr 5:26). Nor does Chronicles recognize the presence of foreigners in the territory of Israel. This is especially surprising for the time of Hezekiah, since we know from other sources, including 2 Kings 17, that foreigners had been imported by Assyria into the region of the North during this period. But there is no hint of any of this in Chronicles. Chronicles does not include the material of 2 Kings 17. According to Chronicles, only

---

[91] *Esra und Nehemia*, 175. These Samaritan colonialists need not be the identical group of 2 Kings 17 but the product of a later, similar deportation, as they themselves admit (Ezra 4:2) and as Isa 7:8 implies. Modern scholarship since Noth and Rudolph views the conflict in Ezra 4, and the important reference to "people of the land" (which often has been equated with Samaritans) as largely an inner-Judean conflict. It is a conflict reflecting theological, economic and social tensions between those who had not been exiled and those who had. This is not the place to dwell on the nature of the historical reality of this conflict, which in parts is absorbed into the Samaritan conflict. The focus of the present examination is on the depiction of the problems and situation in the literature, apart from its historical verities.

[92] *Überlieferungsgeschichtliche Studien*, 175.

Israelites dwell in the North; and Hezekiah considers them pure enough to
participate in his Passover, if they are willing (2 Chr 30:6–9). Nothing in
Chronicles can be construed as anti-Samaritanism because there are, in fact,
no Samaritans in Chronicles!

Williamson reiterates this point. He grants that Ezra 4 plays the crucial
role of depicting and defining the Samaritan conflict and represents a
phenomenon related to 2 Kings 17, i.e., the exile of the North and the impor-
tation of foreigners who become Yahwists. His observations are telling:

> On the theory of unity of authorship, it is therefore extremely surprising
> to find that the Chronicler passes over these matters in complete silence.
> . . . not only does he fail to reproduce 2 Kg. 17 or the alternative traditions
> of resettlement that he is supposed to have included in Ezr. 4, but he even
> goes so far as to make clear that the North was still populated by genuine
> Israelites in the period after the Assyrian conquest (2 Chr. 30:5 . . .),
> without any suggestion of the presence of a new foreign population. In fact,
> the only record that he preserves of the Northern exile is in 1 Chr. 5:26,
> where the two and a half Transjordanian tribes are exiled by
> Tiglath-Pileser.[93]

Chronicles not only neutralizes the presence of foreigners in the North
but also displays a favorable attitude towards foreign participation in the life
of Israel, including mixed marriages:

> . . . the Chronicler nowhere condemns mixed marriages, but if anything
> rather condones them. We find that several of the ancestors of the tribes
> were involved in such marriages: Judah married Bathshua the Canaanitess
> (1 Chr. 2:3); David's sister Abigail bore a son by Jether the Ishmaelite
> (1 Chr. 2:17); Sheshan gave his daughter to his Egyptian slave (1 Chr. 2:34f)
> . . . and so on (1 Chr. 4:17, 8:8). Furthermore, David himself married foreign
> wives (1 Chr. 3:1), as did other influential figures mentioned in the Chroni-
> cler's narrative (cf. 2 Chr. 2:13, 8:11, 12:13, 24:26).[94]

At times Chronicles seems to go out of its way to point to the participa-
tion of foreigners in the life of Israel (2 Chr 2:13–18). As Japhet notes,
Chronicles also recognizes the children of mixed marriages as members of
Israel.

Both Chronicles' view of mixed marriages and its view of Israel are in
complete opposition to those of Ezra-Nehemiah.[95] Ezra-Nehemiah, in contrast to Chronicles, abhors mixed marriages, condemns them unequivocally,
and requires that foreign wives be expelled (Ezra 9–10).[96] Ezra-Nehemiah

---

[93] *Israel in the Books of Chronicles*, 67.

[94] Ibid., 61.

[95] *Ideology of the Book of Chronicles*, 295–299.

[96] It should be noted that Rudolph, who, like von Rad, accepts common authorship for
Chronicles and Ezra-Nehemiah, is troubled by the difference in attitude towards mixed mar-
riages between Ezra-Nehemiah and Chronicles (*Chronikbücher* [HAT 21; Tübingen: Mohr] xxi).
He raises the problem but then leaves it unanswered. The answer offers itself when one

exclusivism extends to politics, making it, as J. D. Newsome, Jr., says, "unyieldingly separatist in its attitudes."[97]

I conclude therefore that "Samaritans," in the sense of Yahwists accused of being of foreign origins, represent indeed a controversial issue in Ezra-Nehemiah. Anti-Samaritan polemic in the way Noth and Rudolph define it takes place in Ezra-Nehemiah. Chronicles, however, has no such polemic and no Samaritans. No foreigners dwell in the land; only Israelites. Some of these Israelites are sinners because they refuse to worship in the proper sanctuary; some of them are true to Yahweh. The latter are always welcome in the community; the former are welcome when they repent. Furthermore, even complete foreigners are welcome. Consequently, anti-Samaritan polemic cannot be attributed to the Chronicler, if the Chronicler is primarily the author of Chronicles. This characteristic applies only to Ezra-Nehemiah. Anti-Samaritan polemic is not common to these two books, and cannot therefore affirm common authorship; it is, in fact, an ideology which sharply separates Chronicles and Ezra-Nehemiah.

Conclusions

A review of the major ideological characteristics which have been attributed to the Chronicler shows that most of the alleged hallmarks of the Chronicler do not occur in both Ezra-Nehemiah and Chronicles. Only one of these, namely the cult, constitutes a possible common emphasis, although even here differences emerge. All other characteristics constitute, in fact, ideological contrasts between the books. Consequently, if by the Chronicler one means the person or group responsible first and foremost for Chronicles, then a different person or group must be deduced for Ezra-Nehemiah.

The Chronicler, as the "author" of Chronicles, places emphasis on David, the cult in Jerusalem, and direct retribution which entails a particular role for the prophets. "He" has an inclusive concept of Israel which embraces all twelve tribes and is open to others who choose to join the true worship in Jerusalem, under the authority of Davidic rulers. Another person or circle, with a different ideology, is responsible for Ezra-Nehemiah. This "author" is not interested in David. "His" concept of Israel is exclusive, limited to Judah, Benjamin, priests and Levites. "He" reflects the tension which is often called "anti-Samaritan polemic," opposes mingling with foreigners, and does not have Chronicles' interest in retribution, nor its emphasis on prophets. The rest of this "author's" distinctive ideology must await a thorough examination of Ezra-Nehemiah (such as Japhet, Mosis, Willi and others have done for

---

separates Chronicles and Ezra-Nehemiah and acknowledges that they are different books with markedly different ideologies.

[97] "Toward a New Understanding of the Chronicler and His Purpose," 207.

Chronicles) without the all too common casting of Ezra-Nehemiah in the image of the Chronicler.

D. The Evidence of 1 Esdras

Scholars frequently invoke 1 Esdras as evidence for the common authorship of Chronicles and Ezra-Nehemiah because in it Ezra 1:1ff. directly continues 2 Chronicles. Thus Zunz writes: "Als die griechische Uebersetzung des sogenannten apokryphischen oder dritten Buches Esra angefertigt wurde, waren unsere Bücher der Chronik nebst Esra und Nehemia sonder Zweifel noch ein einziges ungetheiltes Werk."[98]

Rudolf Kittel, for example, echoes this view:

> Der Umstand, dass Esdr. a, der grosse Teile des Ezrabuches in sein Buch herübernahm, daneben auch Stücke aus der Chronik entlehnte, darf mit Grund dahin gedeutet werden, dass dem Verfasser von Esdr. a beide Bücher schon als zusammengehörig (Nr. 13 z. Anf.)—ob im kanonischen Text oder in einer andern Bearbeitung, tut hier nichts zur Sache— vorlagen. So oder so können wir den Verfasser als Ch bezeichnen.[99]

Pohlmann[100] neatly divides existing theories on 1 Esdras's relation to Chronicles and Ezra-Nehemiah into two basic positions: the Compilation Hypothesis and the Fragment Hypothesis. The Compilation Hypothesis asserts that 1 Esdras is a late compilation out of the earlier material of Chronicles and Ezra-Nehemiah. The Fragment Hypothesis asserts that 1 Esdras is a fragment out of the original work of the Chronicler; the book thus preserves the orignial sequence. Ezra-Nehemiah, according to this position, is a later rearrangement to which Nehemiah traditions had been added.[101] Pohlmann himself advocates the Fragment Hypothesis. He is not directly interested in proving common authorship, but intends to show the priority of 1 Esdras over Ezra-Nehemiah, a priority which implies, for him, the correctness of the Fragment Hypothesis.

In Chapter Five I delve into the relationship among the three books— Ezra-Nehemiah, Chronicles, and 1 Esdras—and expound a theory concerning this relationship. The present section intends only to evaluate 1 Esdras as evidence for common authorship. One can therefore be very brief.

Although 1 Esdras has been frequently summoned as evidence for common authorship, it is inherently self-contradictory to use it as such

---

[98] "Dibre hajamim oder die Bücher der Chronik," 28. Zunz adds: "Der kanonische und der apokryphische Esra beweisen, dass schon in früher Zeit die letzten Theile der Dibre hajamim, da wo die prophetischen Berichte aufhören, als eigenes Buch, das sogar mannigfache Bearbeitungen erfuhr, abgeschrieben und in Umlaut gesetzt wurden" (ibid., 29).

[99] Geschichte des Volkes Israel, V. 3 (Stuttgart: Kohlhammer, 1929) 543.

[100] Studien zum dritten Esra.

[101] Ibid., 15–31.

evidence. The reasons are simple: If, on the one hand, 1 Esdras is indeed the original fragment of the larger work of the Chronicler, as the Fragment Hypothesis claims, then someone else is responsible for Ezra-Nehemiah. 1 Esdras thus becomes evidence against the common authorship of Chronicles and Ezra-Nehemiah. If, on the other hand, Ezra-Nehemiah is earlier, as the Compilation Hypothesis maintains, and 1 Esdras is a later compilation, then it is 1 Esdras—and not the Chronicler—who is responsible for what unity of Chronicles and Ezra-Nehemiah we find in 1 Esdras. This unity, therefore cannot be used to demonstrate a prior common authorship for Chronicles and Ezra-Nehemiah.

It is therefore ironic, even though understandable, that 1 Esdras has been used as evidence for common authorship, indiscriminately invoked by upholders of both Fragment and Compilation hypotheses when it cannot be used this way by either. This is understandable, however, because much confusion has prevailed in the discussion of these three books. Issues have been clouded particularly by the inconsistent and ambiguous use of terms such as "Chronicler," "author," "compiler."

Cross offers a unique approach to this situation by positing Chr_2 and Chr_3. The former comprises Chronicles-1 Esdras and advocates royal ideology; the latter comprises Chronicles-Ezra-Nehemiah and suppresses this ideology presumably because Zerubbabel's movement "was snuffed out and his end ignominious or pathetic."[102] This attractive reconciliation of the data, however, does not demonstrate a single hand for Chronicles and either 1 Esdras or Ezra-Nehemiah. It begins with the premise of the continuity of either (or rather, in Cross's case, both) with Chronicles. Cross does not bring new evidence to bear on such continuity, but attempts to account for the double tradition of 1 Esdras and Ezra-Nehemiah in the face of the antiquity of 1 Esdras. The thrust of Cross's differentiation between these two Chroniclers pertains to 1 Esdras and Ezra-Nehemiah (although he credits the genealogies of 1 Chronicles 1–9 to the hand responsible for Ezra-Nehemiah). He is able to explain their differences but does not bring new evidence to establish their relation to Chronicles. One could just as well argue for the antiquity of two books, Ezra-Nehemiah and 1 Esdras, circulating independently from Chronicles. It is this position that I propose in Chapter Five, where a more detailed analysis of 1 Esdras is undertaken in order to highlight the distinctiveness of both Ezra-Nehemiah and 1 Esdras. For our immediate purpose it suffices to reiterate that, despite scholarly practices to the contrary, 1 Esdras cannot be used as evidence for the common authorship of Chronicles and Ezra-Nehemiah.[103]

---

[102] "Reconstruction of the Judean Restoration," 14.

[103] Williamson also concludes: "I Esdras cannot be used to support the view that Chr. was originally continued by Ezr. 1–10 and Neh. 8. All we can say positively is that by the second century B.C., Chr. was being treated separately from Ezr.-Neh. (as Par. shows). There is nothing

E. Conclusions

This review of the critical opinions indicates that the accumulated force of the arguments against common authorship is more compelling and favors the conclusion that Ezra-Nehemiah and Chronicles are separate books. The oldest extant manuscripts, wherein Ezra-Nehemiah and Chronicles are separated, likewise buttress this conclusion. It is the case that, despite the confident tone of some scholars that "originally Chronicles and Ezra-Nehemiah, in this sequence, formed one work,"[104] there is no ancient manuscript evidence where Chronicles-Ezra-Nehemiah, in that sequence, form one work.

Modern research combines with ancient traditions in calling into question any analysis of Ezra-Nehemiah which relies on Chronicles for its interpretative keys. This opens the way for—nay mandates—a fresh analysis of both books. Several monographs have already done so for Chronicles. One discovers that, indeed, four out of the five recent major works devoted to Chronicles have severed the relationship between Chronicles and Ezra-Nehemiah and treat Chronicles as a separate work.[105] Reassessment has been slower and less steady in the case of Ezra-Nehemiah. Two recent commentaries on Ezra-Nehemiah, by Fensham and Clines, still posit a Chronicler for Ezra-Nehemiah.[106] Fortunately these fine commentaries avoid introjection of Chronicles' ideology into Ezra-Nehemiah and rely in their interpretation primarily on Ezra-Nehemiah itself.

The preceding survey has shown several of the distinctive characteristics of Ezra-Nehemiah. It has become clear that Ezra-Nehemiah is only marginally interested in David, has a vague concept of retribution in comparison with Chronicles, conceives of the prophets differently from Chronicles, confines "Israel" to the South, and forbids marriages with foreigners. These insights have been culled largely by way of contrasting Ezra-Nehemiah with Chronicles. By turning to Ezra-Nehemiah's distinctive structure and themes, one can locate the center of its own ideology and meanings, without depending on Chronicles for highlight. This is the task of the next chapter.

---

from the Greek versions to say whether they were originally joined or always separate, however" (*Israel in the Books of Chronicles*, 36).

[104] P. Katz, "The Old Testament Canon in Palestine and Alexandria," *The Canon and Masorah of the Hebrew Bible* (ed. S. Z. Leiman; New York: Ktav, 1974) 74.

[105] Japhet, *The Ideology of the Book of Chronicles*; P. Welten, *Geschichte und Geschichtsdarstellung in den Chronikbüchern* (WMANT 42; Neukirche-Vluyn: Neukirchener Verlag, 1973); Willi, *Die Chronik als Auslegung*; Williamson, *Israel in the Books of Chronicles*. Only R. Mosis, *Untersuchungen zur Theologie des chronistischen Geschichtswerkes* (Freiburger Theologische Studien 92; Freiburg: Herder, 1973) includes Ezra-Nehemiah in its treatment of Chronicles.

[106] Clines, *Ezra, Nehemiah, Esther*, esp. pp. 25–31; Fensham, *Books of Ezra and Nehemiah*, 3–4.

3
STRUCTURE AND THEMES
OF EZRA-NEHEMIAH

Introduction

Ezra-Nehemiah combines sources, characters, ideas, and events in an intricate—often perplexing—fashion. Many of the book's basic points are relatively simple, common to other postexilic writings as well. They include the restoration of the cult, the rebuilding of the temple and the city, the emphasis on the Torah, the importance of the Levites, and opposition to mixed marriages. What is unique to Ezra-Nehemiah is not so much the substance of what the book addresses but rather the manner in which Ezra-Nehemiah presents these notions. The book appears, at first glance, excessively complex, full of disjunctions, shifts and turns whose purpose is not self-evident.

Scholars draw diverse conclusions from Ezra-Nehemiah's complexity. Some attribute the seeming confusion to unskilled writers, clumsy conflation of sources, accidents of transmission, or ignorance. Others, like Kellermann,[1] perceive Ezra-Nehemiah as the product of complex battles over interpretation which led to the accretion of conflicting materials. Those who seek patterns identify diverse structuring devices. Childs holds that chronology in Ezra-Nehemiah constitutes a sure guide through the book, in spite of certain ambiguities.[2] Japhet divides the book according to particular historical periods.[3]

The complexity of Ezra-Nehemiah gains coherence when one looks at the book's distinctive structure and discerns its major themes. The major repetition of the list of returnees (Ezra 2 and Nehemiah 7) is the clue to the structure. The opening verses of the book, i.e., the edict of Cyrus and the response to it (Ezra 1:1–6), encapsulate the major themes. Ezra 6:14 is a key verse summarizing the book by stating that the house of God was finished in accordance with the decree of God and the decree of three Persian kings. All of these points will be explicated below.

---

[1] *Nehemia*, 89–111.
[2] *Introduction to the Old Testament*, 631–632.
[3] "Sheshbazzar and Zerubbabel," 94.

Like all narratives, Ezra-Nehemiah is a story.[4] "Story" can be defined as "the narrated events and participants in abstraction from text."[5] Discerning events within Ezra-Nehemiah is relatively easy.[6] Grouping them within an overall structure, however, is complicated and subject to different interpretations.

The most useful structural schematization of story for the purpose of describing Ezra-Nehemiah is, in my judgment, the one by the structuralist Claude Bremond, who charts the three formal features of story as follows:

Potentiality (objective defined)
Process of actualization (steps taken)
Success (objective reached)[7]

Bremond's categories allow us to recognize the following structure of Ezra-Nehemiah:

I. Potentiality (objectives defined): decree to the community to build the house of God (Ezra 1:1–4)
II. Process of actualization: the community builds the house of God according to decree (Ezra 1:5–Neh 7:72)
 A. Introduction: proleptic summary (Ezra 1:5–6)
 B. First movement (Ezra 1:7–6:22)
 C. Second movement (Ezra 7:1–10:44)
 D. Third movement (Neh 1:1–7:5)
 E. Recapitulation: the list of returnees (Neh 7:6–7:72)
III. Success (objective reached): the community celebrates the completion of the house of God according to Torah (Neh 8:1–13:31)

---

[4] "Story" in this sense is not a genre definition but a description of one of the three constitutive components of narrative (see Rimmon-Kenan, *Narrative Fiction: Contemporary Poetics*, 3). This use of "story" is to be differentiated from that of Long, for example, for whom it designates a specific genre (see *1 Kings*, esp. pp. 30–31 and 261).

[5] Rimmon-Kenan, *Narrative Fiction: Contemporary Poetics*, 6.

[6] Literary critics debate about the basic components of "events." Rimmon-Kenan defines "event" as "a change from one state of affairs to another" (15). Some literary critics insist on a particular set of relations between the states of affair, such as reversal, opposition, causality, and temporal sequence. G. Prince, cited by Rimmon-Kenan, offers a definition of a minimal story: "A minimal story consists of three conjoined events. The first and the third events are stative, the second is active. Furthermore, the third event is the inverse of the first. Finally, the three events are conjoined by conjunctive features in such a way that (a) the first event precedes the second in time and the second precedes the third, and (b) the second causes the third" (*A Grammar of Stories* [The Hague: Mouton, 1973] 31) [cited by Rimmon-Kenan, *Narrative Fiction: Contemporary Poetics*, 18]. Rimmon-Kenan, however, pares this down to temporality and changes as the basic necessary components (ibid., 18).

[7] "La logique de possibles narratifs," *Communications* 8 (1966) 75. English translation modified. Cited by Rimmon-Kenan, *Narrative Fiction: Contemporary Poetics*, 22.

A. Consolidation according to Torah (Neh 8:1–10:40)
B. Recapitulation: lists of participants (Neh 11:1–12:26)
C. Dedication of the house of God (Neh 12:27–13:3)
D. Coda (Neh 13:4–31)

The first part (I) announces "potentiality" and "objective defined." It is an exhortation and a challenge in the form of a document to the people of God to build the house of God in Jerusalem. It introduces the central character, i.e., the people as a whole, and the central event, i.e., building the house of God.

The second part (II) depicts the "process of actualization" i.e., the building and forming of house and people. The repeated list of returnees, Ezra 2 and Neh 7:6–72, *literally* frames this section. This major repetition re-presents the major character, provides continuity for the section as a whole, and unifies the events in between.[8] The material within this framing device divides into three different stories, each with its own specific "potentiality" (or "objective defined"), "process of actualization," and "success" ("objective reached"). These individual stories are linked to the overall structure by "embedding,"[9] with each one contributing a specific detail to the "process of actualization." I label these three stories "movements" because they present three actual, spatially determined movements from diaspora to Jerusalem. They also are distinct movements in the sense of pertaining to different streams of populations. Each one of these movements actualizes a specific aspect of building the house of God by a group of people; it is thus embedded as a detail of the overall "process of actualization." The three movements are linked to each other by means of "enchainment,"[10] reflected in the chronological arrangement and in the word repetitions which echo an earlier movement in the new.[11] Each movement begins with a setting in the form of preparations "over there" in diaspora, and an introduction of the main characters. Each movement has its task and tension which are satisfactorily resolved by the end of that story.[12] The first movement builds the altar (under

---

[8] A stable character or set of characters is important for differentiating between a genuine event and a series of unrelated episodes. See Rimmon-Kenan, *Narrative Fiction: Contemporary Poetics*, 19.

[9] Rimmon-Kenan, following Bremond, lists three ways in which units combine: "enchainment," "embedding" and "joining." "Embedding" is defined as follows: "Embedding (Bremond's term is 'enclave'): one sequence is inserted into another as a specification or detailing of one of its functions" (*Narrative Fiction: Contemporary Poetics*, 23).

[10] Rimmon-Kenan, defines "enchainment" as "back to back" succession wherein the outcome of one sequence becomes the "potential" or beginning stage of the next (ibid., 23).

[11] Note the repetition of דרש, "to seek," linking Ezra 6:21 and 7:10, and the repetition of פליטה, "remnant," linking Ezra 9:8 and Neh 1:2.

[12] Biblical scholars with literary bent delineate additional characteristics of biblical narrative. Discussing the nature of "Historical Story," Long writes, "Typically, the writer shapes at least a rudimentary plot, i.e., narrative movement from a tension or problem to its resolution" (*1 Kings,*

Cyrus) and the temple (under Darius). The second builds up the community itself (under Artaxerxes), and the third finishes the house of God by restoring the wall (under Artaxerxes). Ezra 6:14 binds the movements thematically. It sums up the central event of the book, stating that the returnees built the house of God according to divine decree and the decree of the three Persian kings.

The recapitulation of the list of returnees combines all of these people and their activities. It reiterates structurally what Ezra 6:14 spells out, namely, that the completion of the house of God spanned the reigns of these three Persian kings. The list also reiterates the fact that the central character in the book is all of these people together. Although a distinct cast of characters dominates each movement, this resumptive repetition combines them all and thereby forms a single cast of characters for the section as a whole (Ezra 2–Nehemiah 7).

The third part (III) depicts "success." The objective has been reached and the community rejoices. The people as a whole, i.e., the central characters, celebrate the success of the completed task, put on the finishing touches, and dedicate the house of God.

The edict of Cyrus (Ezra 1:1–4) introduces and, to an important extent, encapsulates the basic themes of the book by focusing on the people of God, building the house of God, and fulfilling the written edict of God and Cyrus. These three issues — people (עַם), house of God, and written documents — are fundamental to the structure and the message of Ezra-Nehemiah. They correspond to the three major themes in Ezra-Nehemiah: first, the centrality of the community as a whole with a concomitant shift away from the grand heroic exploits of so-called "great men"; second, the expansion of the house of God to encompass not merely the temple, but the city as a whole; third, the centrality of the written texts as a source of authority. These themes combine to articulate a particular ideology which shuns heroes and affirms a life bound by communal effort that gathers together, "inch by inch, the starry worlds," as Adrienne Rich's poem puts it.

The first major theme can be discerned initially from the profusion of lists in Ezra-Nehemiah. The book underscores the importance of the community by its numerous lists of persons. The lists are important structurally and thematically. As documents (such as Neh 7:5–72) they emphasize the written (see the third theme below). But above all, in terms of content, the

---

6). Note also the following definition of "story" in the glossary of Long's book: "A narrative of some literary sophistication that creates interest by arousing tension and resolving it during the course of narration. Its structure is controlled by imaginative plot. The narrator moves from exposition (background and setting for the action) to a problem, sometimes complications in relationships (tension), to a climactic turn of events from which resolution flows. Finally, narrative tension drains away into a concluding sense of rest" (ibid., 261). See also Bar-Efrat (*The Art of Narration in the Bible*, 114) for specific applications to biblical narrative.

lists indelibly impress upon the reader that the real subject of the book is the people—named and unnamed, famous or forgotten—whose presence is memorialized with almost tiresome specificity. These people as a whole ultimately carry out God's charge. The depiction of individual leaders further highlights the book's emphasis on the participating community: outstanding individuals emerge in a manner that finally subsumes them, explicitly or implicitly, to the community as a whole. As a result, success belongs to the people and cannot be reduced to the deeds of a few illustrious men. The people themselves, according to Ezra-Nehemiah, actualize the return and restoration.

The second theme is illustrated by the fact that the house of God is not completed once the היכל or temple itself is finished in Ezra 6:15. The task of building the house of God propels the people's return and restoration. Building activities continue, however, even after the temple has been completed, and must continue until the sanctity of such a house embraces the city as a whole (cf. "holy city," Neh 11:1).

Ezra 6:14 is a retrospective and proleptic summary, encapsulating one of the book's central points: the building was finished "by the command [טעם] of the God of Israel and by the decree [טעם] of Cyrus and Darius and Artaxerxes king of Persia" (Ezra 6:14b). Thus the book in its entirety describes the success of accomplishing what has been set forth in the decree of the God of Israel and the decree of Cyrus, Darius, and Artaxerxes, "king of Persia." The notorious cliché, "I am merely following orders," is carried to its maximum force with the implicit claim that all that transpires in Ezra-Nehemiah is really the following of *one* order. The decree of the God of Israel is unified with the decree of the three named kings. The singular noun "king of Persia" (Ezra 6:14) is appended to all these kings as if they were one. Ezra-Nehemiah implies that all of these speak in a single voice or, rather, issue variations of the same decree. Consequently, Nehemiah and his cohorts, for example, do not initiate new building, but finish, at the time of Artaxerxes, what had begun with Ezra 1:1.

The third theme is reflected in the distinctive role of written documents in Ezra-Nehemiah. Like other biblical books, Ezra-Nehemiah intertwines structure and themes in order to convey its intention. However, in contrast to other biblical books, which utilize documents but acknowledge this only in passing (e.g., Chronicles), Ezra-Nehemiah vividly displays its reliance on reproduced sources. Instead of dismissing this characteristic as a clumsy splicing job, we must recognize it as one of the book's central themes: Ezra-Nehemiah is a book of documents. These documents function as an important structural device. They demonstrate the power or propriety of documents as causative principles and significant forces in human events. The ultimate power behind the documents (Cyrus's edict and the law which is in Ezra's hand) is God. But God's messages, in Ezra-Nehemiah, are transcribed by divinely appointed human subjects (e.g., Cyrus, Moses) into writings which become the definitive forces in the unfolding reality. In *The Histories* of Herodotus the pattern is one in which prophecy/dream propel events and come into fulfillment.[13] In the prophets the prophetic word is actualized. In Ezra-Nehemiah the *written* text comes to be fulfilled.

In sum, Ezra-Nehemiah makes the point that all that transpires from Ezra 1:1 to Neh 13:31 is unified by the command of Israel's God coupled with the command of the three kings. The initial command, stated in Cyrus's decree and reiterated (Ezra 6:2–4), is the basis for all that follows. As the book now stands, the decree is only partly fulfilled in Ezra 6:14–22. The full execution of the task entails three distinct movements, each with its own specific role within the overall project, and with its own distinctive group of participants. The first movement, Ezra 1–6, depicts the fulfillment of the edict up through Darius's time. Two other movements in Artaxerxes' time bring it to completion. Ezra 6:14 is thus a linchpin, informing us of what is yet to come: the completion of the house of God in Artaxerxes' time.

Let us trace the movements of Ezra-Nehemiah as they proceed from documents to their actualization, from the decree of Cyrus to its final fulfillment in the completion of the house of God in Nehemiah 13, from diaspora to Jerusalem, from exile to restoration.

I. Potentiality (Objective Defined):
Decree to the Community to Build
the House of God (Ezra 1:1–4)

The opening notes of Ezra-Nehemiah sound the themes that will be played in a variety of rhythms and keys throughout the book. The first few verses introduce first, the centrality of the community, with the people as a whole, not simply the leaders, as the real subject of the book; second, the building of the house of God; third, the centrality of the written text (and the fulfillment of the written word).

Structure

   A. Setting and divine objective (Ezra 1:1)
   B. Decree proper (oral and written) (1:2–4)
      1. Cyrus's commission from God (1:2)
      2. Exhortation to go up and build (1:3)
      3. Exhortation to neighborly support (1:4)

Cyrus's decree urges each member of God's people to go up and to build the house of God in Jerusalem (note the jussives "let him go up" and "let him build" in Ezra 1:3). The decree defines the objective of the book or, in

---

[13] Van Seters, *In Search of History*, 37.

Bremond's terms, the decree establishes potentiality. What will follow in subsequent chapters is the process of actualization of this potentiality, i.e., the fulfillment of the decree.

The three themes of the book are directly introduced. The decree does not commission specially appointed famous persons but invites any and all of God's people. Such invitation to all the people introduces Ezra-Nehemiah's overriding concern with the community as a whole. The word play of עַמּוֹ, "his people," and עִמּוֹ, "with him" (Ezra 1:3) adds emphasis to people as central subject. Yet Cyrus's decree also poses a challenge: "Whoever is among you of all his people. . . ." (Ezra 1:2) The question "Who are the people of God?" reverberates from beginning to end and is intimately linked to building the house of God.

The task of the people of God is to go up to Jerusalem and build the house of God in Jerusalem (note the repetition of "Jerusalem" in 1:2, 3 [twice], 4). Being the people of God and building the house of God are interdependent. Both people and house of God are to some extent unknown entities, not fully defined at the beginning of the book. They take form in the process that follows.

The first line identifies the real impetus for Cyrus's decree, and for virtually all that follows: "The LORD stirred up the spirit of Cyrus" (Ezra 1:1).[14] This verse also establishes a fundamental *modus operandi:* God works *indirectly.* God prompts humans to action. These promptings issue in decrees, in this case in Cyrus's decree which is both oral (בְּקוֹל) and written (בְּמִכְתָּב).[15] Indirection is also apparent in the delegation of the task from Cyrus to the people. He had been appointed by God to build; he delegates the building task, however, to all those who are God's people, dwelling throughout his kingdom.[16]

---

[14] For a discussion of the expression הֵעִיר רוּחַ and alternate translations of it, see D. L. Petersen, *Haggai and Zechariah 1–8* (OTL; Philadelphia: Westminster, 1984) 58–59.

[15] Williamson elaborates on the oral form of the decree and its relation to prophetic speech (*Ezra, Nehemiah,* 6–7). He considers the written aspect of the decree to be of secondary importance: "וְגַם בְּמִכְתָּב 'and also in writing' is loosely attached. The emphasis falls on the oral proclamation, with this as a parenthetical afterthought" (*Ezra, Nehemiah,* 4 n. 1.d.). The use of וְגַם, "and also," in biblical narrative does not support Williamson's conclusion. In many cases this expression emphasizes the important detail which governs the narrative. See, for example, how Abraham's battle with kings ends with וְגַם אֶת לוֹט אָחִיו ... הֵשִׁיב, ". . . [he] also brought back his kinsman Lot" (Gen 14:16). Since the whole purpose of Abraham's intervention was to release Lot, this restoration can hardly be contrued as an afterthought. Other examples reiterate such emphatic use of וְגַם (see, e.g. Gen 24:14, 19).

[16] The date formula at the very beginning of Ezra-Nehemiah locates all subsequent events in accordance with Persian regnal calendar. Persian royal years will indicate the date of the major movements as they pertain to the fulfillment of this edict. Such dating reference reinforces the impression that a royal command is being carried out. Other cultic events, which will actualize the other controlling document, i.e., the Torah, will follow different temporal markings. The two, however, work harmoniously, as twin expressions of divine command.

For Ezra-Nehemiah, the God of heaven is the power behind the earthly events, stirring humans to action while remaining behind the scenes. God's presence and command continue to find their expression in the written documents. Ezra-Nehemiah focuses on the human or, more specifically, the communal implementation on earth of this divine command. Since building the house of God is finally a human task on earth, as Cyrus declares,[17] the book concentrates on how the people of God build the house of God in accordance with divinely ordained documents.

The opening line is a rare, and therefore significant, excursion behind the scenes, revealing divine purpose: God stirred up the spirit of Cyrus so "that the word of the LORD by the mouth of Jeremiah might be accomplished" (Ezra 1:1). Scholars usually interpret the verse as an allusion to a seventy-year limit to exile (Jer 29:10). Such interpretation relies largely on 2 Chr 36:20–22, where Jeremiah's words are more explicitly defined in conjunction with Cyrus's decree.[18] Ezra-Nehemiah, however, does not make any allusion to these seventy years, either in Ezra 1 or elsewhere. There is no reason to suppose that Chronicles' prescribed limit to exile, so suited to that book's ideology, is intended in Ezra-Nehemiah as well. Jeremiah's word in Ezra-Nehemiah is open-ended, inviting the reader to ponder what precisely will be completed. Such musings are rewarded. As we shall see, other elements in Jeremiah's words, besides the end of exile, come into being. Most prominent among these is the vision of the future in which God's sanctity encompasses the whole of Jerusalem (Neh 11:1).

The written decree empowered by God had set the people of God in motion to go up and build the house of God. Subsequent chapters will describe their adventures in detail by tracing three movements which accomplish the task.

II. Process of Actualization:
The Community Builds the House of God
According to Decree (Ezra 1:5–Neh 7:72)

The "process of actualization" depicts the various steps taken by the community to execute the decree and build the house of God. Cyrus's decree

---

[17] This is in contrast to Zechariah, for example. Petersen (*Haggai and Zechariah -8*, 299) states that Zechariah emphasizes the divine initiative. Ezra-Nehemiah does so also. But this divine initiative is quickly translated into human action and documents which provide guidelines for the divinely initiated human task.

[18] Chronicles explicitly states: "He took into exile in Babylon those who had escaped from the sword, and they became servants to him and to his sons until the establishment of the kingdom of Persia, to fulfil the word of the LORD by the mouth of Jeremiah, until the land had enjoyed its sabbath. All the days that it lay desolate it kept sabbath, to fulfil seventy years. Now in the first year of Cyrus king of Persia, that the word of the LORD by the mouth of Jeremiah might be accomplished. . . ." (2 Chr 36:20–22). The seventy years recur in Zech 1:12, where they refer to a somewhat different scheme (see Petersen, *Haggai and Zechariah 1–8*, 146–151).

precipitates a flurry of activities, a return and reconstruction. The fulfillment of the decree entails three different movements — three movements in space from diaspora to Jerusalem; three movements also in the sense of three different groups and sets of characters; three different Persian kings as well — all bound together in their adherence to divine command and royal decree. Each movement begins in exile and culminates in Jerusalem. Each movement has a similar general structure: preparations "over there" (directly involving the Persian king), introduction of main characters and task, arrival in Judah, and implementation of the decree. The preparations in exile represent compliance with Cyrus's exhortations that the neighbors support the returnees (Ezra 1:4). Each movement focuses upon a specific component of the decree. A conflict invariably hampers the execution of the task; obstacles must be overcome before it is accomplished and the section closes. All three movements are necessary to fulfill the decree(s) of God and the Persian king, and reach the objective of finishing the house of God. Ezra 6:14 sums up these developments: "They finished their building by the command of the God of Israel and by decree of Cyrus and Darius and Artaxerxes king of Persia."

We shall follow these movements in Ezra-Nehemiah by focusing on the three major themes: the centrality of the community, i.e., עַם, "people," with a shift away from leaders; the expansion of the notion of the house of God to include the city as a whole; the centrality of written texts or documents as source of authority. After a brief survey of the structure of each movement, these themes will be discussed correspondingly under the headings: "The People," "The House of God," and "The Documents."

A. Introduction: Proleptic Summary (Ezra 1:5–6)

Structure

1. Report about going up to build (1:5)
2. Report about support from neighbors (1:6)

These two verses are a proleptic summary, stating in embryonic fashion what Ezra 1:7–Neh 7:72 elaborates in detail. They announce the fulfillment of Cyrus's decree. The decree had summoned a people to go up and build the house of God in Jerusalem which is in Judah (Ezra 1:1–4). Ezra 1:5–6 reports that a community rose up promptly to execute this decree, going up to build. To borrow Hillel's famous phrase, "All the rest is commentary." The activities of the three movements from diaspora to Jerusalem (Ezra 1:7–Neh 7:72) are such commentary.

The structure of the introduction largely parallels the decree, stressing thereby the close correspondence between the decree and its fulfillment. The jussives "let him go up" (וְיַעַל) and "let him build" (וְיִבֶן) in Cyrus's edict (Ezra 1:3) become the infinitives "to go up" (לַעֲלוֹת) and "to build" (לִבְנוֹת) in the people's response (Ezra 1:5). The exhortation to neighbors to support the returnees with freewill gifts of silver, gold, goods, and livestock (Ezra 1:4) is matched by the report that the neighbors strengthened the returnees with silver, gold, goods, and livestock (Ezra 1:6).

This introduction specifies that "the people" comprise the heads of fathers' houses of Judah and Benjamin,[19] priests and Levites and every one (לכל) who had been stirred up by God. All of these people are the central subject of Ezra-Nehemiah. What will follow is their story. Thus the group, encompassing various communal categories, is mentioned first, before any individual leaders surface.

As God stirred up the spirit of Cyrus (Ezra 1:1), so does God stir up the spirit of the returnees (Ezra 1:5). The parallel confirms that the response by the community to the decree is prompted by the same divine power responsible for the decree itself, reiterating the connection between decree and fulfillment. In addition, as the proleptic summary of the process of actualization, this repetition consigns all subsequent events in Ezra 1:5–Neh 7:72 to the workings of the same divine initiative.

Having briefly ventured beyond the scenes to attest to God's activities, the narrative resumes its primary concern with mundane reality and focuses on the task at hand, i.e., describing how the people, in fact, build the house of God according to the decree.

B. First Movement (Ezra 1:7–6:22)

Structure

1. Preparations and introduction of the main characters and task (Ezra 1:7–2:67)
   a. Preparations "over there" (1:7–11)
      1) King transfers and returns vessels (1:7–8)
      2) List of returned vessels (1:9–11)
   b. Introduction of main characters: list of returnees (2:1–67)
      1) Heading (2:1–2a)
      2) The list of people (2:2b–65)
      3) List of animals (2:66–67)
2. Initial implementation of the task by the community (Ezra 2:68–3:13)
   a. Arrival (2:68–70)
   b. The building of the altar, temple's foundation, and reestablishment of the cult (3:1–13)
      1) The people build the altar. Reestablishment of cult (3:1–7)
      2) The people set foundations and celebrate (3:8–13)

---

[19] For details of the meaning of this category see J. P. Weinberg, "Das *'beit ābōt* im 6.-4. JH. v.u.Z." *VT* 23 (1973) 400–414.

3. Conflict: disruption of work on the house of God (4:1–24)
   a. Opponents challenge membership and building (4:1–5)
   b. Correspondence opposing building the house of God (4:6–24)
      1) Report about a letter to Ahasuerus (4:6)
      2) Letter to Artaxerxes (4:7–16)
      3) Letter from Artaxerxes (4:17–23)
   c. Result: building activities stop (4:24)
4. Resolution: resumption of the work on the house of God
   (5:1–6:13)
   a. Report about resumption of work (5:1–2)
   b. Correspondence authorizing the building (5:3–6:12)
      1) Letter to Darius (5:3–17)
      2) Letter from Darius (6:1–12)
   c. Results: building activities resume (6:13)
5. Conclusion: completion and celebration
   a. Retrospective and proleptic summary (6:14)
   b. Completion and dedication of the temple; institution of cultic
      procedures by the people (6:15–18)
   c. Celebration of Passover by community (6:19–22)

The first movement depicts a return from Diaspora to Jerusalem and the reestablishment of the cult. The movement opens in Babylon, where preparations are under way for the return in compliance with Cyrus's decree.

The reference to Cyrus (Ezra 1:7 and again 1:8) provides a new starting point after the generalized statement of Ezra 1:5–6.[20] Cyrus's activities constitute the first details of compliance with the decree. The return of the vessels by the king (Ezra 1:7–11) elaborates on Ezra 1:6 in particular, while the list of returnees (Ezra 2:1–67) specifies who the people stirred by God were, elaborating on Ezra 1:5. Together these lists and the sparse narrative linking them constitute the preparations "over there," including (as in the other movements) an introduction of the main characters. The list of returnees presents the people as the main character. The rest of the unit follows the activities of these people as they carry out their primary objective. The central task is the building of altar and temple, built in accordance with the decrees of Cyrus, Darius, and the Torah of Moses. Opposition to building creates the central conflict. The conflict is both triggered and resolved via letters. A resolution finally takes place and the temple is built. Leaders emerge in the process of resolution, only to be also submerged. Accomplishments finally reside with the community itself. A conclusion with a proleptic summary closes the unit. The movement ends with the community as a whole celebrating its success (Ezra 6:16–22).

---

[20] Like most of the major units in the book, this one is linked paratactically with the preceding one with the conjunctive "and" (note Ezra 7:1, Neh 8:1, etc.).

But, as we have observed above, the fulfillment of the decree is not yet complete. Ezra 6:14–15 alerts us to the fact that only a certain phase has been finished thus far. Completion will require more and will take us to other movements in the time of Artaxerxes.

The People

Each movement in Ezra-Nehemiah introduces its main characters early. Ezra-Nehemiah emphasizes the centrality of the communîty as a whole by introducing the entirety of the returning people with great specificity and length. The section begins with lists of returnees: returned holy vessels (Ezra 1:7–11) and, more prominently, returning people (Ezra 2:1–67).[21] These lists, specifying which displaced vessels and people return to their proper place, elaborate on the response to the edict. This beginning introduces us to one of Ezra-Nehemiah's distinguishing characteristics: lists, primarily of people.[22] The extensive list of Ezra 2 makes it clear that the return was a return of a great multitude, composed of the major categories within Judean society (priests, Levites, Israel, gatekeepers, etc.). The people who will build the house of God are the central focus of the book. They are the ones who went up to Jerusalem, in compliance with divine and royal decree, to restore Jewish life. Leaders will emerge (e.g., Zerubbabel and Jeshua); these leaders also fade. The people themselves complete the task and celebrate. They are consequently presented in detail. Ezra-Nehemiah firmly establishes before the readers' eyes the fact that a multiplicity of individuals, families, and classes combine to make up this entity called עַם, the people Israel. It is these people — listed fully with tiresome specificity — whose story Ezra-Nehemiah narrates.

The purpose of the list of returnees is to indicate who is truly important in Ezra-Nehemiah.[23] Josephus, by way of contrast, omits this list from his

---

[21] Vessels, as P. R. Ackroyd suggests, provide continuity ("The Temple Vessels — A Continuity Theme," VTSup 23 [1972] 166–181). They also reflect delegation: Cyrus transfers them to Mithredath, who gives them to Sheshbazzar. Legitimate transfer of power permeates the scene: Yahweh appoints Cyrus; Cyrus appoints the people. Next, Cyrus transfers vessels to Mithredath, who transfers them to Sheshbazzar the prince. Temple vessels are now restored to their original place (Ezra 1:7–11). People likewise return to their place of origin (Ezra 2:1–67). The pattern is the same for both returnees. In each case the book reiterates that these (vessels and people) had been displaced earlier by Nebuchadnezzar (vessels in Ezra 1:7; people in Ezra 2:1), and how they now return to their proper location (vessels in Ezra 1:11; people in Ezra 2:70). This pattern shows that Ezra 1:7–11 belongs with Ezra 2:1–67.

[22] Note "The number of the men of the people (עַם) of Israel" (Ezra 2:2b). For a review of Ezra-Nehemiah's lists, see Talmon, "Ezra and Nehemiah (Books and Men)," 321–322.

[23] The list's historicity, text, and relation to Nehemiah 7 have been thoroughly examined by scholars. See K. Galling, "The 'Gola-List' according to Ezra 2//Nehemiah 7," JBL 70 (1951) 149–158; R. W. Klein, "Old Readings in I Esdras: The List of Returnees from Babylon (Ezra 2//Nehemiah 7)," HTR 62 (1969) 99–107. See also F. Michaeli, Les livres des Chroniques, d'Esdras et de Néhémie (Commentaire de l'Ancien Testament XVI; Paris and Neuchâtel [Suisse]: Éditions

account of the return because, as he admits, he does not wish to distract his readers' attention from the main issues (*Ant.* XI.68). For Ezra-Nehemiah, however, these people and their fate *are* the main issue. The book therefore places this list in a prominent position, providing very definite content for each subsequent occurrence of the terms עם or Israel. Ezra-Nehemiah further emphasizes the importance of this group by repeating these names at yet another strategic position (Neh 7:6–72).

The list itself comprises the various segments of Judean society. It is not insignificant that the list begins with the "lay group" (even though priests and Levites generally receive prominence in Ezra-Nehemiah): "The number of the men of the people of Israel . . ." (Ezra 2:2b). These Israelites count as the majority of the returnees and occupy the larger portion of the list (Ezra 2:3–35). After them come the priests, Levites, singers, gatekeepers, *Netinim* and Solomon's servants (Ezra 2:36–58). Servants, both male and female, follow suit (Ezra 2:65–66). The sequence from priests to Solomon's servants to general servants establishes a flow in descending order, from greater to lesser. The fact that the men of Israel, clearly referring here to laity, are mentioned first underscores their importance. The comprehensiveness of the list implies the return of a whole people.

Communal identity constitutes the first problem as the people confront the necessity of ascertaining who belongs (Ezra 2:59–62). One learns quickly that criteria for membership do exist but also that the exact boundaries of this community of returnees are not yet determined with finality. Temporary measures postpone permanent resolution, at least with respect to the priests (Ezra 2:62–63).[24]

It is not certain who, in Ezra-Nehemiah, heads this massive return. In contrast to 1 Esdras, which places Zerubbabel decidedly at the helm, Ezra-Nehemiah is unclear about precise leadership. Sheshbazzar is named *nāśî'* of Judah in Ezra 1:8.[25] Having briefly mentioned him, Ezra-Nehemiah shifts to the lists of vessels and people, and leaves Sheshbazzar behind. The book does not report any other actions by him until Ezra 5:16, which credits him, retrospectively, with laying the temple foundations. Ezra 3:1–3 mentions Zerubbabel, Jeshua, and others as those who laid the foundations, not naming Sheshbazzar. Eleven men head the list of returning people (Ezra 2:1).

Delachaux & Niestlé, 1967) 256–264, for a convenient comparison of the two lists. A brief review of these positions is included below in my discussion of Neh 7:5–72. What is most significant to note for the present purpose is that Ezra-Nehemiah painstakingly lists many, many people in the book's beginning.

[24] This passage reads: "These sought their registration among those enrolled in the genealogies, but they were not found there, and so they were excluded from the priesthood as unclean; the governor told them that they were not to partake of the most holy food, until there should be a priest to consult Urim and Thummim" (Ezra 2:62–63).

[25] See J. D. Levenson, *Theology of the Program of Restoration of Ezekiel 40–48* (HSM 10; Missoula, MT: Scholars Press, 1976) 62–69 for connotations of the term *nasî'* in the postexilic era.

Zerubbabel is one of them, as is Jeshua; all of them are named without titles or genealogy. To the extent that the return was led by anyone, it is by these eleven or twelve men together.[26] But the book is vague about these proceedings, leaving the reader uncertain about which leaders did what. Such equivocation displays Ezra-Nehemiah's reluctance to dwell on leaders as heroes.

Ezra-Nehemiah is not only vague about leaders in general but about Zerubbabel's specific position in the community in particular. The book does not elevate him above Jeshua, with whom he is usually paired. Zerubbabel's Davidic origin, which Chronicles establishes and Haggai and Zechariah imply, is never mentioned in Ezra-Nehemiah.[27] Nor is he ever called governor, a title which Haggai applies to him (e.g., Hag 1:1). The only named governors in Ezra-Nehemiah are Sheshbazzar (Ezra 5:16) and Nehemiah (e.g., Neh 5:14). When governors are mentioned elsewhere (Ezra 2:63 and 6:7), they remain unnamed. All this is in marked contrast to 1 Esdras, which, in the parallel sections, explicitly attributes governorship, leadership of the return, and laying of the foundation to Zerubbabel (e.g., 1 Esdr 6:28). Attempts to identify Zerubbabel and Sheshbazzar (or Zerubbabel as Sheshbazzar) usually lead to frustrations because they entail reading Ezra-Nehemiah "against the grain," with an interest which Ezra-Nehemiah does not share or deliberately obfuscates. These leaders are important to Ezra-Nehemiah only to a limited degree. The community as a whole and its achievement matter most in this book.

Building the house of God is the central task in this section. Ezra-Nehemiah emphasizes the role of the community as a whole by showing that the building is undertaken by all members of the community. Building the altar makes up the first step in the actual building of the house of God. Once again, as in response to the edict of Cyrus, the initiative comes from the people as a whole: "When the seventh month came, and the sons of Israel were in the towns, the people (עַם) gathered as one man to Jerusalem" (Ezra 3:1). Only then, after the people have already gathered, do leaders crop up and Zerubbabel and Jeshua rise to prominence (Ezra 3:2a). These two figures now emerge jointly (with Jeshua named first). Neither ever acts alone.

---

[26] The parallel in Neh 7:7 mentions twelve men, a number that more appropriately captures the symbolic reconstitution of the people as a twelve tribe system. The emphasis on the twelve runs through Ezra-Nehemiah (e.g., Ezra 6:17). The peculiar listing of only eleven persons in Ezra 2:1 leads Japhet and other scholars to suppose that Neh 7:7 preserves the more original form at this point (see e.g., Japhet, "People and Land in the Restoration Period," *Das Land Israel im biblischer Zeit* [ed. N. Kamp and G. Strecker; Göttingen: Vandenhoeck & Ruprecht, 1983] 112 and 123, n. 45). Another resolution fits the narrative in Ezra 1–6: the list may implicitly include Sheshbazzar, who is clearly part of this return; hence the list refers to twelve men.

[27] See Japhet, "Sheshbazzar and Zerubbabel," for an excellent discussion of the treatment of Zerubbabel in Ezra-Nehemiah.

They usually act as a pair (as is the case here in Ezra 3:2a),[28] and always with others. In other words, they are not leaders who stand apart from their community, nor leaders who alone initiate activities, persuading the community to follow or respond.[29] Zerubbabel and Jeshua always have coworkers. Their entourage in each case proves to be very large, usually including all members of the community. In Ezra 3:2, their coworkers are the cultic personnel and all the rest of the people. Ezra-Nehemiah, in Japhet's words, "attributes the building of the altar to the whole public, the people who had assembled in Jerusalem for that very purpose."[30] They build the altar and restore worship. Zerubbabel and Jeshua are specifically named but not held uniquely responsible.

Similar communal involvement governs the next phase of building the house of God, namely, laying the foundations of the temple (Ezra 3:8-13). Here, too, the community as a whole takes charge:

> Now in the second year . . . Zerubbabel the son of Shealtiel and Jeshua the son of Jozadak made a beginning, together with the rest of their brethren, the priests and the Levites and all who had come to Jersualem from captivity. They appointed the Levites, from twenty years old and upward . . . (Ezra 3:8).

Once again, it is clear that *all* the returned exiles engaged in this process and appointed some of their member for the more specialized tasks. Zerubbabel and Jeshua are prominently named, but act in conjunction with the rest of the people. The founding of the temple is thus initiated by the people as a whole; it is also celebrated by them as a whole.[31]

---

[28] Zerubbabel precedes Jeshua in Ezra 2:1, 3:8, 4:3, 5:2; Neh 7:7, 12:1; Jeshua precedes Zerubbabel in Ezra 3:2. Zerubbabel appears without Jeshua in Ezra 4:2, whereas Jeshua is mentioned without Zerubbabel in Ezra 3:9. We see, thus, that they are almost always together. The single reference to Zerubbabel without Jeshua is counterbalanced by the reference to Jeshua without Zerubbabel.

[29] Cf. 1 Esdras where Zerubabbel, virtually single-handedly, entices the community to return (1 Esdr 3:1–7:15, esp. 4:42–63).

[30] "Sheshbazzar and Zerubbabel," 84. The full quotation is instructive. Japhet writes: "The 'fellow priests' of Joshua are well known to us, but who are the 'kinsmen'—literally: the 'brethren'—of Zerubbabel the son of Shealtiel? Are they other descendants of the Davidic dynasty in Jerusalem, or rather functionaries subsidiary to Zerubbabel? It seems that neither of these suppositions provides a satisfactory solution, and that אחיו is just another expression of the author's tendencies. From his sources, the author knew of two personalities who were leaders of the people: Joshua and Zerubbabel. However, according to his view, the attribution of all action to them does not describe the events as they really occurred. He therefore attributes the building of the altar to the whole public, the people who had assembled in Jerusalem for that very purpose: 'the people gathered as one man to Jerusalem' (Ezr 3:1). The description of the assembled people is accomplished by mentioning its two components: the cult personnel, i.e. Joshua the son of Jozadak and his 'brethren', and all the rest of the people, i.e. Zerubbabel the son of Shealtiel and his 'brethren'" (ibid., 84).

[31] Note the emphasis on the people in the closing section, with three-fold repetition of the term: "But many of the priests and Levites and heads of fathers' houses, old men who had seen

The central conflict in this movement concerns "adversaries" who request permission to participate in the community and in the building, only to be rebuffed by "Zerubbabel, Jeshua, and the rest of the heads of fathers' houses in Israel" (Ezra 4:3). The authority thus lies jointly at the hand of Zerubbabel, Jeshua and the rest of the heads of fathers' houses in Israel. All of them decide who may or may not be part of Israel and build the temple.

Ezra-Nehemiah promotes the centrality of the community by persistently subsuming leaders to the community. This is particularly pronounced as the completion of the temple draws near in the subsequent sections of this movement. Zerubbabel and Jeshua, in conjunction with others, had been named in earlier stages of the work; as Ezra-Nehemiah aptly states: "They began" (Ezra 3:8), along with others. But when the building project is completed, they vanish, just as Sheshbazzar vanished and as Ezra will disappear. Their final appearance is in Ezra 5:1. The correspondence which follows, authorizing the resumption of the building of the temple, does not name them. The intervening negotiations do not mention them. Tattenai and his colleagues negotiate not with Zerubbabel and Jeshua (in contrast to Ezra 4:2) but with the elders who are, according to the narrator, building with God's beneficent eye upon them (Ezra 5:5a). It is the elders who speak with the officials (Ezra 5:9) and recite the "sacred history." It is consequently these elders, along with their unnamed governor, who receive permission from Darius to continue the work. Hence Darius's letter announces: "let the work on this house of God alone; let the governor of the Jews and the elders of the Jews rebuild this house of God on its site. Moreover I make a decree regarding what you shall do for these elders of the Jews for the rebuilding of this house of God" (Ezra 6:7–8a). Zerubbabel and Jeshua have disappeared when or before the task is accomplished.

This first movement of Ezra-Nehemiah illustrates how the returnees build the temple. Two striking particulars differentiate this account from other accounts of temple building in the Hebrew Bible. First, the celebration of completion is relatively mute (to be discussed in the section on the House of God below). Second, in Ezra-Nehemiah the whole community is engaged in the building. This contrasts sharply with 1 Kgs 6:1–8:66 and 2 Chr 3:1–7:11, where clearly the king builds the temple, helped by paid underlings. This contrasts also with Haggai and Zechariah who emphasize the role of leaders in the construction of the temple. Zechariah, for example, proclaims: "The hands of Zerubbabel have laid the foundation of this house; his hands shall also complete it" (Zech 4:9). In Ezra-Nehemiah, however, the community completes the temple.

---

the first house, wept with a loud voice when they saw the foundation of this house being laid, though many shouted aloud for joy; so that the *people* [עַם] could not distinguish the sound of the joyful shout from the sound of the *people's* [עַם] weeping, for the *people* [עַם] shouted with a great shout, and the sound was heard afar" (Ezra 3:12–13).

Most biblical accounts of temple building conform to ancient Near Eastern patterns, where temple building was a task for gods and kings.[32] Ezra-Nehemiah, however, stands apart from all these texts in its insistence that the building was executed by the community. Seen against its larger Near Eastern context, as well as other biblical accounts, the "deviation" of Ezra-Nehemiah underlines the book's bent toward granting the community real power, power elsewhere assigned to kings. It is therefore appropriate that the entire community celebrates the dedication of this building which it, and not simply some royal figure, had erected. The entire returned community then appoints the clergy in accordance with the book of Moses, as Ezra 6:16–18 makes clear.[33]

The dedication of the building takes place in the month of Adar, marked with a celebration by "the people of Israel, the priests and the Levites, and the rest of the returned exiles" (Ezra 6:16), followed subsequently by the celebration of Passover. Celebrations of Passover are frequently invoked as topics common to Ezra-Nehemiah and Chronicles. A comparison between the books' treatment of the celebrations, however, highlights the different ideologies of the books. Chronicles' Passover celebrations are initiated and conducted by kings; they are best described, indeed, as Hezekiah's and Josiah's Passovers (2 Chr 30:1–27; 35:1–19). Ezra-Nehemiah, on the other hand, does not single out any individual leader, placing the community as a whole in charge (Ezra 6:21). Thus, from the movement's beginning to its conclusion, the community initiates activities and the community, finally, celebrates the "feast of unleavened bread seven days with joy" (Ezra 6:22a).

The House of God

As the structure shows, building the house of God is explicitly the central task of this movement. Conflict and resolution pertain to building activities. There is no need, therefore, to demonstrate the emphasis on the house of God. What remains to be shown is the way Ezra-Nehemiah extends the concept of the house in this section to encompass the city as a whole.

We have already observed that it is the people *en masse* who are stirred by God and go up to rebuild the house of God in Ezra-Nehemiah (Ezra 1:5).

---

[32] See A. S. Kapelrud, "Temple Building, a Task for Gods and Kings," *Or* 32 (1963) 56–62. As Kapelrud shows, the various accounts of temple building in the Hebrew Bible (Exodus 25, 1 Kings 6–8, 2 Chronicles 2–7, Ezekiel 40–43) share many features and ideology with ancient Near Eastern literature. Haggai and Zechariah, which Kapelrud does not discuss, also reflect many of these common elements of ancient temple building.

[33] Ezra 6:16–18 states: "And the people of Israel, the priests and the Levites, and the rest of the returned exiles, celebrated the dedication of this house of God with joy. . . . And they set the priests in their divisions and the Levites in their courses, for the service of God at Jerusalem, as it is written in the book of Moses" (cf. also Ezra 3:2–4).

The first movement (Ezra 1:7–6:22), describes how they build the temple in spite of harassment. They erect the altar, lay the foundations of the temple, and eventually complete the house of God according to the decree of Cyrus, Darius, and Artaxerxes (Ezra 6:14). Rebuilding the house of God thus proves to be a task with several stages, spanning the reign of three Persian monarchs: altar, foundation of temple, temple itself and, as I shall argue below, the building of the city wall as well.

An important aspect of the book's definition of the house of God is the distinction the book makes between היכל, "temple," and the house of God. In spite of the all too frequent equation of these terms in the readers' mind, they are not synonymous in Ezra-Nehemiah. An example of a differentiation between the terms is Ezra 3:6–8. Here, having already specified that the foundations of the temple (היכל) have not yet been laid when the cult was first resumed (Ezra 3:6), the book dates the founding of the temple in the following manner: . . . . ובשנה השנית לבואם אל בית האלהים לירושלם (Ezra 3:8)

A literal translation of 3:8 is: "And in the second year of their coming to the house of God, to Jerusalem. . . ." This verse indicates that the returnees arrived at the house of God before the temple had been founded.

Such implicit differentiation between היכל and "house of God" in Ezra 3:8 might appear too fine to merit serious consideration were it not for the fact that other details sustain a similar interpretation. First, the term היכל elsewhere in the Hebrew Bible is also distinguished from the house of God as a whole. Second, the Artaxerxes correspondence helps establish a definition of the house of God which includes the city and the walls. I will develop both points briefly.

The word היכל, both in its original meaning and in the derivative uses in Aramaic and Hebrew, means "palace" and "temple."[34] Ottosson identifies a third meaning in the Hebrew Bible, namely "middle area."[35] In the account of the building of Solomon's temple (1 Kings 6–7 and 2 Chronicles 3–4),[36] היכל does not refer to the temple as a whole but encompasses only a limited area. This is also true of Ezekiel 41. In all these examples the edifice as a whole, which is called בית, is greater than the היכל. Daniel is even clearer in making a distinction between היכל and the house of God, speaking of היכלא די בית אלהא די בירושלם, "the temple of the house of God in Jerusalem" (Dan 5:3). These examples indicate that in the postexilic era היכל

---

[34] היכל is a loan word from Akkadian/Sumerian which could mean in its original languages "large house," "palace," or "temple." In Aramaic it means either "palace" (Dan 4:1, 26, 5:5, 6:19; Ezra 4:14), or "temple" (Dan 5:2; Ezra 5:14f., 6:5). See Ottosson, "היכל," *Theological Dictionary of the Old Testament* (ed. G. J. Botterweck and H. Ringgren; Grand Rapids: Eerdmans, 1978) 382.

[35] Ibid., 383.

[36] See, for example, 1 Kgs 6:2–3.

was not necessarily coterminous with the house of God but sometimes constituted only a portion of the house of God.

The Artaxerxes correspondence (Ezra 4:7–24) implies that for Ezra-Nehemiah itself the house of God encompasses not only this היכל but the city as a whole. It is commonly presumed that this correspondence is misplaced, first, because it conflicts with known chronology (placing, as it does, Artaxerxes before Darius) and second, because it never mentions the temple but objects to the building of the walls of the city.[37] Scholars characteristically interpret the displacement as the book's explanation (or apology) for the building delays, and consider the references to the city walls largely irrelevant to the point made in this context (a point concerned with opposition to the founding of the temple).[38] Williamson recognizes that ". . . our author has consciously given this section a literary setting at variance with its strict historical setting"[39] and explains the passage as a digression.[40]

I suggest, instead, that the specific references to city and walls, far from being subsidiary to the main purpose of the present location of the letters, are crucial to Ezra-Nehemiah's definition of the house of God. They establish, in their present location, a necessary connection between the house of God and the city walls: building the one is tantamount to building the other.

Building the house of God implies, by virtue of these letters, the building of the city and the walls. The tasks are mere extensions of each other. Ezra-Nehemiah shows that this connection is recognized by the opponents who interfere, therefore, in order to prevent such building. This

---

[37] See esp. Ezra 4:12–13. The parallel in 1 Esdr 2:17–18 does refer to the temple.

[38] Myers represents this position: "Having observed that the foundation of the temple was laid in the second month of the second year after the return (iii 8), the writer was forced to explain the long interval between that time and the completion of the structure. Because of his view of the people of Yahweh, he could not, like Haggai and Zechariah, see the reason for the delay in the people's lethargy and indifference. The only reason that commended itself to him was that opponents of the golah had interfered with the work" (*Ezra, Nehemiah*, 34–35). Commenting on Ezra 4:6–16, Myers concludes: "Wrenched from its historical position, this section of the Aramaic record is used by the author to bolster his view as to the reasons for the lack of progress on the work of reconstruction after its spectacular beginning" (ibid., 36). Myers's explanation would be more compelling if Ezra-Nehemiah did indeed bolster the image of the Judeans elsewhere in the book, or if there had been indeed a spectacular beginning. But neither is the case. The community of returnees repeatedly errs and is reprimanded; the tearful response to the rebuilt foundations (Ezra 3.12) implies a pathetic rather than a glorious beginning.

[39] *Ezra, Nehemiah*, 59.

[40] According to Williamson, "It is not difficult to explain why the writer should have wanted to include this digression here. He had just recorded an apparently harsh rejection of an offer to help with the rebuilding of the temple. Here he has sought to justify this by showing how, in the light of history, his earlier designation of this group as 'the enemies of Judah and Benjamin' (4:1) was entirely justified" (ibid., 57).

connection is acknowledged also by the king who stops the construction. In
this manner the particular location of the letters establishes a broad definition of the house of God. Later, when these prohibition orders are
rescinded,[41] this broader concept of the house of God remains the implicit
basis for renewed efforts and subsequent construction.

Put in another way, in Ezra-Nehemiah opposition to building walls and
city is an integral part of the opposition to building the house of God.
Conversely, building walls and city is part of building the house of God. This
implies that building the house of God includes building city and walls.
Having established that vital connection, and having indicated the broad
scope of the house of God, the book informs us that, as a result of the
correspondence, work on the house of God had stopped (Ezra 4:24).

Building activities resume in Ezra 5:1. The היכל is then completed
(Ezra 6:15).[42] One would be tempted to suppose that now the building
project as a whole has been completed and Cyrus's decree has been fulfilled.
But Ezra 6:14 prevents this conclusion by specifying that there is more to
come. It announces: "They finished their building by command of the God
of Israel and by decree of Cyrus and Darius and Artaxerxes king of Persia"
(Ezra 6:14). Completion is thereby projected in a proleptic summary (which
is common in Ezra-Nehemiah) onto the time of Artaxerxes. The reader is
informed that the story of the house of God has not been fully told yet and
is thus prepared for further developments concerning the house of God.
Going up and building in response to Cyrus's decree have not run their full
course with the preceding events; they will continue and be completed by
a decree of Artaxerxes, a decree that is yet to come.

By the time of Ezra 6:14–21 the temple has been built, but this does not
exhaust the definition of a house of God. The ceremony celebrating the
completion of the temple is so cursorily described because only a certain
stage has concluded. The house of God is not yet finished. Three verses mark
the celebration of the dedication of the temple or היכל (on the third day of
Adar, in the sixth year of Darius; Ezra 6:15–18), followed by four verses
depicting the Passover celebration (which comes several weeks later; Ezra
6:19–22). The Passover festivities appear to overshadow the dedication
ceremonies. Such brief treatment of these events stands in sharp contrast to
the celebrations at the end of Ezra-Nehemiah, and to temple dedications in
1 Kings and 2 Chronicles (which span several chapters). The reason is that

---

[41] The Artaxerxes letter, Ezra 4:21, hints at the possibility of a new communication.

[42] Batten, commenting on the Aramaic word שיציא, Ezra 6:15, writes, "The usual rendering,
'complete,' will not serve here unless we dispose of the following עד, which is well attested. We
cannot say 'they finished the house until the 3rd of Adar'; that is no better in Aram. than in
English. But from the root asu we get 'they brought out or continued the work until,' etc." (*Ezra
and Nehemiah*, 151.) This rendition is in accord with the interpretation proposed here. It implies
that only a stage of the building is complete at this point. No finality is indicated.

in Ezra-Nehemiah the final completion of the house of God is yet to come. It is too early for the "grand opening" ceremonies. The latter will take place when the whole task is completed, in Nehemiah 8–13, especially chapters 12 and 13. The temple has been finished, but the house of God is still incomplete.

The incompleteness of the house of God helps explain the strange dimensions for the house of God in Ezra 6:3–5. This passage, which purports to be the copy of Cyrus's edict, now used to legitimate the reconstruction of the house of God by the Judeans, specifies the following dimensions for the house of God: height: sixty cubits; breadth: sixty cubits (Ezra 6:3b).[43] This passage has been subjected to numerous emendations because of the problems it poses. First, the memorandum does not specify the *length* of the house of God; the dimensions remain oddly open-ended. Second, the given dimensions are six times larger than Solomon's temple, and conflict, thereby, with the modest edifice implicit in Ezra 3:12.

Batten therefore bluntly asserts that the dimensions are wrong.[44] Rudolph, along with other scholars, revises the text in light of 1 Kings.[45] The dimensions in 6:3 may be wrong for the temple as such, but they express the view that Cyrus granted permission for a far larger house of God than what was erected as temple. The incomplete dimensions leave much room for growth and expansion.[46] This expansion of the house of God, I suggest, culminates in Ezra's and Nehemiah's activities, during the reign of Artaxerxes, thus reflecting the notion of temple and city composing together the house of God.[47]

---

[43] The Aramaic of Ezra 6:3a is obscure. The Aramaic of Ezra 6:3b is clearer: רומה אמין שתין פתיה אמין שתין (6:3b), translated as follows by the RSV: "its height shall be sixty cubits and its breadth sixty cubits."

[44] Batten writes: "It is certain that we have an omission here. The obscure and corrupt clause must have given the length of the building, for Cyrus would not have given two dimensions and left out the third. The dimensions of Solomon's temple were: 60 cubits in length, 20 in breadth, and 30 in height (1 K. 6²). So that the new temple was six times as big as the old one. These figures are wrong, for the new temple was much smaller than the old one (3¹² Hg.2³)" (*Ezra and Nehemiah*, 142).

[45] Rudolph emends the text and reconstructs it on the basis of Solomonic dimensions (*Esra und Nehemia*, 54). There is, however, no textual basis for this emendation. 1 Esdras follows the MT at this point, as does the LXX.

[46] Ackroyd points out that "the dimensions are incomplete, and such as are given point to a much larger shrine than that of Solomon where we might have expected close correspondence" (*I & II Chronicles, Ezra, Nehemiah*, 235). He concludes that nevertheless, "It is evident here again in this form of Cyrus's edict that the primary emphasis is on the re-establishing of the former temple, a rehabilitation of worship which provides continuity with the past" (ibid., 235). This is correct. But I suggest that more than mere restoration or continuity are established. The decree allows for a greater house of God than was Solomon's. The puny edifice which began in Ezra 3:8–13 only partly corresponds to what has been permitted. The open-ended decree allows for further building.

[47] Cf. other ancient Near Eastern literature such as the Gilgamesh Epic and also Psalm 48.

The Documents

The importance of documents in the first movement is evident when
one observes that both conflict and resolution are propelled by letters.
Documents precipitate and guide the action. Furthermore, a large portion
of Ezra 1:7–6:22 consists of blatantly unintegrated documents. The decree
of Cyrus triggers the chain of events that unravel in the rest of the book. The
restatement of the decree (Ezra 6:3–5) reiterates the continuing significance
of that document in shaping subsequent developments. The eventual linking
of the decree with other documents, appearing alongside it or as an extension, implies that what transpires is essentially the actualization of the
written word. Indeed, all important events in this section happen with
reference to or empowerment by documents.

One such document is the Torah of Moses, working in tandem with royal
decrees in the early part of the book. The edict of Cyrus is still the necessary
background. But building the altar is also governed by what is written in the
Torah of Moses: ". . . they built the altar of the God of Israel, to offer burnt
offerings upon it, as it is written in the law of Moses the man of God" (Ezra
3:2b). The repetition of "as it is written" in Ezra 3:4 stresses the theme of
compliance with the definitive written documents and the fulfillment of the
written word in the life of the community.

Further work ensues, presumably also according to the Torah of Moses,
but linked specifically back to Cyrus. Monies and provisions are given to
workmen "according to the grant which they had from Cyrus king of Persia"
(Ezra 3:7b). This return to the decree of Cyrus marks the end of the initial
phase of the building of the house of God.

Cyrus's decree is invoked in the central conflict of this movement,
undergirding the rejection of the adversaries. Thus the adversaries are told:
"You have nothing to do with us in building a house to our God; but we alone
will build to the LORD, the God of Israel, as King Cyrus the king of Persia
has commanded us" (Ezra 4:3). The claim of "merely following orders"
functions both as a justification for building the house of God and, at the
same time, a means for exclusion from the people of God. The decree
buttresses and defines both house of God and composition of people.

A series of letters follows, signaling, like traffic lights, "stop" and "go" for
the central action of the section, i.e., building of the house of God. The
opposition to building expresses itself in documents which, in turn, refer to
other documents. Ezra 4:6, 7 and 8 all reiterate the fact that letter writing
was the main, and most effective, ammunition used by the opposition. Ezra
4:11–16 reproduces one such letter. This letter, furthermore, urges the king

---

See also M. Eliade, "The World, the City, the House," in *Occultism, Witchcraft, and Cultural
Fashions* (Chicago: University of Chicago Press, 1976) 18–31.

to look for other documents to corroborate and verify its claims.[48] This document generates still another document (Ezra 4:18–22) from King Artaxerxes, acknowledging receipt of the letter, referring to an earlier document as the basis of his present decree, and alluding to a future one as well.[49] The king's letter effectively stops the building (Ezra 4:24).[50]

Documents continue to control the process in the next chapters. The divinely guided voices initiating the next phase (Ezra 5:1) are quickly channelled into written documents which allow the action to materialize (Ezra 5:1–6:14). The pattern of documents invoking other documents and empowering action repeats. Just as obstacles had been generated by documents (Ezra 4:6–24), so too resolution (Ezra 5:1–6:14) comes through documents. The earlier "library search" subverted building activities; a new "library search" reverses the situation. Cyrus's decree is invoked by the builders to explain their activities as continuing from the time of Cyrus to the present (Ezra 5:13). The king is urged by letter (Ezra 5:6–17) to look for this document in his archives (Ezra 5:17). The search is made and a copy of Cyrus's decree is found. Ezra-Nehemiah reproduces a copy of this decree (Ezra 6:3–5) by incorporating it into another letter (Ezra 6:6–12). The work resumes in the wake of the exchange of documents and with the full support of Darius, the present Persian monarch, who not only affirms his predecessor's decree but exceeds him in generosity (Ezra 6:13a).[51]

We see, then, that Ezra 1–6 is practically propelled by written documents. Past and present documents work together, leading to the fulfillment of divine and royal command. The key verse is 6:14, functioning as a linchpin for the whole book. Here the edict of God and the edict of the three kings combine to explain the success of the Judeans, and expand the task even further. Ezra 6:15 indeed reports the completion and dedication of the temple. But the report is prefaced with a statement which unifies the decree of Cyrus with those of Darius and Artaxerxes, and extends it (and the work itself) into completion at some future point. Ezra 6:14 states:

---

[48] The passage reads: "therefore we send and inform the king, in order that search may be made in the book of the records of your fathers. You will find in the book of the records and learn that this city is a rebellious city .. ." (Ezra 4:14b–15a).

[49] Ezra 4:21 states: "Therefore make a decree that these men be made to cease, and that this city be not rebuilt, until a decree is made by me."

[50] Ezra 4:23–24a states: "Then, when the copy of King Artaxerxes' letter was read before Rehum and Shimshai the scribe and their associates, they went in haste to the Jews at Jerusalem and by force and power made them cease. Then the work on the house of God which is in Jerusalem stopped."

[51] The repetition of Cyrus's decree (in spite of the differences between the versions of Ezra 1:2–4 and 6:3–5) binds the intervening events and defines all building activities thus far as an exposition and actualization of the initial written decree of Cyrus. At the same time one notices an extension of the scope of the earlier decree. Each royal decree in turn exceeds its predecessor in privileges and provisions.

ושבי יהודיא בנין ומצלחין בנבואת חגי נביאה וזכריה בר עדוא
ובנו ושכללו מן טעם אלה ישראל ומטעם כורש ודריוש וארתחששתא מלך פרס.

An intriguing transmutation has taken place. Actual completion and
final success must await the execution of the decree of Artaxerxes (טעם)
which is combined with that of Cyrus and Darius and is, at the same time,
consonant with the edict (טעם) of the God of Israel. The singular, "king of
Persia" applies to all three kings as a single unit, as if they spoke with one
voice. Likewise the *decree* of the three kings is spoken of in the singular as
if it were a single decree. Such indeed is Ezra-Nehemiah's point. Divine
command and royal decree, spanning various eras and persons, are, in a
fundamental way, one.

The section closes with celebration and the appointment of priests and
Levites, ככתב ספר משה, "according to what is written in the book of Moses"
(6:18). Nothing of consequence transpires in this movement except by
reference to and authorization of a written document. As royal decree and
divine written word become actualized, one is projected forward, thematically and structurally, towards the next document, the decree of Artaxerxes,
and the completion under Artaxerxes.

C. Second Movement (Ezra 7:1–10:44)

The actualization of the task under Artaxerxes is bifurcated. Two
movements elaborate different components of Cyrus's decree: the one
stresses the "going up" of the people of God (Ezra 7–10), while the other
stresses the "building" (Nehemiah 1–7). The two movements flow in opposite,
yet complementary directions. In this they are like their leaders, who are
contrasted with each other, who will later circumambulate in opposite directions only to come together and complete the circle (see Neh 12:31–40). Ezra
7–10 depicts the process of actualization by Ezra and the children of exile
who, as the lists show (Ezra 8:2–13; 10:18–44), are preoccupied with the
human component of the house of God.

Structure

1. Preparations "over there" and introduction of the main characters
   and task (Ezra 7:1–28)
   a. Narrator's identification of main characters and task (7:1–10)
   b. Artaxerxes' letter identifies main characters and task (7:11–26)
   c. Ezra's response (7:27–28) [first-person report]
2. Initial implementation of the task (8:1–36)
   a. List of returnees (8:1–14)
   b. Assembly and recruiting the Levites (8:15–20)
   c. Further preparations: sanctification (8:21–30)
   d. Journey and arrival (8:31–36)

3. Conflict: concerning purity of community (9:1–15)
a. Report about mixed marriage (9:1–2)
b. Ezra's reaction: mourning and prayer (9:3–15)
4. Resolution: separation from foreign wives (10:1–17) [third-person report]
a. Ezra's action and communal reaction (10:1–6)
  1) Ezra's mourning (10:1)
  2) Response: proposed resolution (10:2–6)
b. Communal assembly to effect separation (10:7–15)
  1) Proclamation of an assembly (10:7–8)
  2) Assembly and decision (10:9–15)
  3) Implementation of communal decision (10:16–17)
5. Conclusion: the separated community (10:18–44)
a. List of people involved (10:18–43)
b. Concluding summary (10:44)

The changed scene (different place, time, and characters), coupled with the loose paratactic ("Now after this. . . ." [Ezra 7:1]) indicates a new section.[52] Like each of the other movements, this one also begins "over there." The focus has shifted from Jerusalem back to a setting in diaspora where preparations are made with the full support of a king (cf. Ezra 1:7). Like the opening scene in the other movements, this one implements, in part, Cyrus's exhortation for neighborly support (Ezra 1:4). The return of Ezra and his companions is analogous to the return under Cyrus, which it parallels, replicates, and extends. The frequency of the root עלה, "go up," in the introduction (Ezra 7:1–10) emphasizes the fulfillment of that aspect of Cyrus's decree.[53] Nehemiah 1–7 will emphasize the other, the building component of the decree. The root עלה is emphasized again by Ezra himself in the section which follows the introduction.[54] The analogy with the earlier return is accentuated by the repetition of this verb and by the form and content of the lists of returnees (cf. Ezra 8:1–14 and 2:1–67): some names and sequences recur, though the numbers are now much smaller.[55]

---

[52] See Long, 1 Kings, 24–25. Batten considers the phrase "And after these things . . ." a "favourite phrase of the Chronicler" (Ezra and Nehemiah, 303). But 2 Chr 32:1, without the conjunctive וֹ, is the sole example of a similar expression in Chronicles. However, "After these things" without the conjunctive וֹ also occurs in other passages in the Hebrew Bible: Gen 15:1; 22:1; 39:7; 40:1; 1 Kgs 17:17; 21:1; Esther 2:1; 3:1. See also Sternberg, Poetics of Biblical Narrative, 144, for classification.

[53] Ezra went up (עלה) (Ezra 7:6); Some of the children of Israel, priests, etc., went up (ויעלו) (Ezra 7:7); and the going up (מעלה) was founded on the first day of the month (Ezra 7:9).

[54] Note עמי, עולים, לעלות, in 7:28–8:1; cf. Ezra 1:5, 2:1.

[55] The specification of twelve families may or may not be significant; see Clines, Ezra, Nehemiah, Esther, 108, and Fensham, Books of Ezra and Nehemiah, 110–111, for different views.

The central characters are Ezra (Ezra 7:1b–6) and the children of exile (Ezra 7:7) who go up. Whereas the central conflict in the first movement concerned participation in building a holy temple, the central conflict here concerns participation in the holy seed (Ezra 9:2), in the building of community itself. This conflict reflects, in some measure, Cyrus's challenge concerning the identity of the people of God. The people themselves, with Ezra's guidance, resolve this problem, and members of the community separate from foreign wives. Once the community has thus purified itself, the narrative turns away again from Jerusalem to diaspora, to a new scene and a new movement.

Two authoritative documents influence events in Ezra 7–10: the Torah of Moses, of which Ezra is a skilled scribe (see Ezra 7:6 and also 7:10, 11, 12), and the letter of Artaxerxes, which authorizes Ezra to implement the teaching of God which is in Ezra's hand (Ezra 7:14). Ezra-Nehemiah quickly establishes Ezra as the book's most important single individual and therefore as the man to watch. Such treatment, at first glance, lures one into thinking about Ezra in heroic terms.[56] But observing how this figure is developed in the book as a whole, and in this section in particular, reveals a remarkable turning of the table of expectations. Ezra is decidedly a model figure. What he exemplifies, however, is a shift from grand and heroic exploits of the individual to another mode of effective leadership in which autocratic tactics are abnegated. One might indeed say that, in contemporary fashion, Ezra-Nehemiah develops Ezra as a protagonist who is an anti-hero. The sharp alternation between Ezra's first person account and a third person account of the events serves, among other things, to recreate the shift away from Ezra to others, literarily as well as thematically.

The book utilizes the character of Ezra to express its dominant themes. The portrait of Ezra as a self-effacing leader, a leader who transfers power and responsibility from himself to the community, corroborates the theme of the centrality of people. The depiction of Ezra as a uniquely qualified priest, commissioned to care for the house of God, reiterates the book's emphasis on the house of God. The portrait of Ezra as a priest whose primary allegiance is to the book of the Torah articulates the centrality of the document.

The People

The second movement demonstrates the centrality of the people through the figure of Ezra and his interaction with the rest of the community and through a central conflict which concerns the community's purity.

Ezra himself is introduced with fanfare unparalleled in Ezra-Nehemiah

---

[56] Ackroyd describes Ezra as a "great hero" to the author of Ezra-Nehemiah (*I & II Chronicles, Ezra, Nehemiah*, 239).

and rare in other biblical books as well. Narrator and king sing his praises before Ezra ever utters a word. Such fanfare establishes Ezra as the most prominent individual in the book. It signals that something momentous is to come and Ezra is at the center of it. Naming Ezra first in conjunction with the king of Persia (Ezra 7:1) and then in conjunction with Aaron the first priest (Ezra 7:5b–6a), the book literally flanks Ezra and his mission by the Persian king and the first priest.

Epithets are heaped upon Ezra. He is favored by God (Ezra 7:6). He is credited with a fourteen-generation pedigree, the longest in the book and the first to exceed a single generation.[57] His priestly credentials are impeccable. His relation to Aaron is underlined by repetition of Ezra's name immediately next to Aaron's role.[58] No other priest in Ezra-Nehemiah is so explicitly linked with Aaron. Such identification sets Ezra up more prominently than any other priest in the book. Although the pedigree shows that Ezra is a priest, Ezra-Nehemiah does not (yet) apply this adjective to him. Instead, the narrator first identifies Ezra as a "scribe skilled in the Law of Moses which the LORD God of Israel had given" (Ezra 7:6), and doubly stresses Ezra's scribal role in Ezra 7:11.[59]

Not only does the narrator testify to Ezra's superlative credentials, but so also does the king. A copy of Artaxerxes' letter (Ezra 7:12–26) follows the narrator's introduction, testifying to the king's unbounded trust in Ezra. Ezra, who already has God's favor on his side, now also receives virtually unlimited powers from the king (see esp. 7:18 and 25–26). All this acclaim, preceding, as it were, Ezra's own appearance draws attention to him in a special way, attesting to his importance. As a result the reader awaits expectantly to see what great things Ezra will do with all his powers. Surprisingly, Ezra refrains from exercising these privileges. Instead, Ezra, who had been vested with great powers, typically transfers power and authority. The heaped

---

[57] Although scholars often refer to the genealogy of Ezra, the term "pedigree" is more accurate, as the following definition attests: "Pedigree is the precise opposite of the Genealogy, which proceeds linearly or collaterally from the early to the late, from ancestor to descendant. In the pedigree a descendant traces his direct lineage to a remote ancestor, naming all the males in the line of descent. The regular formula is 'x son of x son of x son of x son of x son of x,' etc. It is little wonder that ChrH and Ezr-Neh make abundant use of the pedigree, for in the post-exilic era authentic derivation from the founder of the line—especially in the case of priests and Levites—was always crucial to one's status" (S. . . DeVries, courtesy of the FOTL Project).

[58] Note: ". . . בֶּן אַהֲרֹן הַכֹּהֵן הָרֹאשׁ הוּא עֶזְרָא . . ." (7:5b–6a). The rabbis considered the juxtaposition of Ezra's name and Aaron's to be significant: "The Rabbis combine the closing words of v. 5, Aaron, the first Kohen, with the opening words of v. 6, This Ezra, producing the phrase Aaron, the first Kohen, is this Ezra. This homiletically created phrase, the Rabbis remark, 'indicates that Ezra, who ascended from Babylon as the leader of his people, would have been esteemed even over his illustrious ancestor Aaron had the latter been alive then'" (Y. Rabinowitz, The Book of Ezra [New York: Mesorah Publications, 1984] 153–154).

[59] Most translations obscure the double emphasis. The RSV, for example, translates Ezra 7:11 as follows: "the priest, the scribe, learned in matters of the commandments of the LORD and his statutes for Israel."

up credentials only accentuate what Ezra does or, more poignantly, what he does not do. The enormity of privileges demonstrates all the more dramatically Ezra's abnegation of power. Artaxerxes' letter excludes the possiblity that powerlessness or lack of authority can account for what one would call Ezra's "low profile." One is prompted, therefore, to ponder the meaning and significance of Ezra's actions in the face of such prerogatives. His behavior points to Ezra's commitment to placing the people of God and book of Torah — not himself — at the center.

The transfer of power from Ezra to the community is at the heart of this movement. Such transfer takes place in every episode in which Ezra is prominent, and Ezra himself initiates or facilitates it. The opening verses of this section offer a clue to this concern by introducing the children of exile in immediate conjunction with Ezra. As Ezra goes up so also do "some of the people of Israel, and some of the priests and Levites, the singers and gatekeepers, and the temple servants" (Ezra 7:7b). The activities of Ezra (עלה) are directly followed by and thus combined with those of others in the community (ויעלו). The sentence seems somewhat intrusive,[60] but it highlights the inclusion of others along with Ezra as major characters in this section.

Ezra 7:8 reports, proleptically, the arrival in Jerusalem. The syntax here is somewhat awkward. The verse refers to arrival with a singular verb, ויבא. Its subject could be the preceding group, namely Ezra (Ezra 7:6) and those who came up (Ezra 7:7) spoken of as a single body (cf. e.g., Neh 8:9 where this syntax recurs). The subject could also conceivably be the return itself, המעלה, which is mentioned immediately following, and takes a singular, masculine verb.[61] Ezra is not mentioned directly with this verb. This syntactical awkwardness foreshadows a recurrent pattern in Ezra-Nehemiah: Ezra

---

[60] Most commentaries comment on the intrusive nature of this sentence.

[61] The RSV and many other English translations consider Ezra as the intended subject, even though he is not directly mentioned and other subjects intervened. JPS, for example, places vv 7–8 in parenthesis, keeping Ezra as the sole subject. But the MT links the returnees and Ezra, inferring that the arrival is not only Ezra's but that of the others as well; it is these others who more directly stand with the verb. A singular verb with a plural subject is not unusual in the Hebrew Bible in general and Ezra-Nehemiah in particular. (LXX has a plural verb here, eliminating these problems.) To explain such awkward syntax as insertion and leave it at that is to beg the question. Later editors and redactors presumably knew grammar as well as we (for a refreshing challenge to the typical interpretation of "glosses," see J. A. Miles, Jr., "Radical Editing: *Redactiongeschichte* and the Aesthetic of Willed Confusion," *Traditions in Transformation* [ed. B. Halpern and J. D. Levenson; Winona Lake, IN: Eisenbrauns, 1981] 9–31). Textual corruptions can account for a portion of such variations, but there is a tendency to exploit such possibilities far too frequently and often without any textual basis. Awkward shifts or awkward constructions should stimulate us to look for a deeper meaning. In this particular case the text might be indicating that the going up from Babylon began as a plurality of people (ויעלו) (Ezra 7:7), who were unified along the way so that their arrival was that of a single body (ויבא) (Ezra 7:8).

as the disappearing subject. One will notice again and again that Ezra disappears as soon as he accomplishes his tasks.

Ezra's explicit goal is expressly stated and vouched for by the narrator: "For Ezra had set his heart to study the law of the LORD, and to do it, and to teach his statutes and ordinances in Israel" (Ezra 7:10). As do the epithets, so too does the narrator's report prepare the reader for the rest of the narrative. As Fensham states, "Ezra's actions in the rest of the book must be interpreted in the light of this verse."[62] Ezra's primary goals — to study, do, and teach Torah — imply that his behavior in each case can be perceived as an expression of such goals.

Artaxerxes' letter (Ezra 7:11–26) begins the elaboration on the report that had been condensed in Ezra 7:1–10. The letter makes four basic points: First, Artaxerxes grants permission to all of the people to go up with Ezra. Second, Artaxerxes appoints Ezra to oversee or inspect Judah and Jerusalem according to the *dat* of his God (Ezra 7:14). Third, Artaxerxes assures provisions for the care and furnishing of the house of God (Ezra 7:15–24). Finally, Artaxerxes directs Ezra to appoint judges and to teach the *dat* of his God, and authorizes him to inflict severe penalties upon those who violate the *dat* of Ezra's God and the *dat* of the king.

What pertains most to the immediate focus is the fact that Ezra is authorized to appoint, punish, implement, and spend according to his judgment and the book which is in his hand. The letter presumably reflects Ezra's own wishes (see Ezra 7:6b), and this may account for the inclusion of his compatriots and brothers (Ezra 7:18). The greatest powers, however, concentrate in Ezra's own hands. How he uses these powers is our next concern.

The reader has heard about Ezra's credentials, goals and authority first from the narrator and next from King Artaxerxes. Now, at last, Ezra himself appears. His very first words typify him. "Blessed be the LORD, the God of our fathers . . ." (Ezra 7:27a). Ezra first gives thanks and credit to God, the God of "our" fathers. The "we" and the "you" precede the "I" for Ezra. The focus on God comes first. These opening words present what has been called Ezra's memoirs. The memoirs form, generally considered unique to Ezra-Nehemiah in the Hebrew Bible, is even more pronounced in the next movement, with nearly all of Nehemiah 1–6 being Nehemiah's memoirs.[63] For our

---

[62] *The Books of Ezra and Nehemiah*, 101.

[63] Form-critical studies of this genre have focused primarily on the Nehemiah memoirs, whose authenticity is more widely accepted. The Ezra memoirs are usually judged derivative, in imitation of the Nehemiah memoirs. Torrey (*Ezra Studies*) considers Ezra to be a figment of the Chronicler's imagination and the memoirs therefore fiction. Kapelrud's linguistic analysis (*Question of Authorship in the Ezra-Narrative*) leads him to conclude that the same hand is responsible for both the Ezra memoirs and the third person narratives about Ezra. His conclusion is usually interpreted by scholars to mean that the Chronicler composed the Ezra memoirs. Kellermann (*Nehemia*), who does not deny the historicity of Ezra, considers the Ezra memoirs

purpose, the opportunity to "hear" Ezra speak for himself, combined with the third-person perspective (e.g., Ezra 7:1–10 and 11–26) is significant. These strategies enable the reader to assess Ezra's activities from within (i.e., as he sees them) and without (as the narrator presents them). Furthermore, the shift between first-person and third-person account also replicates formally the thematic interplay between Ezra and those around him.

Ezra characteristically includes, invites, and involves (see 8:17–20) others as significant participants in his mission. His first act is to gather companions (Ezra 8:1). He names his companions immediately. We thus have a list in which Ezra himself — and the book — calls attention to the broad communal participation in the event while recording the activities of other individuals. Ezra, as Ezra-Nehemiah presents him, is one who works with others, recognizes their importance, preserves their names, and thereby grants credit where credit is due. Through this list Ezra directly links his own mission and achievements with others. The importance of the larger community thus manifests itself in Ezra's focus on others in the community. His return is not a solitary affair. Others are the important part of his ministry. They occupy the center of his report.

Ezra's concern for broad and full participation similarly shines in the recruiting of Levites (Ezra 8:15–20).[64] Both the fact that Ezra goes out of his way to recruit Levites and the manner with which he does so are telling. The former reflects concern for inclusion (as well as cultic propriety). The latter demonstrates Ezra's recognition of others. After all, one could easily imagine different modes of depicting the gathering of Levites. Ezra could have said: "I did not find Levites and I sent for and acquired some (or so many)." Ezra's own report, however, goes as follows: "Then I sent for Eliezer, Ariel, Shemaiah, Elnathan, Jarib, Elnathan, Nathan, Zechariah, and Meshullam, leading men, and for Joiarib and Elnathan, who were men of insight, and sent

---

to be modelled upon the Nehemiah memoirs by an anti Nehemiah circle in order to disparage Nehemiah. S. Mowinckel (" 'Ich' und 'er' in der Ezrageschichte," *Verbannung und Heimkehr. Beiträge zur Geschichte und Theologie Israel im 6. und 5. Jahrhundert v. Chr. Wilhelm Rudolph zum 70. Geburtstage dargebracht von Kollegen, Freunden und Schülern* [ed. A. Kuschke; Tübingen: Mohr, 1961] 211–233), concludes that literary rather than historical concerns account for the shift in the Ezra narrative between first and third person. For good discussions of the possible genres of the Nehemiah memoirs see Clines, *Ezra, Nehemiah, Esther,* 4–5, Kellermann, *Nehemia,* 4–56, von Rad, "Die Nehemia-Denkscrift," *ZAW* 76 (1964) 176–187, and Williamson, *Ezra, Nehemiah,* xxviii–xxxiii. I examine the literary significance of the memoirs in Chapter Four below.

[64] Ackroyd writes in this connection: "A surprising absence of Levites leads to immediate moves to remedy this deficiency. We may suspect a stylistic device here to underline the point that the true people cannot be such without its proper complement of Levites and their associated servants. The whole ordering of worship depends so fully upon them that existence without them is unthinkable. Se we can find an impressive procedure for obtaining an adequate number of Levites . . ." (*I & II Chronicles, Ezra, Nehemiah,* 248).

them to Iddo . . ." (Ezra 8:16–17a). One notes the specificity of the names of the messengers. Ezra takes care to record these men, their activities, and their decisive role in the project, stating explicitly that they, not Ezra, have brought the Levites (Ezra 8:18).

The transfer of the gifts to Jerusalem provides another important example of Ezra's communal orientation and persistent delegation of power and recognition. As in the return under Cyrus, so too here there are vast treasures for the temple (Ezra 8:24–30). In Ezra 1:8 these had been turned over to Sheshbazzar, prince of Judah. Here Ezra delegates this to twelve priests and Levites.[65]

The particular significance of this episode is that Ezra, himself a priest and therefore holy to Yahweh, carefully transfers the vessels to others and designates them—vessels and people—as holy. Ezra thus tells the priest and Levites: "You are holy to the LORD, and the vessels are holy" (Ezra 8:28a). Holiness has been extended. Moreover, Ezra specifies that these holy treasures should be transferred to the responsible persons in Jerusalem (Ezra 8:29), thereby extending delegation of power even further.[66]

The journey itself receives minimal attention. It is a typical itinerary which telescopes several months and highlights trusting people and protective deity (Ezra 8:22, 31). On the other hand, the book devotes much attention to the events that take place upon arrival. It reports that three days after their arrival,[67] the children of exile ceremoniously transfer the gifts that they brought to the Jerusalem priests. Ezra-Nehemiah specifies that full accounting of the transfer of sacred possessions was made in writing. Once again we have the naming of names in the recording of the events (Ezra 8:33). The handing over of vessels represents continuity of care. It also makes it very clear that, at Ezra's behest, Ezra and these returned exiles grant

---

[65] Fensham suggests that the twelve priests and twelve Levites are in accordance with the Torah division of labor for priests and Levites who carry temple things, as specified in Num 3:8, 31; 4:5–49. See *Books of Ezra and Nehemiah*, 118.

[66] Ackroyd's "The Temple Vessels—A Continuity Theme," traces the ways in which vessels have become a theme of continuity for the Chronicler. It is noteworthy that the vessels in Ezra 8:28, unlike those of Ezra 1:7–11, are not temple vessels returned, but freewill offerings. The parallel in 1 Esdr 8:55 does describe these vessels as holy. In Ezra-Nehemiah, however, they become holy through Ezra's sanctification. Thus, whereas 1 Esdras expresses continuity by means of the vessels, Ezra-Nehemiah is different and has different implications. Sanctification is not viewed as inherited or inherent in these vessels. It is assigned to them by Ezra the priest on the basis of their purpose, i.e., dedication to God and separation. The arena of sanctification has been thereby expanded and extended through Ezra. It will soon spread to the community as a whole.

[67] The date is suggestive, coming so close to that of the Exodus, on the twelfth day of the first month. The Exodus motif has been suggested by K. Koch ("Ezra and the Origins of Judaism," *JSS* 19 [1974] 173–197; cf. Williamson [*Ezra, Nehemiah*, 16–20], who finds the Exodus motif in Ezra 1:1–11). But if present, this motif is veiled. No Passover is mentioned. Moreover, the stress is on the arrival, not the journey.

authority to those who preceded their own "going up" and who are in charge
in Jerusalem. Such deference to others' authority is more dramatic given
Ezra's absolute royal backing, demonstrating vividly that Ezra does not use
his credentials to usurp power. He respects his predecessors, cooperates with
and adheres to existing social and religious structure (all in marked contrast
to Nehemiah). Having done all this, having delegated the task, Ezra
disappears.

The arrival of Ezra and his companions, like other important events in
Ezra-Nehemiah, is marked by a celebration which affirms the oneness of this
people as the totality of Israel. The celebration includes the sacrifice of
twelve animals "for all Israel" (Ezra 8:35). The book also reports that "they,"
i.e., those who returned rather than Ezra himself (the plural subject makes
this quite clear), disseminate royal letters to various officials who, in turn, aid
the people and the house of God. The scene closes with reference to the
documents of the king, with עַם celebrating, and with the house of God
supported (cf. Ezra 1:1–4).

Chapters 9 and 10 describe the central crisis of this movement. It is of
no small significance that Ezra's crisis pertains to the very nature of the
community. What is abhorrent is the mixing of the holy seed with the
peoples of the land. Holiness thus is no longer a matter only for priests and
Levites but for the larger community. Becoming a holy people (Exod 19:6)
is at stake.[68] Ezra admits that the news about mixed marriages was reported
to him. He reacts to the news with self-castigation and a confession to God
in which he includes himself with the transgressors.[69] His confession to God
is a public event, attracting the attention of the devout (Ezra 9:4). Ezra's
moving display stirs the people to repent and to act. Ezra, in his confession,
simply beseeches God, humbles himself, and recounts communal transgressions. His address is to God, but the book makes clear its impact on the
people. The community is affected, and it is from the community that a
course of action issues. Shecaniah, not Ezra, proposes a resolution (Ezra

---

[68] "Separate" is the verb that governs much of what transpires in the next section. The verb
in the *niphal* is infrequent in the Hebrew Bible. Of the ten occurrences, one is in Num 16:21,
two in Chronicles (1 Chr 12:9; 23:13) and the remaining seven are in Ezra-Nehemiah. As in the
other instances, a link has been established previously with the anticipatory נבדלו in 6:21. The
religious connotation of נבדל as demarcation between holy and impure (טמא) has appeared in
6:21 (see Petersen, *Haggai and Zechariah 1–8*, 78–80 for a good discussion of terms for purity
and holiness). Ezra-Nehemiah links separation with becoming holy. This is apparent in Ezra
8:24 (with the verb in the *hifil* form), where priests and Levites are separated and designated
by Ezra as holy. Here, however, separation for holiness is incumbent upon the whole community.
In Isa 6:13 the holy seed refers to the remnant in the land (see Japhet, "People and Land in the
Restoration Period," 107). In Ezra-Nehemiah, however, the returned exiles are the holy seed. It
is their transgression which offends Ezra and is an offense against God (Ezra 9:4).

[69] This is a striking, even humorous, contrast to Nehemiah's reaction to a similar situation (see
below).

10:3). He virtually commands Ezra to take charge, simultaneously expressing communal support for Ezra: ". . . let it be done according to the law. Arise, for it is your task, and we are with you; be strong and do it" (Ezra 10:3b–4; note three verbs in the imperative).[70] Only then does Ezra rise up and assume leadership. This leadership, however, immediately translates into participation by the whole community: "Then Ezra arose and made the leading priests and Levites and all Israel take oath that they would do as had been said. So they took the oath" (Ezra 10:5; cf. the oath almost extorted by Nehemiah from his community, Neh 5:12–13). Ezra ascends to leadership here at the behest of the local community. He takes his mandate from them rather than force them overtly to carry out his preconceived design. He acts as a willing instrument of the community (guided, of course, by the Torah), not as one who compels the community to execute his own vision. Having received communal assent, Ezra engages all its members in a commitment and then withdraws (Ezra 10:6), thereby allowing the community to take charge.

An assembly is then proclaimed.[71] Ezra rises in the assembly, in his priestly capacity this time,[72] reiterates communal transgressions, and then issues a series of directives: "Now then make confession to the LORD the God of your fathers, and do his will; separate yourselves from the peoples of the land and from the foreign wives" (Ezra 10:11). These are Ezra's only direct commands in the book.

The communal response is delightfully revealing. A resounding "Yes" comes first. Fensham rightly underscores this with an exclamation mark: "The whole congregation responded with a loud voice: 'Yes! We shall do as you say!' But. . . ."[73] The "but," however, is followed by a counterproposal, to which Ezra consents. The larger community then carries out the task.[74] Ezra

---

[70] In Ezra 10:3 אֲדֹנִי is introduced. The MT refers to God whereas LXX and 1 Esdras seem to have read this as a reference to Ezra's counsel (1 Esdr 8:90). The slight change in vocalization reflects sharp differences between Ezra-Nehemiah and 1 Esdras. The MT makes Ezra a leader by virtue of carrying out God's Torah and communal voluntary commitment. He has made no proposal for a solution but mainly demonstrated proper behavior. Shecaniah is the one who has given advice. Only God has given guidance. The MT is thus consistent in its portayal of Ezra and insists that the proposal came from Shecaniah not Ezra. 1 Esdras, on the other hand, is more interested in the "great men" model of history and thus credits Ezra himself with a solution. The different readings illustrate two different ways of perceiving how history takes shape.

[71] The unspecified "they" who proclaim it are the subject of the next verses (Ezra 10:7). Exclusion threatens whoever does not assemble. The most natural referent of the verb is those who took the oath earlier, i.e., the leading priests and Levites and all Israel of Ezra 10:5; "they" could also be the leaders and elders mentioned later in Ezra 10:8. In either case a group, not Ezra himself, declares an assembly.

[72] Note "Ezra the priest" (Ezra 10:10).

[73] *The Books of Ezra and Nehemiah*, 137.

[74] Possibly in spite of some dissenting voices which Ezra 10:15 may be reflecting. 1 Esdr 9:14, in contrast to Ezra 10:15, expresses an unqualified affirmation of Ezra. This can be explained as Ackroyd suggests, that for 1 Esdras, "a tradition of opposition was felt to be unacceptable. Ezra

10:16 is grammatically awkward, but its awkwardness only highlights the text's determination to emphasize the communal involvement in the proceedings: "Then the returned exiles did so. And there were selected [literally "separated"] Ezra, men, heads of father's houses according to their fathers' houses . . ." (Ezra 10:16a).[75]

The movement ends with a lengthy list of people. Ezra had received a unique introduction. His own report of his activities, however, began with a list of companions. Lists of names, thereby, frame his actions. Having begun with Ezra, the movement ends with a community that has separated itself in accordance with the Torah. The community both initiated and executed its own purification, assisted by Ezra. We indeed have here "a kind of democratic instrument."[76] Ezra himself is portrayed as guiding the movement *from* himself *to* these other members of the community. The alternation between first- and third-person narrative in this section exemplifies this as well. The "I" voice gives way to the communal. The final reported speech in this section is the community's (Ezra 10:12–14).

Ezra the teacher who came equipped with unlimited powers and the highest rank of holiness demonstrates how these must be used. He acts by including appropriate partners as much as by excluding foreigners. Each one of his activities corroborates the importance of sharing authority and prerogatives. The final episode exemplifies his willingness and ability to heed directives of the community. If Ezra is a leader, and the leader par excellence for Ezra-Nehemiah, he achieves this status by listening to the community as much as by making the community listen to him. His is a dialogical process. Ezra thus exemplifies a shift from the image of the fearless hero at the head of the pack to a guide who places responsibility in the hands of others and places them in the center of his report.

---

could only, on this view, have met with wholehearted support" (*I & II Chronicles, Ezra, Nehemiah*, 259).

[75] My translation. The awkwardness is caused by the absence of any conjunctions between Ezra, the plural verb "they separated," and the plural noun "men." The RSV follows LXX and 1 Esdr 9:16 "Then the returned exiles did so. Ezra the priest selected men, heads of fathers' houses. . . ." Characteristically, 1 Esdras places more authority in Ezra's hands than MT Ezra-Nehemiah does. The most likely meaning of Ezra 10:16 is a description of the formation of a committee, separated for a holy task, hence יבדלו. Once again textual difficulties in the MT insist on a communal activity, whereas 1 Esdras insists on the unique position of Ezra as leader. Williamson, even though he follows 1 Esdras rendering, also acknowledges Ezra's communal orientation in Ezra-Nehemiah: ". . . we would not expect him personally to decide the disputed cases, but rather to initiate a course of action that would encourage the community's own leaders to accept responsibility" (*Ezra, Nehemiah*, 144 n. 16a).

[76] Fensham, *Books of Ezra and Nehemiah*, 137. Fensham sums up the event: "Ezra was in the background, maintaining a low profile, but the moment the decision was made by the exiles, he started to execute their plans. Ezra was a good diplomat and did not enforce his opinions on the exiles. He gave his views and waited for them to decide. We have here the traces of a form of democracy" (ibid., 141).

The House of God

Ezra 6:14 has prepared the reader for the completion of the house of God under Artaxerxes by stating that the house had been completed in accordance with the edict of Cyrus, Darius, and Artaxerxes. The reference to Artaxerxes at the opening of this movement (Ezra 7:1) triggers an expectation that this completion is imminent.

Artaxerxes' reign comprises two distinct movements. The completion of the wall in the third movement marks, as I propose below, the completion of the house of God. But steps towards its completion are undertaken in this second movement as well. The book's concern for the house of God is introduced in Artaxerxes' letter (Ezra 7:11–26). The house of God looms large in the letter, standing at the very center (Ezra 7:15–24), flanked by Ezra's credentials and the king's law, and serving as a focal point.[77] The letter echoes Cyrus's decree[78] and extends it by specifying rights, privileges, and provisions for this house of God, which exceed considerably both Cyrus's and Darius's. Ezra now has virtually unlimited funds for the house of God and the cult.

The letter indicates, in addition, that the generous provisions for the house of God, along with the vessels, are intended to complete, somehow, the house of God (Ezra 7:19). We thus note the word השלם, "to complete" or "to finish," in Ezra 7:19. Most translations obscure this point by rendering השלם here as "hand over," following the LXX (παραδος).[79] But this is not what the MT has. The verb most naturally means here what it means elsewhere in Ezra-Nehemiah, namely, "to complete." The root שלם in the *hifil/hafel* forms occurs in Ezra-Nehemiah in strategic places (Ezra 5:16; Neh 6:15a). In Ezra 5:16 it refers to the house of God which had been under construction since Cyrus, indicating that completion is at stake: "and it is not yet finished [נשלם]." In Nehemiah 6 the Hebrew form of the verb refers to the walls: "So the wall was finished [ותשלם] on the twenty-fifth day of the month Elul" (Neh 6:15a). Outside of Ezra-Nehemiah one finds the Aramaic form of the verb in Daniel's interpretation of the king's dream: " . . . God has numbered the days of your kingdom and brought it to an end [והשלמה]" (Dan 5:26b). The meaning in all these instances (bracketing Ezra 7:19 for the moment) is quite clear and consistent. There is every reason to suppose that the meaning is the same in Ezra 7:19 as elsewhere, i.e., to complete. Ezra is authorized to bring some kind of completion to the house of God. Such completion at the time of

---

[77] The authenticity of this letter is usually doubted on account of its generous — in fact almost unlimited — funding for the house of God. See, however, Fensham for a defense of authenticity in *Books of Ezra and Nehemiah*, 103–104.

[78] We find once again the permission to return (with the word-play that we encounter in Cyrus's decree; Ezra 7:13; cf. Ezra 1:3). The monarch, once again, expresses a desire to carry out the will of the God of heaven, presenting himself as a divine instrument (Ezra 7:23; cf. Ezra 1:2). Freewill offerings, authorized by Cyrus, are again elicited and offered (Ezra 7:15–24; note esp. v 16; cf. Ezra 1:4).

[79] Thus the RSV says: "The vessels . . . you shall deliver before the God of Jerusalem."

Artaxerxes was envisaged in Ezra 6:14 and granted in this document. Vessels and law in Artaxerxes' letter appear to be a part of this completion with which Ezra is entrusted.

Other suggestive details imply that work on the house is still necessary. Ezra's thankful response to the Artaxerxes' letter is a case in point. Ezra acknowledges all of the measures specified in that letter as the "adorning of the house of Yahweh" (Ezra 7:27). Fensham observes the use of the term "adorn," פאר, in Third Isaiah, especially Isa 60:7, 13, where "the term has some definite eschatological overtone,"[80] and wonders: "Is it possible that Ezra, by using the same terminology, wanted to show that the pronouncements of Isaiah were fulfilled?"[81]

This possibility is intriguing in ways that Fensham does not develop. He connects this verb with the renovation of the temple (as in Isa 60:13). It should be noted, however, that Third Isaiah is not exclusively concerned with the temple but reflects the same clustering of terms that one finds in Ezra-Nehemiah: temple, city, walls. Glorification and restoration in Third Isaiah refer to Zion or Jerusalem as a whole. Additional terms also link Ezra-Nehemiah with Third Isaiah.[82] Such allusions support Fensham's suggestion that a restoration like that of Isaiah 60 does lurk in the background of Ezra-Nehemiah. Ezra-Nehemiah very likely wants to show that certain types of prophetic pronouncements are fulfilled. But the restoration envisioned, in both Ezra-Nehemiah and Third Isaiah, is not limited to the temple but to the city as a whole.[83]

Ezra's confession likewise implies that more than the temple is needed to complete the house of God. Ezra speaks of God having already granted יתד במקום קדשו, literally referring to a "tent peg in his holy place" (Ezra 9:8). Given that the temple is already standing, the possession of but a tent peg

---

[80] Fensham writes: "*To adorn* . . . is used in the latter part of Isaiah (55:5; 60:7, 9, 13) as well as in Ps. 149:4. In all these cases the Lord is the subject of the verb. The objects in these sentences are the temple (Isa. 60:7, 13), the people of God (Isa. 55:5; 60:9), and the meek (Ps. 149:4). In Isaiah the term has some definite eschatological overtones. The references in Isaiah to the temple are of interest" (*Books of Ezra and Nehemiah*, 109). See also Clines who writes that "The idea of beautifying the temple by supplying a rich sacrificial cult may be founded on Isa. 60:7" (*Ezra, Nehemiah, Esther*, 107).

[81] *Books of Ezra and Nehemiah*, 109.

[82] Ezra's gathering of others (Ezra 7:28) uses the same root as Isa 60:4. The great riches that Ezra's caravan brings to Jerusalem may be a reflection of Isa 60:6–7. The reference to the holy city in Isa 60:14b is particularly suggestive (even though the terminology is not identical with that used in Neh 11:1): ". . . they shall call you the City of the LORD, the Zion of the Holy One of Israel."

[83] Ezra-Nehemiah ultimately diverges from Third Isaiah's vision as it pertains to Jerusalem's relation to the world. This is encapsulated best in the image of the gates. Isa 60:10–11 speaks of gates perpetually open whereas Ezra-Nehemiah finally closes its gates (Neh 13:19). Cf. also Zech 2:9.

in God's holy place strongly suggests that the important structure, the "tent" itself, is still incomplete (see also Ezra 9:9).

Ezra 7–10 implies that building the house of God is not limited to structures in stone but refers to the process of building the community itself.[84] An allusion to this is contained in Ezra 7:9. Both the noun for the "return" and the verb "to found" carry architectural connotations. "To found," יסד, used in Ezra 7:9, refers elsewhere exclusively to concrete, architectural foundings, as, for example, in Ezra 3:6 and 3:12, where it refers to the foundations of the temple. The irregular use of this verb in Ezra 7:9 establishes an analogy between the two "foundings." Likewise, the participle used for the return in Ezra 7:9, מעלה, literally "the going up," occurs elsewhere in the plural, referring also to concrete, structural elements such as stairs (Neh 3:15; 2 Chr 9:19). This language suggests that Ezra's return and subsequent activities are perceived in distinctly architectural terms; Ezra is also engaged in a building project. One can say that one movement during the time of Artaxerxes focuses on the human component of the house of God in preparation for its completion, whereas the other (which follows) focuses on the physical component. Both dimensions are necessary and combine to complete the house of God.

The Documents

Ezra-Nehemiah's emphasis on documents appears in two major ways in Ezra 7–10: first, in the connection between Ezra and a document, i.e., Ezra as scribe of the book of the Torah; and second, in the way one document (Artaxerxes' letter) empowers another (the law in Ezra's hand). This latter point also replicates Ezra-Nehemiah's pattern wherein documents precipitate action, propel the story, and propagate other documents.

The emphatic bonding of Ezra with the book of Torah in the introduction exemplifies the significance of documents. Ezra, who is the book's outstanding character, is defined by the narrator first of all as a ספר מהיר, "scribe skilled in the Law of Moses which the LORD God of Israel had given" (Ezra 7:6). The emphasis on Ezra's scribal orientation might surprise those who would expect a priest with such superlative credentials to be primarily associated with the cult; it highlights, however, the emphasis on the book.

Epithets designating Ezra as scribe multiply, exemplifying Ezra-Nehemiah's interest. As Sternberg, for example, demonstrates, epithets in biblical narrative are not merely reported for the sake of realism but lay the ground for narrative development and emphases.[85] Epithets are "a tickling

---

[84] This theme appears in Second Isaiah as well, where Zion is both people and place.

[85] Sternberg observes that in the Hebrew Bible all formal epithets "... enter into tight relations with the patterns that surround them, fulfilling at least one role beyond direct characterization. That invariable function consists in laying the ground for plot developments, so as to enhance their predictability or at least their intelligibility after the event. Ostensibly

bomb, sure to explode into action in the narrator's (and God's) own good time."[86] In Ezra's case epithets recur, supplied by the narrator (Ezra 7:6, 11) and king (Ezra 7:12). All of them reiterate forcefully his scribal affiliation. The double emphasis in the repetition of the root ספר in Ezra 7:11 is particularly noteworthy: לעזרא הכהן הספר ספר דברי מצות יהוה.[87]

Ezra's epithet as a skilled scribe of the book leaves the modern reader with several uncertainties. The implications of מהיר are not clear.[88] Nor is the term ספר, "scribe," wholly understood.[89] It is not self-evident whether a scribe in this context is an official title or a profession and what precisely it entails. Scribes appear elsewhere in the Hebrew Bible, but their range of authority and expertise is not clear.[90] Shaphan (2 Kgs 22:3) is definitely a scribe, but his expertise does not include the book of the Torah, since he is not at all prepared to deal with the book when it is found (2 Kings 22). Baruch is also a scribe (Jeremiah 36). Beyond the obvious connection between scribe and book, not much is certain.[91]

Despite uncertainties about the full connotations of ספר מהיר, one can elucidate Ezra-Nehemiah's own emphases by means of a comparison with other biblical references. The term "scribe" in the Hebrew Bible occurs frequently in the absolute form, as in 2 Kgs 22:3. Occasionally it appears in the construct form, as in Ezra 7:6. 2 Kgs 12:11 mentions the scribe of the king, as does the parallel in 2 Chr 24:11. Jer 52:25 speaks of the scribe of the commander of the army. The scribe in the Hebrew Bible is paired, several times, with a priest, while at the same time differentiated from the priest (2 Sam 8:17; 20:25; 2 Kgs 12:11 and 2 Kings 22). Such functions are in accordance with the roles of scribes in the ancient Near East as royal functionaries

---

descriptive of the statics of character, all these epithets are implicitly proleptic within the dynamics of action. Not even the most idiosyncratic trait fails to cohere, sooner or later, with the processes of history" (*Poetics of Biblical Narratives*, 331).

[86] Ibid., 339.

[87] As noted earlier, the RSV, like most translations, obscures the double emphasis, rendering the verse as follows: "Ezra the priest, the scribe, learned in matters of the commandments of the LORD."

[88] The various English translations reveal the ambiguity of the term. RSV translates it as "skilled." Batten speaks of "a ready scribe in the law of Moses" (*Ezra and Nehemiah*, 304). Fensham has "a secretary well versed in the law of Moses" (*Books of Ezra and Nehemiah*, 97). 1 Esdras, which alternately describes Ezra as "scribe" and as "reader" further diffuses the picture.

[89] See Fensham, *Books of Ezra and Nehemiah*, 72, and Ackroyd, *I & II Chronciles, Ezra, Nehemiah*, 241, for good discussions of the terms.

[90] See KB, 665–666 for the range of usages.

[91] If the prophet is associated with the mouth/ears (Ezra 1:1; cf. Isa 6:7, Ezek 2:8, Jer 1:9), the scribe is associated with the hand/eye. The hand replaces the mouth as the conveyor of meaning. This shift in emphasis may lie also behind the repetition of "hand" in Ezra 7:7, 9, 14, 25, 28.

or trained writers/readers subservient to kings or to whoever hires them.[92]

Ezra, however, is the scribe of the words of the commandments of Yahweh (Ezra 7:11), as well as a scribe skilled in the Torah of Moses which Yahweh gave (Ezra 7:6). This is a unique function in the Hebrew Bible. Whatever the uncertainty about terminology, the definition of his role within Ezra-Nehemiah is thereby made clear: his master is neither king nor prophet, nor military prince, but the words of Yahweh, the Torah of Moses. Ezra is a scribe at the service of a book; his primary affiliation and primary allegiance are to the Torah. If one glides too swiftly over Ezra's description as a scribe of the Torah, it is largely because the very success of the innovation made in this postexilic era has blunted our sensitivity to Ezra-Nehemiah's peculiar synthesis. Whatever priestly Torah may have meant for the prophets or preexilic writers, here it is a book and its priest is first and foremost a scribe. This is the first and only occasion in the Hebrew Bible where the two functions are explicitly combined or rather fused. One of Ezra's chief contributions in Ezra-Nehemiah may in fact be this fusion.[93]

---

[92] For a discussion of scribes in ancient Near East see D. J. Wiseman,"Books in the Ancient Near East and in the Old Testament," *The Cambridge History of the Bible,* V.1 (ed. P. R. Ackroyd and C. F. Evans; Cambridge: University Press, 1970) 30–47, esp. pp. 35–42. Wiseman writes: "Until the Exile the scribal profession was largely separate from the priesthood which had its own secretaries and scribes, and in this Israel was in line with her neighbours" (ibid., 38). See also C. H. Kraeling and R. Mc. Adams, ed., *City Invincible, A Symposium on Urbanization and Cultural Development in the Ancient Near East* (Chicago: University of Chicago Press, 1960).

[93] What precisely is this book of the Torah in whose service stands Ezra the scribe? Scholars debate about the actual scope and content of Ezra's law (See Klein, "Ezra and Nehemiah in Recent Studies," 366–368, for a good summary of the issues). The purpose of the following discussion is to ascertain what Ezra-Nehemiah implies and not what the historical realities were.

The first twelve verses of the second movement employ different terms that can be construed as references to the book of the Torah (and others will appear later). It is "the law of Moses which the LORD the God of Israel had given" (Ezra 7:6). It is "the law of the LORD" (Ezra 7:10). It is also "the commandments of the LORD and his statutes for Israel" (Ezra 7:11). One can detect original differences among all of these appellations. R. Rendtorff ("Esra und das 'Gesetz,'" *ZAW* 96 (1984) 165–184), for example, skillfully differentiates among various strata and documents. Some scholars, therefore, argue against a naive equation of these various terms — and those used in the Artaxerxes' letter — with the Torah, since the terms referred originally to diverse documents and teachings. Ezra-Nehemiah in its present form, however, effectively equates all these documents, largely through repetitive linking with Ezra, both in the introduction (Ezra 7:1–10) and in Artaxerxes' letter. Thus, for Ezra-Nehemiah, the Torah of Moses is the Torah of Yahweh; it is the words of the commandments of Yahweh; and it is, finally, the תרה of Ezra's God.

This equation of the terms is developed by means of a series of usages. Ezra is introduced as a scribe of the Torah of Moses, which Yahweh, the God of Israel, has given (Ezra 7:6). The narrator informs the reader that "Ezra had set his heart to study the law [תורת] of the LORD, and to do it, and to teach his statutes and ordinances in Israel" (Ezra 7:10). The narrator next identifies Ezra as "Ezra the priest, the scribe [ספר], learned [ספר] in matters of the commandments of the LORD and his statutes for Israel" (Ezra 7:11b). The commandments of the LORD and his statutes are equated with the Torah of Moses which the LORD the God of Israel had given (according to Ezra 7:6). The very first line of Artaxerxes' letter is an Aramaic parallel,

This riveting together of Ezra and the book of the Torah places the written document in the forefront, together with Ezra. It implies that where Ezra is, so also is the book whose scribe he is. The prominence of Ezra goes hand in hand with the prominence of the book.

The function and content of Artaxerxes' letter (Ezra 7:12–26) serve likewise to exemplify the importance of documents. Like other documents in Ezra-Nehemiah, the letter propels activities, thus governing the flow of the movement. Set at the beginning of the account, before Ezra himself appears on stage, the letter reflects the recurrent pattern in which unfolding events are the fulfillment of documents.[94]

An even more pointed emphasis on documents occurs within the letter itself. In the first place, the letter authorizes Ezra to implement the law of his God. In the second place, it enforces the law of the king and the law of Ezra's God in tandem and equates them, by inference, as the authoritative documents for Judah, and for the rest of Ezra-Nehemiah.

The emphasis on the law of Ezra's God is particularly strong in both the frame and center of the letter. Ezra is addressed by the king as "the priest, the scribe of the law of the God of heaven" (Ezra 7:12). His mission is to inquire about Judah and Jerusalem "according to the law of your God, which is in your hand" (Ezra 7:14). Artaxerxes' instructions to his officials stress the importance of that law (Ezra 7:21–23). And finally, the conclusion of the letter reiterates the importance of the law with a double emphasis:

> And you, Ezra, according to the *wisdom of your God which is in your hand,* appoint magistrates and judges who may judge all the people in the province Beyond the River, all such as know *the laws of your God;* and those who do not know them, you shall teach. *Whoever will not obey the law of your God and the law of the king,* let judgment be strictly executed upon him. . . . (7:25–26)

Fensham's translation of v 26, although not literal, captures the implications: "Everyone who does not comply with the law of your God—*it is also the law of the king*—let judgment be diligently meted out to him: death,

---

designating Ezra as the scribe of the רֹת of the God of heaven (Ezra 7:12). This רֹת is something in Ezra's possession: ". . . according to the law [רֹת] of your God, which is in your hand" (Ezra 7:14b). Ezra is also identified as scribe of the law of the God of heaven in Ezra 7:21. The repetition of "in your hand" in v 25, this time attached to the "wisdom of your God," implies still another equation, adding yet another appellation for and understanding of the Torah. The inevitable inference is that all these labels apply to one basic thing, i.e., Torah whose scribe Ezra is.

94 One should note in this connection that the report about the letter (Ezra 7:6b) precedes the report about the return (Ezra 7:7a). As in the case of Cyrus's decree—and in order to parallel it—the narrator also vouches for divine participation in this occasion. This letter, somewhat like Cyrus's decree, has God's backing in some definite even though nebulous fashion: "for the hand of the LORD his God was upon him" (Ezra 7:6b).

corporal punishment, confiscation, or imprisonment."[95] In Artaxerxes' letter, the bottom line (literally and metaphorically) is that the law of the God of heaven is also the law of the king.

This letter of Artaxerxes positions the law of Ezra's God as an authoritative document in tandem with the law of the king. As in Ezra 6:14, Ezra-Nehemiah envisions no tension between the two.[96] The Torah of Moses and the command of the king work together. The one supports the other. Adherence to the one implies adherence to the other. Heavenly ruler and earthly ruler collaborate for the sake of the house of God. Having combined these sources of authority and having established the dual affirmation of the Torah, Ezra-Nehemiah can now leave the emphasis on the דת of the earthly king behind and proceed with emphasis on the book of Torah, which this king has already sanctioned as his will. This book of Torah, this document, will henceforth govern communal life.

D. Third Movement (Neh 1:1–7:5)

Nehemiah 1–7 describes the building of the wall of Jerusalem by Nehemiah and the Judeans, despite external and internal opposition. The section begins with an internal superscription (cf. Isa 2:1) which introduces yet another document. Nehemiah's first-person report narrates how Nehemiah learns about his people's plight, wrests permission to come to the rescue, goes up to Jerusalem, and mobilizes the Judeans to build the wall. Opposition to Nehemiah threatens the project, but the builders overcome it and complete the restoration of the wall. The completion of the wall marks the completion of the architectural component of the house of God under Artaxerxes. The scene is set for gathering all of these movements to celebrate the communal achievement.

Structure

1. Preparations "over there" and introduction of the main characters and task (Neh 1:1–2:8)
   a. Superscription (1:1a)
   b. Nehemiah's identification of main characters and task (1:1b–2:1) [first-person report]

---

[95] *Books of Ezra and Nehemiah,* 102 (emphasis added). On sheer grammatical ground רתא די אלהך ודתא די מלכא does not have the emphasis which Fensham includes. The two "laws" are connected by the conjunction "and." Nevertheless, Fensham is correct as far as the implications of this verse are concerned. Williamson detects here the beginning of a careful distinction between "church" and state (*Ezra, Nehemiah,* 105–106). Even if that be true, the thrust of the passage remains unchanged: the "laws" are harmoniously linked.

[96] Whedbee draws attention to this lack of tension between "politics and piety" in his "Ezra and Nehemiah: A Tale of Torah and City, Politics and Piety."

      1) Setting and occasion (1:1b–3)
      2) Nehemiah's request from God (1:4–11a)
      3) Nehemiah's request from the king: identification of the task
         (1:11b–2:8)
  2. Initial implementation of the task (2:9–3:32)
    a. Nehemiah's arrival (2:9–11)
      1) Delivering letters; getting an escort (cf. with Ezra) (2:9)
      2) Objections of Sanballat and Tobiah (2:10)
      3) Arrival (2:11)
    b. Nehemiah's first activities in Jerusalem (2:12–20)
      1) Lone inspection of the walls (cf. with Ezra) (2:12–15)
      2) Nehemiah and the Judeans (2:16–18)
    c. Opposition: responses of Sanballat, Tobiah, and others
      (2:19–20)
    d. Building the wall: list of builders (3:1–32)
      1) Sanctification (3:1)
      2) List of builders and their accomplishments (3:2–32)
  3. Conflict: obstacles to building the wall (3:33–5:19)
    a. Obstacles from without: cycles of harassments (3:33–4:17)
      1) First stage of building (3:33–38)
      2) Second stage of building (3:39–4:17)
    b. Obstacles from within: economic oppression (5:1–19)
      1) The cry of oppressed people (5:1–5)
      2) Nehemiah's reaction and restoration of equity (5:6–13)
      3) Nehemiah's activities as governor (5:14–19)
  4. Resolution: completion of the wall (6:1–15)
  5. Conclusion: final preparations of the city (7:1–5)
    a. Appointment of cultic personnel (7:1–3)
    b. Repopulation measures (7:4–5)

The change of scene (Jerusalem in Ezra 10; Susa in Neh 1:1), time, and major characters all separate this section from the preceding one. But the incomplete date formula (Neh 1:1) establishes a connection with the preceding material despite the other sharp markings of separation, with Ezra 7:7–8 as the last complete date. Both movements (Neh 1:1–7:5 and Ezra 7–10) belong to the reign of Artaxerxes and receive his assistance. They are bound together yet distinct; together they complete the house of God under Artaxerxes, as has been reported in Ezra 6:14.

Ezra-Nehemiah thus links the sections. It also links the figures of Ezra and Nehemiah, first implicitly, through parallels and contrasts, and later explicitly, by joining their actions. In this section the contrast between them is pervasive, with the preparations "over there," the introduction of the main characters, and the initial execution of the task in Nehemiah 1–7 all virtually reversing those of Ezra 7–10.

Building the wall is the central task and the source of conflict in this section. Nehemiah 1–7 describes how Nehemiah and the Judeans build the wall, just as Ezra 1–6 describes how the returned exiles build the altar and temple. The unit is punctuated by reports of the different stages of building (reminiscent of the stages of building in Ezra 1–6): Nehemiah 3 lists the builders and their specific activities; Neh 3:38 reports that half the wall had been finished. Neh 6:1 reports that the whole wall, except for the doors, was complete. Neh 6:15 records the completion date. The final touches are described in Neh 7:1–3. As in the earlier movement so too here, the conflict is precipitated by adversaries. There is a striking similarity between Ezra 4:1–5 and Neh 2:19–20 with their exclusions of opponents from participation in the building. Nehemiah rebuffs his adversaries, saying: "The God of heaven will make us prosper, and we his servants will arise and build; but you have no portion or right or memorial in Jerusalem" (Neh 2:20). This echoes the earlier response to the adversaries in Ezra 4:3b: "You have nothing to do with us in building a house to our God; but we alone will build to the LORD. . . ." Nehemiah's retort, which otherwise stands as a non sequitur, gains some clarity when we perceive it as a parallel to the rejection of the adversaries' offer in Ezra 4. Obstacles from within complicate matters (Nehemiah 5) but these conflicts are satisfactorily resolved and the section concludes.

The People

The emphasis on community in this movement is conveyed through the particular characterization of Nehemiah and by demonstrating that the community accomplishes the central task of this section, namely, building the wall. I have argued that Ezra-Nehemiah shifts the focus from the heroic individual as the most significant actor to the larger group, and, finally, to the community as a whole. The figure of Ezra in Ezra 7–10 appeared initially to challenge that assertion. But, as we have seen, Ezra-Nehemiah emphasizes the centrality of the people precisely through its portrayal of Ezra. Nehemiah, at first glance, emerges as the great hero, particularly if we listen only to his words. But a closer inspection shows that Ezra-Nehemiah subverts Nehemiah's self-glorification. This is accomplished, on the one hand, through the contrast with Ezra and, on the other hand, by means of the slight discrepancy between the narrator's emphases and Nehemiah's own assertions. In this fashion Ezra-Nehemiah preserves Nehemiah's memory ("Remember me. . . .") while deflating his heroic aspirations. If Nehemiah is a would-be hero, Ezra, as his counterpart, is an anti-hero. The book pays the highest homage to the anti-hero, thereby commenting indirectly on the would-be hero as well.

The very structure of their introduction establishes the implicit contrast between the two men by presenting them from the beginning in an inverted or reversed form, like counterpoint in music. Setting their introductions next to one another illustrates this contrast: Ezra's introduction consists of preparations "over there" and an introduction of the main characters and task (Ezra 7:1–28):

    a. Narrator's identification of main characters and task (Ezra
       7:1–10)
       1) Setting (Babylon) (7:1a)
       2) Ezra's pedigree (7:1b–5)
       3) Ezra's mission, credentials, and goal (7:6–10)
    b. Artaxerxes' letter identifies main character and task (7:11–26)
    c. Ezra's response (7:27–28) [first-person report]

Nehemiah's introduction also consists of preparations "over there" and an introduction of the main characters and task (Neh 1:1–2:8):

    a. Superscription (Neh 1:1a)
    b. Nehemiah's identification of main characters and task (1:1b–2:1)
       [first-person report]
       1) Setting and occasion (Susa) (1:1b–3)
       2) Nehemiah's request from God (4–11a)
       3) Nehemiah's request from the king: identification of the task
          (1:11b–2:8)

    Ezra, one observes, is introduced at length. First the narrator provides details about Ezra's pedigree, mission, and full royal backing, reporting that the king granted Ezra according to his request (with such requests taking place "off stage," outside the reader's field of vision). Next, Artaxerxes' letter fully reproduces what was granted. Ezra himself speaks only after others have testified on his behalf; his first words are thanksgiving to God. In sum, the initial introduction of Ezra takes the form of a pedigree, a location, a report of Ezra's credentials and motives, a report of royal benevolence with the full transcript of Artaxerxes' letter as the example of such benevolence, followed finally by Ezra's own voice in thanksgiving.

    In Nehemiah's introduction, on the other hand, the narrator provides the barest details. Instead of Ezra's fourteen-name pedigree there is only Nehemiah's father's name (Neh 1:1) and no hint as to what family or tribe Nehemiah belongs to. This is an odd omission in a book so conscious of genealogical matters. Nehemiah speaks first, and speaks constantly. His actual requests from God and king are fully reproduced, while the responses to the requests, i.e., Artaxerxes' letters, are only briefly acknowledged. The text focuses on the scene of Nehemiah's request, while omitting to transcribe the letter itself. Nehemiah's address to God in petition typifies his relation to God and contrasts him with Ezra's. Nehemiah's intentions are alluded to (Neh 1:11) but their content is hidden from the reader until Neh 2:5. Put simply, what is background in the introduction of Ezra is foreground with Nehemiah and vice versa, like the play of light and dark in M. C. Escher's drawings. As a result, there is a stress on complementarity as well as on differences.[97]

Having established a relationship with and a contrast to Ezra, the book allows Nehemiah to press himself forward as a hero while undercutting Nehemiah's own self-adulation. Kellermann, observing this undercutting, speaks of it as the degradation of Nehemiah.[98] "Cutting down to size" is a more apt description. This is achieved through the contrast with Ezra and through an oblique commentary on Nehemiah's own reports. Chapter Four presents a fuller discussion of the book's portrait of Nehemiah. Here I shall illustrate the undermining of Nehemiah's report with one brief example: the builders of the wall. Nehemiah's asserts that he built the wall: "Now when it was reported to Sanballat and Tobiah and to Geshem . . . that I had built the wall . . ." (Neh 6:1). But the narrator of Ezra-Nehemiah already preceded with a list which fully reports who, in fact, built the wall (Neh 3:1–32). The two accounts are not mutually exclusive. The sequence with which the information is dispensed in the book, however, with its concrete emphasis on the actual builders (Neh 3:1–32), makes Nehemiah's own declaration appear somewhat hollow and definitely exaggerated.

Nehemiah's articulated concern for the welfare of the people contributes to the emphasis on the community even when Nehemiah's own unsolicited solicitations make him a bit suspect. Nehemiah's initial inquiry pertains to the fate of the Judeans who had remained in the land (note the repetition of אשר נשארו מן השבי in Neh 1:2 and 1:3).[99] Without losing oneself in the quagmire of the historical problems, it is possible, and profitable, to assert a few things about these Judeans, limiting ourselves to descriptive and literary claims. The Judeans continue to be Nehemiah's primary community, just as

---

[97] Kellermann lists numerous parallels between Ezra and Nehemiah. He points out that both men hold high position in court, rely on the good hand of God, bring others with them, receive royal letters. Kellermann mentions differences at Nehemiah's expense: Ezra could boast of special letters and funds; he foregoes military escort and trusts God; his battle with mixed marriages is more severe. See *Nehemia*, 95.

[98] Ibid., 92.

[99] Interpreters frequently equate these Judeans with the early returnees and survivors of more recent calamities. See, for example, Fensham, *Books of Ezra and Nehemiah*, 151. Vogt, however, notes that the Masoretic punctuation implies that the "survivors" or "remnant" are those who have never left the province of Judah. Arguing that other factors besides philology and grammar must be weighed in translating the passage, Vogt concludes that historical considerations indicate that the remnant for Nehemiah most probably includes both those who had returned and those who had never left the land. See *Studie zur nachexilischen Gemeinde in Ezra-Nehemiah*, (Werl: Dietrich, Coelde, 1966) 44–45. Clines holds a similar view: "The inquiry concerned not only descendants of those who had not been taken into exile but also returned exiles" (*Ezra, Nehemiah, Esther*, 137). Japhet, on the other hand, asserts that for Ezra-Nehemiah, only the returned exiles are members of Israel and excludes the possibility that the book here refers to Judeans who have never left ("People and Land in the Restoration Period," 113–117).

the children of exile are Ezra's primary community. The distinction between
the groups is apparent in the distribution of the terms. The fact that the
names in the list of builders in Neh 3:1–32 do not coincide with previously
named groups and individuals contributes to the conclusion that Nehemiah's
cohorts, "the Judeans," constituted a somewhat different group from Ezra's
"children of exile."[100] Each movement thus preserves a focus on a different
segment of the population.[101]

The groups eventually combine. As we shall see, the most frequent use
of the term "people" occurs in Nehemiah 8, where it is used fifteen (!) times
in eighteen verses—a section where Nehemiah and Ezra, and their groups,
converge. The fact that Ezra-Nehemiah retains terminology with some consistency for different movements implies a recognition of diversity in its
concept of עם. Boundaries between groups are not erased. Unity is not a
fusion but a braiding of diverse strands or, more in tune with the structure
of the book, unity is the harmonious orchestration of different instruments
and melodies.

The list of builders (Neh 3:1–23) is an example of the emphasis on the
community, incorporated into Nehemiah's account. The list accomplishes
several important things pertaining to the thesis. It challenges Nehemiah's
report (that he got everything done) and simultaneously credits the community with the central task of this section, i.e., building the wall. Such a list
of builders is an important example of how other members of the larger
community, and not only Nehemiah, are memorialized. The tedious explicit-
ness of who did what imprints upon the reader's mind the community's
dominant role in the actual building. Nehemiah had asked and was granted
permission to build the city (Neh 2:5b). Building cities, like building temples,
was a royal prerogative in the ancient Near East. Ezra-Nehemiah, however,
credits named members of the community with the actualization of this task.
The list is one of the ways in which Ezra-Nehemiah transfers to the people
a power and a role that elsewhere belongs to leaders.

---

[100] Rudolph (*Esra und Nehemia*, 121) observes that the majority of names in Nehemiah 3 do
not occur in the previous lists and concludes from this that Ezra's return followed Nehemiah's.
But I suggest instead that this difference is an indication that Nehemiah's entourage and
supporters drew upon a different segment of population, probably those who never left and did
not therefore need to return.

[101] Vogt charts the distribution of the terms for the community (Israel, people, Judah, *gōlâ*,
congregation) in Ezra-Nehemiah, showing that different terms predominate in different
segments of the book, associated with different persons. "*Gōlâ*" and "Israel" are most common
in the Ezra traditions; "Judah" and "Judeans" are most common in the Nehemiah memoirs. Only
the term עם, "people," occurs in both the Ezra memoirs and Nehemiah memoirs in comparable
distribution (*Studie zur nachexilischen Gemeinde*, 21). For Vogt this distribution confirms the
view that we have different sources represented. The more important conclusion for the present
purpose is that we have different terms and therefore different segments of the community
associated with the different persons.

The list is also a symbolic reflection of the book's understanding of building processes. Descriptions of building activities can take many forms. They could focus on size, origin, and cost of material, duration of labor, numbers of people, shape of the reults, etc. But Ezra-Nehemiah focuses on names of people in relation to the scope of the task: "so and so built this and that section." The builders, not simply the description of the wall, matter.[102] Sections have been parceled out to different groups and families. Their individual efforts are jointly enshrined in stone. In this sense the building process mirrors graphically Ezra-Nehemiah's concepts of community, text, and history. Great events, like large edifices, are the product of many distinct and distinguishable efforts. Credit goes to individuals and groups responsible for definable segments of the whole. Demarcations are not obliterated. The list of builders exemplifies, as Williamson points out, a unity that is not uniformity by incorporating a diversity of interests and a variety of involvements.[103] The individual input is retained in a visible fashion, not swallowed into an anonymity. The "we" and the "I" both exist, with neither overpowering the other. This is how Ezra-Nehemiah perceives activities of the restoration. This is how Ezra-Nehemiah perceives community; this is also how the book is shaped.[104]

The House of God

The house of God is both the most important and most intricate aspect of this section. The central significance of the wall in this section is clear. Nehemiah comes to build the wall, requesting permission with much fear and trembling. The process of building itself is the glue that holds the narrative together, as the discussion of the structure shows. Less overt, however, is the transformation that takes place. I suggest that in Ezra-Nehemiah, the building of the wall is an extension of building the temple. This shift, extending temple-like sanctity to the city as a whole, best explains some of the peculiarities in Ezra-Nehemiah that have puzzled critics.

---

[102] See Clines, *Ezra, Nehemiah, Esther,* 159, for a good summary of K. Kenyon's archeological reports with details of the actual shape of Nehemiah's wall.

[103] Williamson writes, "We may note, for instance, that some participated on the basis of family association, others as individuals, some in district associations, some on the basis of their standing or position within the community, and yet others because of professional association" (*Ezra, Nehemiah,* 212).

[104] When the wall is complete, the community appoints functionaries to stand at its gates (Neh 7:1–3). Thus Fensham writes as follows on Neh 7:1–3: "The appointment in v. 1 was probably made by representatives of the people, the one in v. 2 by Nehemiah as governor (the same verb is used for the appointment by the king), and in v. 3 it was made by the two officials elected by Nehemiah. So the three verbs have different shades of meaning" (*Books of Ezra and Nehemiah,* 209). The situation is analogous to Ezra 3:8, still another indication of the communal involvement in these events.

The implicit connection between temple and city walls had been brought into effect in the Artaxerxes correspondence (Ezra 4:7–24), wherein it has been established that the house of God and the city walls are coextensive. This same connection persists in the present section. It is indicated to some extent by the parallels between the building accounts in Nehemiah 1–7 and Ezra 1–6 (note the discussion of "structure" above) and in other suggestive details. Let us look at some examples.

Nehemiah asks of the king: ". . . send me to Judah, to the city of my fathers' sepulchres, that I may rebuild it" (Neh 2:5b). His statement is quite blunt and bold, with no hint of trickery. We must suppose that the king is cognizant of what he had granted, wine and woman notwithstanding, even though present readers, from this distance, may not be fully clear what Nehemiah's request to build the city presumes upon from the king's point of view.[105] The reader is aware of the fact that Artaxerxes had in the past prohibited the building of the city (Ezra 4:21). Propitiously, the last part of that earlier letter left a loophole, anticipating a new decree able to reverse the prohibition. The new letters obtained by Nehemiah (Neh 2:7–9) implicitly utilize that loophole, reverse the earlier decree, and allow the resumption of the work.

Nehemiah's work essentially continues the work on the house of God, commanded by God through Cyrus, extended in light of Ezra 4–6 to encompass the city and the wall, now authorized by Artaxerxes. Work on the house of God is explicitly indicated in Nehemiah's request from Artaxerxes.[106] The gates are the final physical element in Nehemiah's restoration of the house of God (Neh 7:1). The fact that the house of God is being built explains why sanctification is the first step in building the walls. The actual building begins as follows: "Then Eliashib the high priest rose up with his brethren the priests and they built the Sheep Gate. They *consecrated* it [קִדְּשׁוּהוּ] and set its doors; they *consecrated* it [קִדְּשׁוּהוּ] as far as the Tower of the Hundred, as far as the Tower of Hananel" (Neh 3:1).

Several observations about Neh 3:1 are in order. The double reference to consecration is of special importance. Some scholars consider this reference too odd to be correct and emend the text. Rudolph, for example, emends it in light of Neh 3:6, reading קֵרוּהוּ.[107] Myers, likewise translates this as "repaired."[108] L. H. Brockington reads קֵרְשׁוּהוּ.[109] Fensham rightly

---

[105] Ancient Near Eastern writings indicate that city building was a royal prerogative. In that case Nehemiah is arrogating to himself a rather ambitious role. Later accusations (Neh 2:9 and 5:5–7) imply precisely that. Nehemiah's trepidation is therefore quite natural. He risks being suspected of usurping privileges too great.

[106] Nehemiah asks for timber for the "gates of the fortress of the temple, and for the wall of the city and for the house which I shall occupy" (Neh 2:8).

[107] *Esra und Nehemia*, 114.

[108] *Ezra, Nehemiah*, 107

[109] *Ezra, Nehemiah and Esther* (Century Bible, New Series; London: Nelson, 1969) 111. So too Williamson, *Ezra, Nehemiah*, 195 n. 1a).

challenges such emendations (which are not supported by the LXX).[110] But as Clines observes, the references to consecration are nevertheless strange.[111]

The consecration seems less strange when we construe it as a sanctification by the high priest of the project as a whole. This is the first time in Ezra-Nehemiah that the high priest is specifically designated as such. It is not an accident that his credentials are flaunted in connection with the building of the wall. They are emphasized in order to illustrate fully the religious significance of the task.

This religious significance also explains the appointment of singers and Levites to guard the gates of the city (Neh 7:1 and later in 13:22). Here too puzzled scholars resort to emendation of the text in order to eliminate a seemingly nonsensical action. Even Fensham, who cautiously resists emendation elsewhere, comments as follows on this reference:

> Scholars regard these words as a gloss which crept in from vv. 43ff. This is quite probably correct because the appointment of singers and Levites at the gates seems indeed strange. *Singers and Levites were appointed for service at the gates of the temple and not for the gates of the city.*[112]

The reference ceases to be strange when one realizes that for Ezra-Nehemiah the house of God has been expanded as far as the city wall. Therefore those usually assigned to the temple entrance are now appointed to guard the wall.

The reference to the Tower of Hananel in Neh 3:1 is also important. The precise location of this tower is not certain. From Zech 14:10 one gathers that it marks the northernmost point of the wall; no more has been ascertained about it.[113] The Tower of Hananel is mentioned in only a few texts. In addition to Ezra-Nehemiah (Neh 3:1 and 12:39), it recurs in Jer 31:38 and Zech 14:10. In both Jeremiah and Zechariah it appears in texts replete with promises of salvation and eschatological expectations, in the context of final restoration.

---

[110] Fensham comments: "If we accept this emendation, we must also accept that *qiddešûhû* later in this verse is a scribal error. However, two scribal errors of the same word in the same sentence seem unlikely" (*Books of Ezra and Nehemiah*, 173).

[111] "It is strange that the builders should be said here to have *consecrated* it when it is only in 12:27–30 that we read of the consecration of the wall; but perhaps they are different ceremonies (here *qdš*, 'to set apart as holy', whereas in 12:27–30 *hnk*, 'to dedicate', and *thr*, 'to purify'). If we can suppose that this section of the wall also formed part of the temple enclosure, a double consecration may be intelligible; elsewhere, the priests did not 'consecrate' their work (vv. 21f.)" (*Ezra, Nehemiah, Esther*, 131).

[112] *Books of Ezra and Nehemiah*, 209 (emphasis added). Other scholars who hold this view are: Rudolph (*Esra und Nehemia*, 138), Myers (*Ezra, Nehemiah*, 141), and Brockington (*Ezra, Nehemiah and Esther*, 127). See also Clines who writes about the singers and Levites: "Since they have nothing to do with the security of the city, most commentators (and NEB) delete these words as a scribal, or more probably, editorial, gloss (cf. vv. 43ff., where in any case the gatekeepers guard the temple, not the city, gates)" (*Ezra, Nehemiah, Esther*, 178).

[113] So Clines, *Ezra, Nehemiah, Esther*, 150.

In Jeremiah the reference occurs at the end of the "Book of Comfort." The relevant quotation is as follows:

> Behold, the days are coming, says the LORD, when the city shall be rebuilt for the LORD from the tower of Hananel to the Corner gate. And the measuring line shall go out farther, straight to the hill Gareb, and shall then turn to Goah. The whole valley of the dead bodies and ashes, and all the fields as far as the brook Kidron, to the corner of the Horse Gate toward the east, shall be sacred (קֹדֶשׁ) to the LORD. It shall not be uprooted or overthrown any more for ever (Jer 31:38–39).

In Zechariah the reference comes in the final chapter of the book, following (again) "Behold, a day of the LORD is coming, when . . ." (Zech 14:1), in a passage describing peaceful and restored Jerusalem, with almost Edenic associations (Zech 14:8):

> The whole land shall be turned into a plain from Geba to Rimmon south of Jerusalem. But Jerusalem shall remain aloft upon its site from the Gate of Benjamin to the place of the former gate, to the Corner Gate, and from the Tower of Hananel to the king's wine presses. And it shall be inhabited, for there shall be no more curse; Jerusalem shall dwell in security. (Zech 14:10–11)

The chapter, which concludes the book, closes with the extension of altar-like sanctity to every house in Jerusalem and Judah.[114]

Even when we suppose that nothing more than architectural reality accounts for the repeated references to the Tower of Hananel, it remains significant that this reference is always associated with completed restoration. The Tower of Hananel is also mentioned in that context in the dedication and celebration of Neh 12:39. This use, combined with the consecration in Neh 3:1, gathers around it associations and expectations that extend beyond mere architectural information. Such clustering of associations casts the sanctification and the repair or restoration of the Tower of Hananel as the enactment of a larger theological-salvific vision. We may see here one of the ways in which Ezra-Nehemiah understands the fulfillment of the word of Jeremiah (Ezra 1:1). Ezra-Nehemiah is concerned with the actuality of the prophetic word, but translates it into concrete and not eschatological terms. The rebuilding of the wall is one such actuality; it leads to the later sanctification of all that is within its boundaries. The project as a whole has been sanctified. The city as a whole is now guarded by those who previously guarded the temple (Neh 7:1). It is after such completion of the house of God that the city as a whole will be declared holy (Neh 11:1, 18). It is this

---

[114] The final verses are as follows: "And on that day there shall be inscribed on the bells of the horses, 'Holy to the LORD.' And the pots in the house of the LORD shall be as the bowls before the altar; and every pot in Jerusalem and Judah shall be sacred to the LORD of hosts, so that all who sacrifice may come and take of them and boil the flesh of the sacrifice in them. And there shall no longer be a trader in the house of the LORD of hosts on that day" (Zech 14:20–21).

completion that at last fulfills the decree of God and of Cyrus, Darius, and Artaxerxes (Ezra 6:14).[115]

The Documents

This section reiterates the importance of written documents less vigorously than do the sections which precede and follow. The heading in the form of superscription, "The words of Nehemiah son of Hacaliah" (Neh 1:1a), indicates that what follows is a document.[116] The section closes by pointing to yet another document which Nehemiah reproduces in order to determine present population procedures (Neh 7:5). The perpetuation of documents thus persists in this movement. In between these markers we find documents emphasized in Nehemiah's request for letters from the king, and the use of letters in the conflict with opponents.

Nehemiah, having been granted permission to build, boldly requests that the king's words be transcribed into letters (Neh 2:7–8a). Nehemiah's interaction with opponents also takes place through letters. Sanballat, in his attempt to ensnare Nehemiah (according to Nehemiah's assessment of the motive), sends letters. "In the same way Sanballat for the fifth time sent his servant to me with an open letter in his hand. In it was written, 'It is reported among the nations, and Geshem also says it, that you and the Jews intend to rebel . . .'" (Neh 6:5–6a). The interaction with other opponents also takes the form of letters:

> . . . the nobles of Judah sent many letters to Tobiah, and Tobiah's letters came to them. For many in Judah were bound by oath to him, because he was the son-in-law of Shecaniah. . . . Also they spoke of his good deeds in my presence, and reported my words to him. And Tobiah sent letters to make me afraid (Neh 6:17–19).

The most significant use of documents in this section occurs at the conclusion, when Nehemiah resorts to a written document in order to resolve the population problem. One reads, "Then God put it into my mind to assemble the nobles and the officials and the people to be enrolled by genealogy. And I found the book of the genealogy [ספר היחש] of those who came up at the first, and I found written in it. . . . " (Neh 7:5) The following section, Neh 7:6–72, reproduces the document in toto. Here the prescription for settling the rebuilt city requires a document to which Nehemiah turns. Just as Cyrus's decree was recalled earlier to provide a model and authority

---

[115] We are now in a position to understand Josephus's version of Nehemiah's activities. According to Josephus Nehemiah asks the king: ". . . permit me to go there and raise up the wall and complete the building that remains to be done on the temple" (*Ant.* XI.v.6). Nehemiah 1–7 suggests that Nehemiah and the Judeans have completed the house of God.

[116] As G. M. Tucker points out, superscriptions presuppose that the words "have already been committed to writing" ("Prophetic Superscriptions and the Growth of a Canon," *Canon and Authority* [ed. G. W. Coats and B. O. Long; Philadelphia: Fortress, 1977] 65–66).

(Ezra 5:13–6:5), so now the "book of genealogy" is recalled as a "voice" from the past to guide the present. It prepares the restored community for the celebration of its completed house of God.

E. Recapitulation: The List of Returnees (Neh 7:6–72)

This section constitutes one of the most striking aspects of Ezra-Nehemiah and its major repetition. This written list (note: "I found written in it," Neh 7:5b), recapitulating the names of the returnees, is practically identical with Ezra 2. The resumptive repetition of Ezra 2 in Nehemiah 7 clamps together everything and everyone in between, i.e., the earlier movements and characters from Ezra 2 to Nehemiah 7. The repetition welds diverse groups into a unity, into עם, a "people." This document also effects a unity of past events with the present via the written mode. Previous generations become partners in present events through this document.

Structure

1. The names of returnees (Neh 7:6–60)
   a. Heading (7:6–7a)
   b. Israelites (7:7b–38)
   c. Priests (7:39–42)
   d. Levites (7:43)
   e. Singers and gatekeepers (7:44–45)
   f. Cult personnel (7:46–60)
      1) *Netinim* (7:46–56)
      2) Solomon's servants (7:57–59)
      3) Summary (7:60)
2. Conflict and resolution: problem ascertaining membership (7:61–65)
3. Summary of returnees (7:66–68)
4. Report of contributions (7:69–71)
5. Conclusion (7:72)

The list of returnees is the major structuring device of Ezra-Nehemiah. The three movements of the return and reconstruction are held together internally through the linchpin of Ezra 6:14 and externally through the repetition of the list of returnees in Ezra 2 and Nehemiah 7. The list reiterates, both formally and thematically, the major concerns of the book. The formal aspect is reflected in the repetition that unifies the movements, articulating their confluence into a decisive entity known as עם. The thematic aspect is expressed through the content of the repetition and in the specific manner in which the list is embedded into its context.

Three steps help discern the full implications of this list. First, one must examine the content of the list (especially as it pertains to the thesis of this work). Second, it is necessary to look at what this section accomplishes by virtue of being a repetition. Third, it is necessary to analyze how the list is embedded in the present context and what this entails in terms of its meaning and function.

The first step can be brief, since the list's content has already been discussed in connection with Ezra 2. The list of returnees focuses on people, recording them according to class, families, geography and numbers, and occasionally by profession. It includes a wide range of categories of persons who now form the people of Israel and who have returned to their home. The list is headed by twelve men, their number presumably reflects a new configuration to retain, in symbolic fashion, the earlier twelve-tribe division. The emphasis on people expresses vividly the book's emphasis on the centrality of the community as a whole. The list also briefly mentions the earliest activities of the returnees. The community's action concerning the house of God reflects the book's preoccupation with the house of God. The list itself is a written document, recalled by Nehemiah in order to solve a problem. In this sense the list reiterates the book's emphasis on documents.

The second step requires some discussion of the ways repetitions function in narrative. The list of returnees in Nehemiah 7, which closely parallels Ezra 2, constitutes the most striking repetition in the book of Ezra-Nehemiah. This repetition is one of the most distinctive aspects of the book. For scholars who rely on literary-source criticism, repetitions most often signal insertions; they become occasions for dissecting the text and distributing its components to different sources rather than potential clues for apprehending the text's present meaning. This approach characterizes most studies of Ezra-Nehemiah, even when undertaken by scholars who have applied new literary tools to other biblical works. As a result, Ezra-Nehemiah's most outstanding repetition typically turns into evidence for the initial independence of the books of Ezra and Nehemiah. Talmon's view is representative: "If indeed Ezra and Nehemiah at one time were two separate works written by different authors, this could help in explaining the duplication of some events and the literary units in both, such as the list of returning exiles (Ezra 2 = Nehemiah 7)."[117]

According to contemporary literary criticism, however, repetitions are significant vehicles for the text's intention. Recent literary studies confirm, and amply demonstrate, the ingenious and sophisticated use of repetition in biblical narrative in particular to convey meaning.[118] Contemporary literary criticism, consequently, invites us to consider this dramatic and weighty

---

[117] "Ezra and Nehemiah (Books and Men)," 318. Elsewhere historical and textual questions and implications preeminently occupy discussions of these lists. See, for example, Galling, "The 'Gola List' According to Ezra 2//Nehemiah 7," and Klein, "Old Readings in 1 Esdras."

[118] See Alter, *Art of Biblical Narrative*, 88–113; Sternberg, *Poetics of Biblical Narrative*, 365–440.

repetition of the list of returnees in terms of its significance for the book's overall intention. Repetition in literature serves no single function.[119] One cannot, therefore, apply an automatic or mechanical interpretation to this particular repetition. Specific meanings have to be teased out. One thing can be asserted with confidence: the list, by virtue of being an overt and major repetition, is important as a distinctive *literary* strategy. It articulates, thereby, something central to the book as a whole. Our task is to determine what this might be. I identify at least six important points that the repetition of the lists articulates.

First, structurally speaking, repetition as an inclusio unifies material.[120] Inclusio, like chiasm, constitutes one of the major devices for defining units in ancient literature. As H. Van Dyke Parunak observes, "An inclusio is a three-membered (A B A) chiasm whose outer members are short, compared with the center member."[121] As an inclusio, as well as a chiasm, repetition signals conclusion of a unit.[122] The weighty repetition of the list in Ezra-Nehemiah, as a literary technique, defines the structure of the narrative. It establishes boundaries and compresses all the material that has been "bracketed" within the repetition. The repetition of the list frames the intervening material, binding it more closely together, forming a unit from Ezra 2 to Nehemiah 7.

The vise of the two lists compresses the three movements of restoration into a unity and establishes their relationship. Each movement retains its own distinctive population and accomplishments: the first movement rebuilds the temple; the second movement, with Ezra, brings the Torah, refurbishes the house of God, and purifies the community; the third movement of Nehemiah and the Judeans builds the wall. The three movements, three groups, and three tasks are now joined and made to flow together into the next stage. It is no mere accident that Neh 8:1 reports, for the first time in Ezra-Nehemiah, that "*all* the people gathered as *one*." This "all" indicates the efforts and participation of all who preceded this gathering; it encompasses, in particular, all who are embraced within the repeated lists.

---

[119] See J. H. Miller, *Fiction and Repetition* (Cambridge: Harvard University Press, 1982), esp. pp. 1–21.

[120] See H. V. D. Parunak, "Oral Typesetting: Some Uses of Biblical Structure," *Bib* 62 (1981), esp. p. 158 n. 8. Parunak later adds: "The notion of the inclusio as a segmenting device has been discussed extensively in the literature. The more important works are listed in B. Porten, 'The Structure and Theme of the Solomon Narrative (I Kings 3–11)', *HUCA* 38 (1967) 94 note 2" (ibid., 158 n. 9).

[121] Ibid., 158.

[122] Ibid., 158. See also p. 168. Parunak calls attention to the fact that repetition can not only mark a unit but also indicate secondary material (158–161). He therefore distinguishes between what he calls internal and external inclusios and develops guidelines for differentiating between the two. Ezra 2 through Nehemiah 7 clearly fits the definition of demarcated unit rather than peripheral material.

Second, repetition indicates emphasis. Repetitions most frequently occur in order to stress something important. Biblical narrative, as well as other ancient and modern literature, characteristically repeats ideas, information or phrases that are significant (note the repeated stories of creation and the ten commandments, etc.). In Ezra-Nehemiah, the repetition then emphasizes the significance of the persons named in the lists. The repetition keeps numerous persons and names firmly before the readers' eyes, drawing attention to the multitude that constitutes the people of Israel. Josephus, as *via negativa*, helps us appreciate the import of the lists and of their repetition. His own account of the return omits the list of returnees with the following rationale: "But I have thought it better not to give a list of the names of the families lest I distract the minds of my readers from the connexion of events and make the narrative difficult for them to follow" (*Ant.* XI.iii. 10).

The difference from Ezra-Nehemiah's strategy could not be more telling. Josephus, in a rush to continue his main story line, refuses to linger on what for him comprise the less important details, i.e., the lists. Ezra-Nehemiah, however, keeps the readers' mind *precisely* on such lists because they are the bearers of the narrative line. It is the names in this duplicated list (and other such lists) that disclose the characters whose adventures are recounted. For Ezra-Nehemiah, the people, not simply their illustrious leaders, are the main characters in the book. By repeating, the book underscores this point, emphasizing the role of the people as a whole.

Third, as an emphasis on the people as a whole, the list also expresses Ezra-Nehemiah's view as to the wholeness of the people. Chronicles, by way of contrast, assumes the twelve-tribe schema for Israel even after the demise of the northern kingdom. Consequently, Chronicles includes members of the northern tribes in the return (e.g. 1 Chr 9:3). Ezra-Nehemiah offers a different notion as to who Israel is. For Ezra-Nehemiah, as Japhet, for example, has shown,[123] only the returned exiles now constitute Israel. These comprise the Judeans, Benjaminites, priests and Levites (Ezra 1:5). By enumerating the composition of the people twice, Ezra-Nehemiah stresses the nature of this reconstituted community and continuity with the early return.[124]

Fourth, the repetition bridges past and present. Talmon has shown that resumptive repetition can convey contemporaneity of events.[125] Something akin to this happens here. The repetition of Ezra 2 and Nehemiah 7 links people and events of the past with those in the present. Nehemiah 7 literally brings the earlier returnees into the present and combines them as participants in the subsequent event(s): namely, celebration and dedication. All that

---

[123] "People and Land in the Restoration Period," 112–8; so too Williamson, *Ezra, Nehemiah*, 32.

[124] See also Gunneweg, "Zur Interpretation der Bücher Esra-Nehemia," 156.

[125] "The Presentation of Synchroneity and Simultaneity in Biblical Narrative," *Scripta Hierosolymitana* 28 (1978), esp. p. 17.

transpired between the "brackets" (i.e., the two lists) now joins with what follows. The structure suggests that all the groups have had a specific role in the "process of actualization." All the people thereby gather together to celebrate "success." Just as the later rabbis saw "all Israel" standing at Sinai, including all those who followed since Moses, so Ezra-Nehemiah, by repeating Ezra 2 in Nehemiah 7, makes all those who preceded take part in the ensuing celebration of the reading of the Torah and the dedication of the walls, i.e., in the completion of the house of God and its dedication. Celebration waits until such conjoining takes place. The list at this juncture not only stresses the importance of the people as a whole but also unites them in time and place.

Fifth, the repetition suggests the broadening of communal participation. This meaning can be gathered from looking at differences in details, since repetition sometimes draws attention to important differences by establishing an initial commonality followed by variations.[126] One detects within the lists slight differences in names and numbers which are most easily explained as textual corruptions.[127] The more obvious difference concerns the reports of the initial activities in the land (Ezra 2:68-9; Neh 7:69-71). These differences include variant details of who did what, and who contributed what. The amount of contributions differs. The most dramatic differences are the priests' garments and gold darics.[128] As for the contributors, Ezra 2 mentions only "some of the heads of families" (Ezra 2:68) whereas Nehemiah 7 mentions the heads of the ancestors' houses, the governor, but also *the rest of the people* (Neh 7:71). The rest of the people contribute as much as the heads of the houses and much more than the governor.[129] Galling explains these variations on the basis of historical issues,[130] whereas Japhet grounds them in ideology.[131] From our perspective, one may conclude that the differences cited express in Nehemiah 7 the broader participation of the populace in the task of building.[132] Not only are the leaders involved but the people as a whole make substantial contribution.

Sixth, and more speculative, interpretation of the repetition implies that the list sets equivalencies between Torah reading and sacrifices. This

---

[126] See Berlin, *Poetics and Interpretation*, 76-79.

[127] See Klein, "Old Readings in 1 Esdras."

[128] There are 597 priests' garments in Nehemiah 7, against 100 in Ezra 2; 41,000 gold darics in Nehemiah 7 against 61,000 in Ezra 2.

[129] Unless the priestly garments were valued in 10,000 gold darics (which seems unlikely), the governor's contribution is the smallest. That of the heads of the ancestors' houses and that of the rest of the people appear to be comparable. The numbers themselves are large and imply a great deal of wealth being contributed to the project.

[130] "The 'Gola List' According to Ezra 2//Nehemiah 7."

[131] "People and Land in the Restoration Period," 112 and 123 n. 46.

[132] See Clines, *Ezra, Nehemiah, Esther*, 60-61 for an interesting attempt to reconcile these numbers.

interpretation is based on the recognition that repetitions establish at times analogies, equivalencies, or substitutions between those things that follow, to which the repetition points.[133] Ezra 2 immediately leads to the building of the altar and to worship. Nehemiah 7 directly leads to the ceremony of the reading of the Torah. This arrangement suggests a relation between altar building and Torah reading. One could postulate that here we find an earlier version of a view that later becomes normative, i.e., that the study of Torah replaces the offering of sacrifices. Such a conclusion is attractive all the more when one notes how rare and briskly reported are the sacrifices in Ezra-Nehemiah, especially after Nehemiah 8. The idea is indirectly supported by the location of the reading of the Torah in Nehemiah 8. As H. L. Ellison has suggested, "In the choice of site we have Ezra's deliberate proclamation that the Torah was greater than the Temple and its sacrifices, indeed that the Torah as such was above anything it might contain."[134] This use of the repetition to replace cult with Torah is too subtle, however, to constitute a major focus. At best one can argue for a beginning of such analogies and possible shift in cultic orientation which later generations utilized.

The third step in elucidating the list entails looking at the ways the list of Nehemiah 7 is embedded in its context. The seams which bind Nehemiah 7 to its surrounding reveal the confluence of the preceding (unified) material through the list.

Traditional assessment of the list in Nehemiah 7 in relation to its context usually focuses on questions of priority vis-à-vis Ezra 2. The seemingly tight connection in Nehemiah 7 is generally used to argue that Nehemiah 7 is prior to Ezra 2.[135] On the other hand, Kellermann argues for a closer integrity of Ezra 2 with its context, and grants therefore priority to Ezra 2.[136]

---

[133] See, e.g., Sternberg's discussion of "Repetition with Variation: Forms and Functions of Deviance," *Poetics of Biblical Narrative*, pp. 390–393.

[134] *From Babylon to Bethlehem* (Atlanta: John Knox, 1979) 47.

[135] Clines's view is representative of this position: "Which, then, is its original place: Ezr. 2 or Neh. 7? In Neh 7, the concluding verse (73b) [Heb: 72b] is followed naturally by 8:1; but the same verse, with slight variations in Ezra (3:1), is not well suited to the context: in the book of Nehemiah as it stands 'the seventh month' belongs to a stated year (445/4 BC.), but in Ezra there is no indication of the year. It would therefore appear that in Ezr. 2 the editor has copied the list, together with the linking final verse, from its place in the Nehemiah memoirs" (*Ezra, Nehemiah, Esther*, 44–45).

[136] Having excluded the likelihood that both lists go back to a common source, and concluding therefore that one depends on the other, Kellermann resolves the question of priority in this fashion: "Meine Entscheidung fällt für Esr 2:80 im ehron Zusammenhang Esr 1–6;90, denn die erzählende Schlußnotiz über die Niederlassung der Gola im Lande (Neh 7:72 Esr 2:70), die wegen des Impf. cons. וישבו kaum zur Liste gehört haben kann, ist allein im Zusammenhang der ersten Heimkehr sinnvoll. Der Chron kann dort das Ereignis der Heimkehr in seiner großen Bedeutung für die Kultgemeinde und ihre Reinheit nicht mit einem Nebensatz wie Esr 1:11b abgetan haben. Die Notiz über die Volksversammlung in Jerusalem Esr 3:1 setzt eine entsprechende über die Niederlassung der Heimkehrer, d. h. aber den Text Esr 2:1, 70 voraus. Esr 3:9a könnte auf Esr 2:40 zurückverweisen. Mit der Priorität von Esr 2 innerhalb des

Such inconclusive debates, which mix historical and literary questions, serve to illustrate the complexities and ambiguities in the text. They reveal, in this particular case, that both Ezra 2 and Nehemiah 7 are in some respects well integrated into their respective contexts and that, in others, they stand apart from their surrounding.

The list in Nehemiah 7 is especially perplexing. The beginning of the list is clear. Nehemiah reports: "Then God put it into my mind to assemble the nobles and the officials and the people to be enrolled by genealogy. And I found the book of the genealogy of those who came up at the first, and I found written in it" (Neh 7:5). The phrase, "and I found written in it" (וָאֶמְצָא כָּתוּב בּוֹ) is an unambiguous clue that what follows is a quoted document. The conclusion of the quotation, however, is obscure. There are no indications that one thing has ended and another one has begun. The shift from the quoted document about the past to the report about later events is so subtle that scholars break the units in different ways, often concluding with Neh 7:72a. Neh 7:72b becomes attached to the subsequent chapter (e.g., the RSV, where Neh 7:73b, which translates the MT Neh 7:72b, is printed with the next paragraph).

No formulaic language or any other literary markings indicate the conclusion of the unit. The last identified speaker/writer was Nehemiah (Neh 7:5). One would have expected him to resume once his quotation concluded, possibly in Neh 7:72. Yet it is not self evident where the list does conclude. One cannot immediately determine whether the report about the gathering on the first day of the first month belongs still to the document which has been introduced and quoted, i.e., the book of genealogy, or whether it is a resumption of Nehemiah's own memoirs. Only further reading yields the necessary conclusion that *neither* is the case. The reference to Ezra in Neh 8:2 indicates that the scene belongs to the more recent time, in the reign of Artaxerxes, wherein all subsequent events transpire.[137] This confirms the view that Nehemiah's quotation of the older document had come to conclusion at an earlier point.

One might seek to argue that Nehemiah has resumed his memoirs, somewhere before Neh 8:2. However, the reference to Nehemiah in the third

---

chron Werkes ist die ursprüngliche Zugehörigkeit von Neh 7:6–72 zu der zeitlich früheren NQ [Nehemia Quellen] ausgeschlossen, denn eine Wiederholung dieses Protokolles durch den Chron läßt sich kaum vorstellen" (*Nehemia*, 25).

[137] The exact date is obscure. If Neh 7:72b belongs to the subsequent assembly, then the date appears to be the seventh month of the twentieth year of Artaxerxes (see Neh 6:15). But Nehemiah 13 frustrates the attempt to accept this date by its repeated references to "that day," which refer, in their present context, to the celebration of the dedication of the walls. It also mentions, however, Nehemiah's activities after his return at least twelve years later (Neh 13:6). Perhaps all that we can conclude from this is that the book is not interested in ascertaining this date in its vertical dimension but prefers to focus on the cyclical dimension of the ritual season.

person (Neh 8:9) implies that the depicted episode in Neh 8:2–12 cannot be an entry in Nehemiah's memoirs. A definite transition occurs between Nehemiah 7 and 8, but the exact location of that transition is unclear. The customary scholarly designation of Nehemiah 8 as part of the Ezra material acknowledges the transition. The arrangement in 1 Esdras, where the parallels to Nehemiah 8 follow the parallel to Ezra 10, indicates to many scholars that this material has been dislodged from its original position, which was initially after Ezra 10.[138]

What is striking in the relation of Nehemiah 7 and Nehemiah 8 is the remarkable *seamlessness* of this particular transition. Such seamlessness is all the more astonishing in a book so rife with obvious seams. It is at this juncture that "confluence" appears as the most apt description. A probable explanation of this peculiar confluence of the texts — peculiar all the more in view of Ezra-Nehemiah's rough transitions elsewhere — is that it expresses syntactically what is also expressed through the repetition: the confluence of persons and events embraced in the preceding section into the present event of Nehemiah 8–12. Like a funnel through which sand flows, so does Nehemiah 7 channel persons and events from Ezra 2 through Nehemiah 7 into the final celebration which comes next to conclude the book.

III. Success (Objective Reached):
The Community Celebrates the Completion of the
House of God According to Torah (Neh 8:1–13:31)

The confluence of the movements leads to celebration of success by the united people. The objective has been reached. The community completed the house of God in full accordance with Yahweh's command and the Persian edicts. All roads have led to this. What began at different times and different places, with different people, now converges in Jerusalem. The movements come togther, flow into a grand symphonic finale, replaying the individual motifs and instruments of earlier movements in a fullness of polyphonic orchestration.

The structure of the finale is as follows:

A. Consolidation according to Torah (Neh 8:1–10:40)
B. Recapitulation: lists of participants (11:1–12:26)
C. Dedication of the house of God (Neh 12:27–13:3)
D. Coda (Neh 13:4–31)

The very first line opens on the note of a (finally) united people: "And all the people gathered as one man into the square before the Water Gate;

---

[138] See Pohlmann, *Studien zum dritten Esra*, 127–143 for a thorough discussion of this point; cf. Williamson's critique in *Israel in the Books of Chronicles*, 22–25.

and they told Ezra the scribe to bring the book of the law of Moses which the LORD had given to Israel" (Neh 8:1). For the very first time in Ezra-Nehemiah *all* the people gather *as one man.* The united community begins the celebration of its success with the rigorous implementation of the Torah (Neh 8:1–10:40), dedicating itself fully prior to dedicating the stone walls. Final preparations (Neh 11:1–12:26) include the recapitulation of names and the accounting of settlers, linking the present with the book's beginning (cf. Neh 12:1 and Ezra 2:1). The dedication ceremony itself (Neh 12:27–13:3) is marked by the purification of walls and people and unmitigated joy. The book closes with a coda (Neh 13:4–31).

A. *Consolidation According to Torah (Neh 8:1–10:40)*

The celebration of success begins with the rededication of the people themselves to the Torah and to the house of their God. Nehemiah 8 places the book of the Torah (literally) at the center of a united people who proceed to implement the Torah. This section shows how the written text governs communal life, generating action, celebration, commitment to the house of God, and leading to the emergence of yet another document.

Structure
1. First reading and implementation of Torah (Neh 8:1–12) [third-person report]
   a. Assembly (8:1–3)
   b. Reading of Torah (8:4–8)
   c. Implementation: celebration not lamentation (8:9–12)
      1) Instructions to people (8:9–11)
      2) Celebration by all the people (8:12)
2. Second reading and implementation of Torah (8:13–18)
   a. Assembly around Ezra and Torah (8:13)
   b. Reading (8:14–15)
   c. Implementation: celebration of Succoth (8:16–18)
      1) Celebration of Succoth (8:16–17)
      2) Daily reading of Torah (8:18)
3. Third reading and implementation of Torah (9:1–37)
   a. Assembly (9:1–2)
   b. Reading (9:3)
   c. Implementation: the great prayer (9:4–37)
      1) Preparations (9:4–5a)
      2) The great prayer (9:5b–37)
4. The result: a *written* pledge to Torah and house of God by community (10:1–40)
   a. List of participants (10:1–29)
      1) Heading (10:1)

2) List of participating signatories (10:2–28)
3) Summary of the rest of the people (10:29)
    b. List of commitments to the Torah and house of God
    (10:30–40)

The section elaborates on three assemblies (note the repetition of אסף, "gather" in Neh 8:1, 8:13, 9:1, beginning each unit) in which the reading of the Torah takes place (Neh 8:1, 8:13–14, 9:3). It concludes, in the fourth part, by reproducing a *written* pledge (Neh 10:1) by all the people (Neh 10:1–29) to observe the Torah (Neh 10:30b), with detailed obligations for the house of God (Neh 10:31–40). There is an incremental progression, with an ever intensifying display of commitment by the community. These units, linked through enchainment, function both as the culmination of what preceded and as a necessary prelude to declaring of city holy (Neh 11:1).

The People

Intense emphasis on the people as a whole marks the opening scene (Neh 8:1–12) and sets the tone for the rest of the book. The people remain unequivocally in the foreground to the end of the book, except in the Coda. The word עם, "people," occurs thirteen times in the first twelve verses.[139] The expression *"all* the people" occurs nine times in these verses.[140] Each reference describes the people as actors or subject. Such density of repetition has no parallels in Ezra-Nehemiah. This emphasis on the people united as one comes only with the confluence of the three movements and reflects the importance of their convergence. "A people" means "those who together form an entity, a whole, and whose members are united by 'fellow-feeling' as brothers and comrades."[141] In Ezra-Nehemiah this entity is most fully actualized when the three distinct movements have been combined.

The people gather at no one's coaxing (Neh 8:1). No leader declares an assembly. The book implies a spontaneous ingathering of the community. The people instruct Ezra to bring the book of the Torah. They, not Ezra, initiate the action and remain the central actors in what follows. Ezra is at the people's service, helping them satisfy their eager interest in the Torah. The public reading of the Torah, initiated by the people, includes all members of the community: men, women, and children.[142] They are attentive (Neh 8:3) and responsive (Neh 8:6, 9). They are the subject of the first

---

[139] The thirteen references to people are: Neh 8:1, 3, 5 (3 times), 6, 7 (twice), 9 (3 times), 11, 12.

[140] These nine references are: Neh 8:1, 3, 5 (twice), 6, 9 (twice), 11, 12.

[141] R. B. Y. Scott, *The Relevance of the Prophets* (Rev. ed., London: Macmillan, 1968) 24–25.

[142] According to Williamson, Ezra chose to read the Torah "in an easily accessible public place away from the sacred precincts of the temple, so that none might be barred from attending, and to associate laymen with him in the whole enterprise (v 4)" (*Ezra-Nehemiah*, 297).

line and last line of the first scene; the section ends with their celebration (Neh 8:12).

Ezra-Nehemiah's emphasis on the community in this section manifests itself not solely in this manifold repetition of "people" and "all the people," but also in the actual depiction of the leaders: as soon as the single, outstanding leader emerges at the behest of the community, he quickly gives way to a plurality of leaders, then vanishes, letting the community carry on the task.

The most prominent leader is Ezra who embodies here, as elsewhere, a brand of leadership that enhances the role of the community. Ezra, having been summoned by the people (Neh 8:1b), immediately surrounds himself with coworkers. The full identity of Ezra's companions is not clear even though we have their names. Williamson, who argues that these persons are probably laymen, concludes:

> If these deductions are correct, the fact that Ezra chose members of the laity to assist him with the reading will be highly significant. Coupled with the choice of location (see *Comment* on v 1), Ezra was boldly proclaiming that the Torah was for all the people, not just for a few privileged by either birth or particular ability.[143]

These people and/or the Levites read and instruct the people with Ezra, as the plural verb ויקראו, "and they read," (Neh 8:8) shows. A multiplicity of leaders issues instructions to the people in Neh 8:9. The passage begins with a singular verb, ויאמר, "and he said" (Neh 8:9a), followed by several names as subjects of the verb: "Nehemiah, who was the governor, and Ezra the priest and scribe, and the Levites who taught the people said [ויאמר] to all the people . . ." (Neh 8:9; see also ויאמר, "and he said," for a plural subject in Neh 8:10).

The awkward syntax and the variants in the LXX and 1 Esdras have led some scholars to conclude that much in Neh 8:9 in the MT is an insertion.[144] Two things, however, can be said in favor of the MT at this point. First, the use of plural subject with singular verb is not impossible in Biblical Hebrew, and common in Ezra-Nehemiah;[145] it recurs in Neh 9:4 as well. Second, the

---

[143] *Ezra, Nehemiah*, 289.

[144] The LXX mentions Nehemiah in this place without "the governor"; 1 Esdr 9:49 has "the governor" without naming Nehemiah (see also 1 Esdras 5:40, where Nehemiah and the governor are differentiated). Insertion is supposed by Rudolph (*Esra und Nehemia*, 148), In der Smitten (*Esra*, 43), Clines (*Ezra, Nehemiah, Esther,* 185), and Ackroyd (*I & II Chronicles, Ezra, Nehemiah,* 296). Fensham, however, differs: "From this we may deduce that at an early stage the name Nehemiah occurred in the Hebrew text. In spite of the difficulty with the singular of the verb, we take the position that both Nehemiah and Ezra are mentioned in this text and that not enough textual-critical evidence can be presented to delete either name" (*Books of Ezra and Nehemiah,* 218).

[145] Cf. e.g., C. Brockelmann, *Hebräische Syntax,* (Neukirchen, 1956) 5 [cited by Fensham, *Books of Ezra and Nehemiah,* 218 n. 23]. Note also Williamson's comment (on Ezra 4:7): "a sg verb before a multiple subject is common in these books" (*Ezra, Nehemiah,* 54 n. 7b).

deliberate association of the activities of Ezra and Nehemiah, whatever their historical relation, is fundamental to the *present* structure of the Ezra-Nehemiah. This is the purpose of the persistent interspersing of the work and words of the one with those of the other.[146] Consequently, the naming of both figures in such an important occasion is not extrinsic but intrinsic to the book.[147] As the passage stands in the MT, it expresses a unity of leadership. Ezra-Nehemiah is at pains to show that Ezra and Nehemiah, despite their different tasks and different "clientele," different movements and different history, nevertheless combine their effort in this momentous gathering. Both of them issue instructions in one voice, as it were (Neh 8:9). Both will later parade. Each has an inextricable part in the other's life's work.

From named leaders and their cohorts (Neh 8:9), leadership shifts to the Levites who speak next—alone this time (Neh 8:11). Ezra and Nehemiah are left out from these latter instructions. A delegation of power from the singular to the plural appears to have transpired.

The second-day reading (Neh 8:13–18), like the first, begins with a gathering, but of a smaller group who comes to "Ezra the scribe" (i.e., Ezra in his scribal capacity) to learn Torah (Neh 8:13). The section provides an important glimpse into the process wherein the Torah replaces the individual leader. The narrator reports that "they found it written in the law . . ." (Neh 8:14). The "they" refers to "the heads of fathers' houses of all the people, with the priests and the Levites" (Neh 8:13) who have come to Ezra to become enlightened. The text does not say, "Ezra told them," nor "Ezra showed them," but states that *they* themselves now find the commandments in the Torah. Much to one's amazement, Ezra has disappeared, giving way to the book. The people themselves immediately execute the written injunction which they found and joyfully celebrate Succoth. Again, the initiative has come from the people themselves; the results—finding the commandment and carrying it out—are likewise enacted by the people.

This second implementation of the Torah closes with the statement: "And day by day, from the first day to the last day, he read from the book of the law of God. They kept the feast seven days . . ." (Neh 8:18). The singular verb וַיִּקְרָא, "he read," without an immediately identifiable subject, has led many scholars to insert Ezra's name, even though such textual emendation is not supported even by the LXX. The MT, however, implies that Ezra has accomplished his task and then vanished, leaving the

---

[146] See also Childs, *Introduction to the Old Testament*, 635.

[147] The variation in 1 Esdr 9:49 can be easily understood in light of that book's overall tendencies. By only mentioning the governor, without a name, the book allows the reader to suppose that the person intended is the last named governor, i.e., Zerubbabel. The separation between governor and Nehemiah in 1 Esdr 5:40 likewise expresses 1 Esdras' emphasis on Zerubbabel as *the* governor.

community holding the book, as it were.[148]

The third assembly (Neh 9:1–37) also involves a reading of the Torah (Neh 9:2b–3a).[149] The initiative, once more, rests with members of the community and not with a leading individual. Moreover, as the ceremony progresses, no single individual rises up to conduct it. The people remain the subject of the verbs, as they have been in the two previous units. They stand up, they confess, they read the Torah. Only then do certain Levites rise up to what approximates a leadership role. One notes that they do so jointly.[150] Again, the plural subject has a singular verb. וַיָּקָם, "he rose" is followed by the plural subject of several Levites in Neh 9:4, implying here, as in each of the previous units, a unison of voices. Ezra himself is not named in MT Nehemiah 9.

A lengthy prayer, Neh 9:5b–37, dominates this section and constitutes a third implementation of Torah. The shift into the prayer in the MT obscures the identity of the speakers, who could be either the Levites or the people as a whole.[151] The exhortation by the Levites to bless (Neh 9:5), and the pattern of antiphonal recitation in the earlier gatherings (Ezra 3:11; Neh 8:5–7), together with the emphatic identification of the community in the attached pledge (Neh 10:1), imply that the speakers of the prayer are the whole community.[152]

The ceremony represents, as Clines says, "a popular reaction to the reading of the law, not a service conducted by Ezra."[153] The prayer itself articulates the centrality of the community in several decisive ways. First, the fact that this longest prayer in the book comes from the community grants the people the most prominent voice. Second, the community's role is highighted within the prayer itself in that this recitation of Israel's history focuses on the community, not on some famous leaders. Only Abraham is named. The formative events in Israel's life, such as the Exodus and Sinai, are envisioned as encounters between God and Israel, without reference to

[148] The singular verb with plural subject may reflect here, as it most probably does in Neh 8:9, a unity.

[149] It occurs on the 24th day of the month. Note how "that month" (Neh 9:1) links this to the preceding chapter. Indeed, the section Nehemiah 8–10 is tightly held together.

[150] One also notes that several of these Levites have been Ezra's partners in the first reading (Neh 8:4, 7).

[151] The LXX specifies Ezra as the speaker of the prayer. Many scholars and translations follow the LXX. See, for example, Ezra 9:6 in the RSV. The correct location of this prayer is disputed. Some scholars place it immediately after Ezra 10, or after Ezra 9. See Myers, *Ezra, Nehemiah*, 165–166, and Fensham, *Books of Ezra and Nehemiah*, 222–223 for an outline of the major views.

[152] This is clearly the case in Neh 10:1, which speaks of "our princes, our Levites, and our priests." Myers associates the prayer with Chronicles, calling it a favorite method of the Chronicler, pointing to David's prayer (1 Chr 29:10–19) and Jehoshaphat's (2 Chr 20:6–15) (*Ezra, Nehemiah*, 166). Chronicles, however, places prayer in the mouth of individual leaders, usually kings. Ezra-Nehemiah's most impressive prayer, on the other hand, is spoken by the community.

[153] *Ezra, Nehemiah, Esther*, 189–190.

famous men, not even Moses.[154] Third, the breadth of knowledge of Israel's traditions that the prayer exhibits speaks well for the chanting community. As Myers observes, "The author of our prayer psalm drew upon a wide knowledge of the theology and traditions of his people, skillfully weaving into it elements of instruction, exhortation, and confession."[155] Such breadth of knowledge testifies loudly that the people have learned well from their teacher. Having learned Torah, having read the book of the Torah (Neh 9:3), the people demonstrate a new competence, a new understanding of what they have read, and prove able to translate these into commitment and action. This recitation of the people's history, meaningfully aware of the relationship between God and Israel, is also, thereby, another example of implementing the Torah.

The fourth unit (Neh 10:1–40) reproduces a written pledge by the community, in which the community as a whole vows to follow the Torah. As the community's response to (stressed by וּבְכָל זאת, "because of all this," [10:1]) and rectification of a history of violations (acknowledged in Nehemiah 9), the pledge becomes yet another facet of having learned Torah well. The pledge, like the prayer, brings the primacy of the community to the fore in a variety of complementary ways. The literary setting of the pledge, the nature of the pledge as an interpretive process of Torah, the dynamics of this event as a covenant ceremony, and the details of the list of participants—all contribute to make the community the central and decisive actor. Each of these ways needs to be examined in greater detail.

Scholars dispute over the original setting of the pledge but usually concur that this chapter is dislocated.[156] Clines would place this chapter after Nehemiah 13, stating: "There can be little doubt ... that these halakot are *ad hoc* responses to problems encountered by Nehemiah in his so-called second governorship; for all the items except the sabbatical and remission year correspond to elements of Nehemiah 13. . . ."[157] Ezra-Nehemiah, however, presents the reforms as neither Ezra's nor Nehemiah's but as the spontaneous response of a repentant community. The particular setting of the pledge thereby subsumes the implementations by Nehemiah to the prior communal decision. In Ezra-Nehemiah, the community formulates

---

[154] The absence of the temple and David constitutes an important difference from Chronicles. See Fensham, *Books of Ezra and Nehemiah*, 230, esp. n. 9.

[155] Myers, *Ezra, Nehemiah*, 169–170. No single source can account for this seeming patchwork of biblical quotations. Myers lists numerous parallels to other books, showing that they reflect the prayer's affinity with wide ranging material in the Bible.

[156] Clines, for example, writes, "There can be little doubt therefore, as most scholars agree, that this chapter belongs chronologically after Neh. 13. . . ." (*Ezra, Nehemiah, Esther*, 199).

[157] "Nehemiah 10 as an Example of Early Jewish Biblical Exegesis," *JSOT* 21 (1981) 114. This makes the present arrangement all the more interesting in that the pledge precedes Nehemiah's self-attested reforms. The book, we would say, reverses historical development and thereby grants different meaning to the events and their relationship.

obligations in writing (Nehemiah 10), and Nehemiah then carries them out (Nehemiah 13). Nehemiah, despite his own self-assertions, is finally merely executing communal orders.

The substance of the pledge, not only its setting, corroborates the centrality of the community as a whole. The pledge itself is, as Clines observes, "an example of early Jewish biblical exegesis."[158] Clines notes exegetical innovations in the pledge and considers the pledge a product of Ezra's appointment of magistrates and judges, in accordance with the letter of Artaxerxes (Ezra 7:25), and evident already in Neh 8:13-15. One can take Cline's insights even further by noting that the book expands the basis of the alleged source of these innovations. Ezra-Nehemiah does not attribute the pledge to any individual nor to any officially constituted body of uniquely appointed persons (by God, king, or priests), but to the community as a whole, with specific signatories who represent the various strata, followed by all the rest (Neh 10:29-30).[159] The list of signatories broadens the circle of delegation to the utmost, being dominated not by Nehemiah, priests, or Levites, but by lay persons. The oath itself includes the community as a whole.

The pledge of communal tax is particularly illuminating as an emphasis, within the pledge, upon the community. Nowhere else in the Bible is there a command of annual "temple tax." There is mention of an occasional taxation for the tabernacle in Exod 30:11-16 and 38:25, and for temple repair under Joash (2 Kgs 12:4-15; 2 Chr 24:4-14). Temple provisions have been the prerogative and responsibility of kings during the monarchy, a practice which was implicitly continued by the Persian kings, as the decrees of Darius and Artaxerxes indicate.[160] In Neh 10:33, however, the people introduce a permanent tax for the house of God.

Clines credits Nehemiah with this innovation. Ezra-Nehemiah, however, does not. It shows, instead, communal decision as well as communal obligation. This difference is extremely important. Support for the house of God

---

[158] "Nehemiah 10 as an Example," 111.

[158] Even though the list opens with Nehemiah the governor we ought not thereby grant him too great an honor, since the list may go from lesser to greater, as the Levites and priests are at the end.

[160] Clines writes: "The present pledge may reflect economies in the imperial budget, or perhaps the sheer difficulty of extracting money from the satrapy treasurers (Ezr. 7:21) when three other provincial governors were determined to thwart Nehemiah in every way possible (cf. 4:7). Alternatively, this could be a sign of a reviving sense of national independence. Certainly, by making support of the temple everyone's responsibility rather than the concern simply of the local or imperial government, Nehemiah gave his community a focus and a sense of solidarity. The conception of this pledge, which plainly derives from Nehemiah (cf. 13:30f.), is thus all of a piece with his other great achievement, the building of the wall, the military significance of which was overshadowed by its function as a monument to national unity" (*Ezra, Nehemiah, Esther*, 207).

is now voluntarily assumed by the people as a whole. Such innovation, ascribing to the community what hitherto was royal or gubernatorial prerogative, also ascribes to the community new power.

The names in the list of signatures further attest to the significance of the community as a whole. To begin with, the majority of the names are of lay people, showing the growing importance of that group in the leadership of the community. Second, the meticulous naming of names functions here, as in other lists in the book, to preserve, credit, and memorialize numerous individuals responsible for the accomplishments of the return and reconstruction. Characteristically, Ezra-Nehemiah does not simply resort to a perfunctory statement that "all the people signed this," but records the names of many of them. Third, the names themselves show a braiding of different movements of peoples in the community. Eighty-four names occur in Neh 10:2–28. The list is then expanded to include all the rest of the community in the most comprehensive manner possible (Neh 10:29–30). Most of the names of priests and Levites in this list are familiar from other lists.[161] But some new names appear as well. Fourteen of the family names occur in Ezra 2, Nehemiah 7, and Ezra 8, specifying people who have gone into exile. Some are those who built the walls (Nehemiah 3).[162] The majority, however, are different.[163] The combination of names suggests that the diverse groups have joined hands and hearts in an oath to care for the house of God.

The relation of the pledge to covenant ceremonies highlights the centrality of the community from another perspective. Covenant ceremonies occur elsewhere in the Bible. They invariably describe the event in terms of leaders and some general inclusive labels for the rest of the community. Ezra-Nehemiah, however, names the participants in the central event and underscores its democratic process. Dennis J. McCarthy's analysis of covenant renewals shows Nehemiah 10's uniqueness as a democratically focused covenant (at times, one might add, almost in spite of McCarthy's own interpretation). McCarthy notes the Assyrian *adû* in the background of the covenant renewal ceremonies in Chronicles and Ezra-Nehemiah, and lists several of its common elements with biblical patterns.[164] He concludes,

> All this, the form and attitudes surrounding it, is wonderfully adapted to expressing the basic religious concepts of Chronicles-Nehemiah. The

---

[161] See A. Jepsen, "Nehemia 10," ZAW 66 (1954) 87–106, and Myers, *Ezra, Nehemiah*, 174–180.

[162] Some of their names are: Parosh, Pahath-moab, Meshozabel, Hallohesh, Ananiah, Baana(h), Harim, Hanahiah, Hashabanah.

[163] Myers writes as follows on this expansion: "The list of laymen is expanded far beyond that of Ezra ii and Neh vii. . . . This expanded list represents the growth of the community by the addition of those who had not gone into exile or who had returned to the land from hideouts during the Babylonian invasion. Also included are families that were probably new but developed as separate branches from older ones" (*Ezra, Nehemiah*, 177).

[164] "Covenant and Law in Chronicles-Nehemiah," *CBQ* 44 (1982) 36–39.

concentration on loyalty to a society's lord was admirably fitted to a society which the LORD had made and wished to keep his very own. His earthly representative was the Davidic king, and this representative bound the society to the LORD by oath in covenant-renewal, though in need another authority could substitute.[165]

Nehemiah 10, however, differs sharply from Chronicles and the Assyrian examples in the absence of leaders and the primacy of the larger community. McCarthy observes the absence of a leader in Nehemiah 10, but overlooks the implications. He writes, "Here the leader never really reassumes the initiative, though Nehemiah does sign first."[166] Such reference to reassuming initiative is misleading because the initiative in Nehemiah 10 or even Nehemiah 8 never came from leaders. Initiative rested throughout with "the people." The pledge in Nehemiah 10 is dramatically different from other covenants by virtue of being a voluntary act by the people.[167] What had been the concern of the state and the king becomes now the concern of the congregation.[168]

Every aspect of Nehemiah 8–10 incessantly reiterates the central significance of the people as a whole. This people is composed of groups and individuals, often named and identifiable. It is they who seek the Torah, implement it, and initiate reforms. The success of the restoration is indisputably theirs.

The House of God

The completion of the wall serves as the occasion for the ceremonies in Nehemiah 8–10, a time of renewed commitment to the Torah, interpreted as a renewed commitment to the house of God. For Ezra-Nehemiah this occasion signifies the completion of the house of God. The house of God is, therefore, literally the final word(s) in this section (Neh 10:40).

In order to appreciate the role of the house of God in this section, it is necessary to observe that neither היכל nor "house of God" appears in Nehemiah 8 and 9.[169] A unique sanctity nevertheless permeates the assembly

---

[165] Ibid., 40.

[166] Ibid., 34. McCarthy also notes: "Then the people, not the leader, 'make a covenant written of a sealed document,' 10:1. (The rough Hebrew may mark a join between sources, but this does not diminish the important fact: the chapters *are* joined. On the contrary, the struggle to put two sections together shows that the compiler—if any—found the sequence so necessary to his idea of covenant-renewal that he paid the price of clumsiness to express it)" (ibid., 34).

[167] M. Weinfeld notes the contrast with preexilic law: "a shift occurred in 'the dialogue,' the main speaker is now the commanded one and not the commander. The regulations of the renewed congregation and especially those concerned with organizing the cultic community (Neh x) are indeed styled in the first person plural" ("The Origin of the Apodictic Law," *VT* 23 [1973] 73).

[168] Ibid., 73.

[169] Ezra-Nehemiah locates the assembly in front of the Water Gate, which, as far as we can

when the Torah is read, as the reference to bowing down to God (Neh 8:6) indicates. Nor does the recital of Israel's history in Nehemiah 9 mention the temple. The silence over the temple indicates that the older temple does not hold great significance for this book. I suggest that one reason for such silence is that the older temple does not fully correspond to Ezra-Nehemiah's notion of the house of God and therefore does not merit great emphasis.

Whereas the first three scenes of Nehemiah 8–10 (Neh 8:1–12; 13–18 and 9:1–37) ignore the house of God, Nehemiah 10 reverses this tendency. It is, in many ways, a counterpart to Neh 8:1–12, with this difference: as "people" was the *Leitwort* of Neh 8:1–12, the "house of God" is the *Leitwort* of Neh 10:33–40. Neh 10:30 declares primary commitment to the Torah; the rest of the chapter spells out this commitment largely in terms of commitment to the house of God.[170] The expression "house of *our* God" recurs eight times in the seven verses of Neh 10:33–40,[171] with every single verse reiterating the concern for the house of God. It is, indeed the final word of the section, which closes as follows: ולא נעזב את בית אלהינו, "We will not neglect the house of our God" (Neh 10:40).

Commentaries, in their discussion of Nehemiah 10, invariably focus on the provisions themselves, on the biblical sources for these various stipulations, and on their practical implications.[172] The unique emphasis on the house of *our* God is frequently overlooked. The expression בית אלהינו, "the house of *our* God," is extremely rare outside of Ezra-Nehemiah, occurring only in Joel 1:16 and Ps 135:2. A close parallel, and a suggestive analogue, is 1 Chr 29:2, 3 where "the house of my God" in David's mouth highlights the difference between the two books. Ezra-Nehemiah, however, uses "the house of our God" eight times in Nehemiah 10. It appears also in Neh 13:4 and Ezra 8:25, 30, 33; 9:9. In Ezra 8 and 9 Ezra uses this expression. In Nehemiah 10, Ezra's "inclusive" language is reiterated by the community as a whole. Ezra-Nehemiah shows that once the wall is complete and the Torah is properly understood, the people as a whole reclaim the house of God as theirs.

Scholars frequently compare Nehemiah 8–10, or portions of it, with other public assemblies, especially those in Chronicles. The Torah readings of Nehemiah 8–10 have been judged, since Zunz, as similar to Chronicles, with similarities ascribed to the Chronicler's hand. Clines, writing about Neh

---

ascertain, is not a landmark associated with temple. See Clines, *Ezra, Nehemiah, Esther,* 156. This is in contrast to 1 Esdr 9:6 and 41, which associate the reading of the Torah with the temple.

[170] The pledge specifies the following commitments: 1) avoidance of mixed marriages (Neh 10:31); 2) Sabbath observances (Neh 10:32); 3) provisions for the house of God (Neh 10:33–40).

[171] The verses are: Neh 10:33, 34, 35 ("to the house of our God, the house of our fathers"), 37 (twice), 38, 39, 40. There is also the house of Yahweh (Neh 10:36).

[172] See, for example, the discussions on Nehemiah 10 in Batten, *Ezra and Nehemiah;* Clines, *Ezra, Nehemiah, Esther;* Myers, *Ezra, Nehemiah;* Rudolph, *Esra und Nehemia.*

8:4–8, lists some of the parallels usually invoked in such comparisons between Ezra-Nehemiah and Chronicles:

> As may be expected, this ceremony is parallel at several points with the Chronicler's account of the reading of the 'book of the law' under Josiah (2 Chr. 34:14–32) and especially with the account of Solomon's assembly (2 Chr. 5–7). Here the occasion is the seventh month (v. 2; cf. 1 Chr. 5:3 [sic. Clearly Clines means 2 Chr 5:3], the reader stood on a platform (v. 4; cf. 2 Chr. 6:13), the people stood at the blessing (v. 5; cf. 2 Chr. 6:3), and dispersed with joy (v. 12; cf. 2 Chr. 7:10).[173]

Clines himself retains a measure of agnosticism as to the source of these similarities,[174] implying, nevertheless, like most scholars since Zunz, that Chronicles' account of the dedication of Solomon's temple is similar to Neh 8:1–12 or Nehemiah 8–10.

The very frequency of such assertions invites a closer examination of these accounts. A comparison between Chronicles and Ezra-Nehemiah, however, taking into account the material in 1 Kings, dispels any real parallels. Instead, it largely illustrates the differences between Ezra-Nehemiah and Chronicles, and highlights more vividly Ezra-Nehemiah's distinctive perspective.

Such a comparison reveals, in the first place, that Clines's examples practically exhaust the possible parallels. Yet these parallels finally fail to exemplify a unique relation between Chronicles and Ezra-Nehemiah because they go back to 1 Kings. Standing at the blessing (2 Chr 6:3; Neh 8:5) goes back, in Chronicles, to 1 Kgs 8:14. The seventh month also goes back to 1 Kings. In 2 Chronicles it marks the time of the dedication of the temple (cf. also Ezra 3, which forms the better parallel with 2 Chronicles 5–7). In Ezra-Nehemiah the occasion marks the reading of the Torah, granting sanctity to the Torah, not to the temple. If anything, one could argue for the substitution of emphasis from temple to the book of the Torah in Ezra-Nehemiah — a shift of emphasis foreign to Chronicles. In the second place, some of Clines's similarities prove to be differences on close inspection. The platform of 2 Chr 6:13 is a כיור נחשת. Neh 8:4, however, speaks of a מגדל, a wooden "tower." In the third place, telling differences can be discerned. One notes the differences in the shape of the narratives, in comparative length, in the nature of the participants and their roles, and in the content of the messages. Indeed, aside from the fact that both celebrations occur in the seventh month, that Levites appear to have an important role, an elevation of sort is used (a circumstantially dictated detail), and that people

---

[173] Clines, *Ezra, Nehemiah, Esther,* 183.

[174] Clines adds, "These parallels need not imply that one account was the literary prototype of the other; sufficient causes for the details of each ceremony arise from the historical situations. But we cannot know to what extent the details of such ceremonies were traditional in the Chronicler's day or to what extent he projected the customs of his own time back on to earlier occasions" (ibid., 183).

rejoice, nothing is common to the two accounts. The usual association of the two in so many scholarly works, from Zunz to Clines, is therefore surprising.

Structural outlines of the temple dedication in 1 Kings and 2 Chronicles clearly illustrate the differences with Nehemiah 8–10.

The dedication of Solomon's temple, 1 Kings 8

    I. Introductory setting: Solomon gathers an assembly (1 Kgs 8:1–2)

    II. The transfer of the ark (8:3–11)
- A. Priests carry ark (8:3–4)
- B. Solomon and Israel witness and sacrifice (8:5)
- C. Details of the ark itself (8:6–9)
- D. Report of God's presence (8:10–11)

    III. The dedication ceremony (8:12–64)
- A. Solomon's speech (8:12–61)
  1. Concerning promises to David (8:12–21)
  2. Concerning David and God's responsiveness to the house (8:22–53)
  3. Closing invocation (8:54–61)
- B. Sacrifices (8:62–63)
- C. Solomon sanctifies the court (8:64)

    IV. Conclusion (8:65–66)
- A. Summary (8:65)
- B. Dismissal of assembly in joy (8:66)

This report is preceded by several chapters with detailed descriptions of construction, dimensions, and furnishing of the temple, preparations having begun in 1 Kgs 5:9.[175]

The temple dedication in 2 Chronicles

    I. Introductory setting: Solomon gathers an assembly (2 Chr 5:1–3)
- A. Solomon completes the work (5:1a)
- B. Solomon brings David's holy vessels (5:1b)
- C. Solomon assembles elders, etc. (5:2)
- D. Assembly in the seventh month (5:3)

    II. Transfer of the ark and holy vessels (5:4–14)
- A. Levites carry the ark (5:4–5)
- B. Solomon and congregation witness and sacrifice (5:6)
- C. Details of the ark itself (5:7–10)
- D. The activities of cultic personnel (5:11–13)
  1. Priests' role (5:11)
  2. Roles of Levites and singers (music) (5:12–13)

---

[175] For details see Long, *1 Kings*, 76–108. My structural outline largely depends on his.

  E. Report of God's presence (5:14)
III. The dedication ceremony (6:1–7:7)
  A. Solomon's speech (6:1–42)
   1. Concerning promises to David (6:1–11)
   2. Concerning David and God's responsiveness to the house
    (6:12–39)
   3. Closing invocation (6:40–42)
  B. Divine response (7:1–3)
  C. Sacrifices and singing (7:4–6)
  D. Solomon sanctifies the court (7:7)
IV. Conclusion (7:8–10)
  A. Summary (7:8–9)
  B. Dismissal with joy on twenty-third day (7:10)

  The structures of 1 Kings 8 and 2 Chr 5:1–7:10 are very similar. The latter expands the role of David and the role of the Levites, and heightens divine participation (2 Chr 7:1–3).

  No amount of maneuvering would form Nehemiah 8–10 into a comparable structure; it stands in stark contrast to both Chronicles and Kings, especially in terms of participants. Chronicles and Kings report the activities of kings, with the people as mere followers or background scenery. King Solomon is the most visible and vocal subject. Ezra-Nehemiah, on the other hand, is about the community, with the community as a whole as the central actor and speaker. Not only do the central roles differ, but much else shows either a reversal or a contrast. The temporal pacing, for example, varies. The temple dedication focuses on a single day. Nehemiah 8–10 specifies activities that span several weeks. If one were to narrow the basis of comparison between the two events to Neh 8:1–12, then the differences only intensify. Numerous other details differentiate the accounts as well. The terminology for the elders in 2 Chronicles follows 2 Kings in using terms which never occur in Ezra-Nehemiah.[176] 2 Chronicles emphasizes sacrifices (2 Chr 5:6), describes venerated objects with care (2 Chr 5:7–10), reports the activities of sanctified priests in detail, as well as the role of Levites and singers (these details echo Ezra 3. Cf. 2 Chr 5:13 with Ezra 3:8–13), and climaxes with the presence of God's glory (2 Chr 5:14). The final part of the dedication (2 Chr 7:1–22) is marked by fire and glory (2 Chr 7:1–3) over and above the less theophanic emphasis of 1 Kings 8.

  These details remind one how much is absent from Ezra-Nehemiah: no pomp and circumstance, no description of the Torah itself, either visually or in terms of content (hence the scholarly debates about Ezra's Torah) and, most striking, no cloud of God's glory. Ezra-Nehemiah has no theophany

---

[176] Note נשיאי האבות, ראשי המטות, זקני ישראל (2 Chr 5:2). Ezra-Nehemiah on the other hand speaks instead about ראשי בתי האבות, שבי ישראל, ראשי האבות.

anywhere. Bowing down in Neh 8:6 nevertheless acknowledges God's presence, but without glory.

An important difference stands out in the prayers that dominate the scenes. 2 Chr 6:1–42 is a long prayer by Solomon, the monarch whose voice dominates all these chapters. The contrast with the comparable long prayer in Nehemiah 9 is illuminating. First, Chronicles places the recitation of history and prayer in the king's mouth. Ezra-Nehemiah gives the prayer to the people. Second, Chronicles underlines the importance of the temple and the Davidic house, whereas Nehemiah 9 mentions neither David nor temple. These differences compound to accentuate the contrast between the accounts.

To the extent that Solomon's temple dedication, either in 1 Kings or 2 Chronicles, prompts comparison with Nehemiah 8–10, or even Neh 8:1–12, it does so by way of contrast. If the temple dedication were indeed a model for Ezra-Nehemiah, it is a model that the book repudiates, turning each emphasis on its head and establishing a new center—people and the book of the Torah—to replace king and temple.

The tendency to compare Nehemiah 8–10 with the dedication of the first temple has one thing in its favor. It captures the sense that, for Ezra-Nehemiah, this event in the latter part of the book is indeed the proper dedication of the new house of God. This house of God has required the activities of several generations. It is the work of community and not king; therefore the community offers the great prayer. It has required human as well as architectural restructuring, and it now encompasses the city as a whole.

The Documents

This section articulates the authority of the written document through its structure which is organized around documents, and by the way documents hold the community's center of attention. The book of the Torah had received full royal imprimatur in Ezra 7. It alone is now recognized as the source of instruction. The Torah is therefore read publicly and interpreted publicly. It is from the Torah that behavior issues and to the Torah that the community turns for further instructions (Neh 8:13).

People and Torah are intimately bound in our section. This is apparent when the very first thing the assembled people do is ask Ezra to bring the Torah. The first scene (Neh 8:1–12) devotes itself to a rather detailed account of the public reading of the Torah. It is also replete with repetition of "book" and "Torah" (Neh 8:1, 2, 3, 5, 8). The section shows four implementations of the Torah (Neh 8:1–12; Neh 8:13–18; Neh 9:1–37 and Neh 10:1–40), each demonstrating not only how the reading was done but, more to the point, how it should be done and *that* it should be done. One notes, above all, the public, communal character of the Torah reading. Access to the Torah, to its content and implications, is to be made available to all people, men, women and whoever is capable of understanding (Neh 8:3). Conversely, the Torah takes a primary place in public worship. Worship becomes "Torah-centric." Ezra leaves. Torah remains. That which is written continues to be carried out, as the repetition of "the written" in Neh 8:14 and 8:15 stresses, without Ezra's explicit presence.

Nehemiah 8–10 can be characterized as a flowing out and a flowing into documents. Three readings of the Torah issue in a written pledge, Nehemiah 10, in response to an awareness prompted by the readings of the Torah. The content of the pledge is an oath to observe the Torah (Neh 10:30). This pledge is tightly knit with what preceded in a causal relation. The connection is awkward and has encouraged the separation of the two chapters. But as McCarthy points out,

> The rough Hebrew may mark a join between sources, but this does not diminish the important fact: the chapters *are* joined. On the contrary, the struggle to put two sections together shows that the compiler—if any— found the sequence so necessary to his idea of covenant-renewal that he paid the price of clumsiness to express it.[177]

The pledge expresses a marvelously unconditional commitment by the people, with a generosity of spirit worthy of the divine, and a subtlety worthy of an Ezra. As in Ezra's confession, nothing is requested. The history of transgression and God's חסד has been recited, the present misery depicted, and a commitment in writing made by the whole people.

This pledge, אמנה, often labelled "covenant," and understood as a covenant ceremony spanning Nehemiah 8–10, has been compared with covenant renewal ceremonies in Chronicles. Scholars from Zunz to Clines allude to similarities particularly between Nehemiah 8–10 and the famous reading of the law under Josiah (2 Chronicles 34). But a closer inspection of the two readings shows no real parallels. Differences in structure, content, and emphasis stand out. One searches in vain for any common denominator above and beyond the mere fact of a public reading followed, at some interval, by a festival (Passover for Chronicles; Succoth for Ezra-Nehemiah). Ezra-Nehemiah shares these features with 2 Kings 23 as well, discounting thereby any unique relationship between Chronicles and Ezra-Nehemiah on this matter.[178] Chronicles' own modifications of 2 Kings at this point actually accentuate differences with Ezra-Nehemiah: 2 Chronicles minimizes the impact and import of the Torah by having the greater bulk of Josiah's reforms *precede* the discovery of the book (2 Chr 34:3–7), whereas 2 Kings shows them as a result of the implementing of the book (2 Kgs 23:4–20). In this

---

[177] "Covenant and Law in Chronicles-Nehemiah," 34.

[178] One should note the difference between 2 Kings and 2 Chronicles pertaining to the Levites. 2 Kgs 23:2 speaks of "priests and prophets" whereas the parallel in 2 Chronicles 34:30 has "priests and Levites."

Chronicles goes counter to the emphases of Ezra-Nehemiah.

McCarthy sums up the important differences among covenant renewal ceremonies in these books. He notes that in Ezra-Nehemiah, in contrast to Chronicles, "there is emphasis on a written law. This is not alien to Chronicles, but the change of emphasis is notable. The Chronicler honored 'the book of the law,' but it is at the very heart of Ezra-Nehemiah."[179] Ezra-Nehemiah also differs from Deuteronomy. In Deuteronomy, the people pledge themselves to God (see Deut 26:17–19).[180] In Nehemiah 8–10, the pledge is to the Torah itself; the emphasis on the book is thereby heightened.

The confluence of persons and movements in Nehemiah 8–10 is matched by the intensified linking of the people and book and people and the house of God. The commitment to the one is tantamount to a commitment to the other. The community, having coalesced—as a community, around the Torah, and in relation to the house of God—embodies the goals of Cyrus's decree. It had gone up and built the house of God in Jerusalem which is in Judah. It has also demonstrated who are the people of God.

B. Recapitulation: Lists of Participants (Neh 11:1–12:26)

Lists weave characters together in relation through time and space, knotting threads together. Thus Nehemiah 11 links people and land, while Nehemiah 12 braids the present day with the beginning of the book, recording the network of cult personnel that span the unified era, from Zerubbabel and Jeshua (Neh 12:1) to Ezra and Nehemiah (Neh 12:26). The recapitulation is another indication that the three movements of the return and restoration constitute a single event for the book.[181]

Structure

1. Settlers in Jerusalem and its environs (Neh 11:1–36)
   a. Settlers in the holy city (11:1–19)
      1) Procedure: settling of holy city (11:1–2)
      2) Lists and pedigrees of settlers (11:3–19)
   b. Lists of surrounding settlements and population (11:20–36)
      1) A general report (11:20–21)
      2) Lists (11:22–36)
2. Cultic personnel (12:1–26)

---

[179] "Covenant and Law in Chronicles-Nehemiah," 35.

[180] As McCarthy observes, "In Deuteronomy the first step is a pledge whose object is a personal relationship, the law a guide for living out that relationship. In Nehemiah the law itself is the object of the pledge. The commitment seems to be to the law, not to a person who guides a relationship by directives or 'law'" (ibid., 26).

[181] The fact that the concluding recapitulation links the conclusion to the beginning of Ezra-Nehemiah, and not to events in Chronicles, shows that Ezra-Nehemiah is a self-standing book and not the continuation of of Chronicles.

   a. Lists of priests and Levites (12:1–9)
   b. Genealogies (12:10–11)
   c. List of priests (12:12–21)
   d. List of Levites (12:22–25)
   e. Conclusion (12:26)

Each section in the finale of Nehemiah 8–13 is closely related to the preceding one in causal as well as temporal relation. The casting of lots in Neh 11:1, for example, echoes the casting of lots in Neh 10:35. Links with Neh 7:4 readily appear in the resumption of city population at the beginning of Nehemiah 11. But Nehemiah 11–12 is not a mere continuation of an interrupted report. Its binding allusions do not reach solely to Nehemiah 7 but connect, instead, to the beginning of the book, since Neh 12:1 directly refers to Ezra 2:1. Moreover, as will be discussed below, a decisive transformation has taken place in the intervening chapters, making the present account of Nehemiah 11 and 12 not a resumption but a culmination.

Composed almost entirely of lists of persons, this section focuses overtly on the people. The book of the Torah and the house of God remain background rather than foreground. Lists and pedigrees, woven together with a minimum of narrative, capture the final details of the restoration and its significance by recounting important participants in the return and restoration.

One must consider Nehemiah 11 as one of the ways the community as a whole implements the immediately preceding pledge. Settling the city constitutes the first step in demonstrating that the people will not forsake the house of God. Nehemiah had approached the task at an earlier point (Neh 7:4); scholars, therefore, incline to consign Neh 11:1–2 to the Nehemiah memoirs, and thereby credit him with the subsequent procedures.[182] Ezra-

---

[182] Rudolph writes that the beginning of Neh 11 "bilden den Abschluß des Berichts 7⁴⁻⁷²ᵃ, von dem sie jetzt durch die lange nachchronistische Einschaltung von 7⁷²ᵇ–10⁴⁰ getrennt sind. Schon in der Einleitung zu Esr 2 (S. 11 f.) wurde gezeigt, daß kein Grund besteht, sie der Denkschrift Nehemias abzusprechen, daß aber damit zu rechnen ist, daß vor 11¹ ein Satz verlorn ging, in dem Nehemia davon sprach. . . ." (Esra und Nehemia, 181). Despite Rudolph's disclaimer, much ground for doubting Nehemiah's role here exists. Nehemiah, to begin with, is never identified in this section, nor does he play any other role whatsoever. There is no textual evidence that his name dropped off or that earlier copyists/scribes thought it might have. Style and content bear no resemblance to the Nehemiah memoirs (see Kellermann, Nehemia, 43). In addition, the procedure contradicts Nehemiah's own intention to repopulate Jerusalem on the basis of the list of returnees (Williamson, Ezra, Nehemiah, 345). Clines holds a middle position: "It is by no means certain that these verses are from Nehemiah's memoirs: they are not in the first person form, and they do not mention Nehemiah. But since 7:1–5 is intelligible as Nehemiah's preparations for this synoecism, 7:4 especially demanding a sequel like 11:1f., it is not unreasonable to suppose that Nehemiah's memoirs recounted some such incident, even if the present wording is not Nehemiah's" (Ezra, Nehemiah, Esther, 211). Ezra-Nehemiah, however, is unequivocal about the people's role in this section.

Nehemiah, however, portrays the repopulation of the holy city as the voluntary act of the people themselves. The report is given by a third person narrator who assumed the role with Nehemiah 8, and who refers to Nehemiah in the third person (Neh 8:9). Nehemiah neither speaks nor acts in this section. The narrator states that the princes have already settled in Jerusalem (Neh 11:1a) and that the rest of the people cast lots in order to determine who else among them should populate the holy city (Neh 11:1b). One out of ten moves into the city with the people's blessings (Neh 11:2).

Two models provide illuminating background for this method of repopulating a city. First, one notes the echoes of the settlement of the land at the time of Joshua ben Nun. Allusions to that era occur in Neh 8:17, which directly refers to Joshua, in the list of cities of Neh 11:25–36 which resembles Joshua 15, and in the method of distribution which replicates, for example, Joshua 15. Second, the *synokismos*, i.e., the Greek method of forcibly moving population, presents another relevant model which scholars recognize in these proceedings.[183] Both of these models finally serve, not to explain Nehemiah 11–12, but to throw Ezra-Nehemiah's emphasis on the community as a whole into sharper relief. First, in the book of Joshua, the leaders, especially Joshua himself (e.g., Josh 14:1–2), are usually responsible for casting lots and distributing the land. In Neh 11:1–2, on the other hand, the people themselves, not a leader, determine the proceedings. The subject of the verbs "cast lots" and "blessed" is "the rest of the people" (Neh 11:1) or simply "the people" (Neh 11:2). The role of the community, in contrast to its leaders, is emphasized all the more by the specificity of the text, which states that the princes dwelt in Jerusalem, and the rest of the people cast lots (Neh 11:1). The "rest of the people" thus excludes the princes. Second, the *voluntary* nature of the Judean settlement (note "the people blessed all the men who willingly offered to live in Jerusalem," Neh 11:1b–2) contrasts with the mandatory nature of the *synokismos*.

The lists themselves also emphasize the importance of the community as a whole. There are two general types of lists in this section, lists of settlers, some with their pedigrees (11:3–36), and lists of cultic personnel (12:1–26). The lists convey, here as elsewhere, the book's persistent attention to the many persons responsible for the restoration, underscoring the communal role in the events. Nehemiah 11 and 12, however, articulate something new as well: lengthy pedigrees. Although Fensham, for example, refers to these pedigrees as typical postexilic phenomena,[184] this is actually the first time in Ezra-Nehemiah that lengthy pedigrees appear, apart from Ezra's own pedigree in Ezra 7.[185] Such sudden clustering at this juncture requires an explanation.

---

[183] This practice, if Clines is right, would be a novelty for Israel. See Clines, *Ezra, Nehemiah, Esther,* 179.

[184] Fensham, *Books of Ezra and Nehemiah,* 244.

[185] There are two Judean pedigrees going back to Perez (Neh 11:4b–5), each with seven

The purpose of these pedigrees appears to be rooted in the transformation that has taken place. Listing pedigrees is prompted by the unique, newly established holiness of the city, which the designation of Jerusalem as עיר הקדש, "holy city" or "city of holiness" (Neh 11:1, 18) reflects. "Holy city" is an infrequent term in the Hebrew Bible, occurring only here in Neh 11:1 and 11:18, and in Isa 48:2, 52:1, and Dan 9:22. Rudolph suggests that "Nehemia dachte bei diesem Namen wohl in erster Linie an den Tempel (vgl. 10:40b): Jerusalem war 'die Stadt des Heiligtums.' "[186] But Neh 11:1 implies more than that. It indicates that the city as a whole is now holy, by virtue of its history, action, and relation to God. Rudolph's linking this holiness with Neh 10:40b is apt because the city as a whole is now perceived as a house of God. Holiness has been extending in Ezra-Nehemiah, from vessels (Ezra 1), to priests (Ezra 8), to seed (Ezra 9:2), to gates (Neh 3:1), and now to city. The completion of the wall and the rededication of the people are factors in this holiness.

The voluntary settling by one out of ten, together with the lists and pedigrees in Nehemiah 11 which follow directly, need to be understood in light of this new holiness.[187] One must observe that the the last item in the pledge was the commitment of the community to tithing for the house of God (Neh 10:38–40). The volunteering of one tenth of the population is a form of tithing for Jerusalem, the holy city, the house of God.[188] The long pedigrees in this section deliberately recall the only previous long pedigree, i.e., Ezra's. Pedigrees for Judah and Benjamin become relevant for the same reason that priestly pedigrees mattered earlier: legitimation. In a holy city, purity of laymen is as important as purity of priests. Jacob Neusner points out that the Pharisees advocated the same degree of purity for a person at home, around the table, as for a priest at the altar.[189] Ezra-Nehemiah in its understated but very concrete way reflects a similar process. Credentials and legitimation hitherto concerning only priests now concern all the inhabitants of the holy city. The connection between these pedigrees and holiness is

---

names; the Judean pedigrees bypass David's name. There is a Benjamin pedigree with eight names (Neh 11:7), some priests' (Neh 11:11 with six names; Neh 11:12b with seven; others are shorter), and some shorter Levites' pedigrees.

[186] Rudolph, Esra und Nehemia, 181.

[187] Affinities between these lists and various parallels, especially 1 Chronicles 9, have been explored carefully by many scholars without reaching a consensus. Rudolph considers 1 Chronicles 9 to be dependent on Nehemiah 11 (ibid., 183). Myers, on the other hand, argues that in spite of the similarities between Nehemiah 11 and 1 Chronicles 9, "neither list was copied from the other; there are too many differences. Schneider may be right in surmising that both were copied from archival material" (Ezra, Nehemiah, 185).

[188] See Ackroyd for suggestive interpretations of the symbolism of this mode of settlement (I & II Chronicles, Ezra, Nehemiah, 309–310).

[189] Neusner, Between Time and Eternity (Encino, CA: Dickenson, 1975), esp. pp. 28–32.

emphasized by the repetition of "the holy city" (Neh 11:1 and 11:18), surrounding the pedigrees, literally, with a frame of holiness.

Lists and pedigrees link people next with territory. The list in Neh 11:25–35 expands the geographical boundaries of the restored community by spreading the population over an area greater than before. These territorial boundaries of Nehemiah 11 are themselves a problem and a revelation. Unlike the other lists in Ezra-Nehemiah, which correspond in significant measure to archeological data, the list of settlements in Nehemiah 11 has been described by Ephraim Stern as "utopian."[190] It expresses the book's intent to depict expanded boundaries for the restored community, united and settled, at last, upon its land.[191]

As the book closes, Neh 12:1–26 explicitly retraces the threads back to Ezra 2:1, recapitulating lines of cultic personnel back to those who came up in the first wave of return.[192] The loose ends of the tapestry are thus tied together. The network of priests and Levites unifies the earlier and later periods into a single, continuous, event: the actualization of Cyrus's edict. Having begun in the days of Zerubbabel and Jeshua (Neh 12:1; cf. Ezra 2:1), the list concludes with the days of "Joiakim the son of Jeshua son of Jozadak, and in the days of Nehemiah the governor and of Ezra the priest the scribe" (Neh 12:26). This articulates, as did the three movements of the return, the oneness of the intervening generations and activities.

Mapping the era by the network of cultic personnel reiterates the book's emphasis on people. A human chain spans and unifies the days of the earliest return and this time of celebration. Such recapitulation, like credits at the end of a movie, reminds us who some of the important figures are and have been, going back to the beginning of the book.

The lists of priests and Levites in Neh 12:1–26 pose many historical and textual problems that have remained unresolved.[193] Prominent among them is the near repetition of many of the names. The list of the earliest priests (Neh 12:1–7) is suspiciously like the list of the later priests (Neh 12:12–21). Rudolph has suggested that the compiler had lists of priests for the time of

---

[190] E. Stern observes significant difference between the list of place names in Nehemiah 11 and the rest of Ezra-Nehemiah's lists. He concludes that Nehemiah 11 is "a utopian plan showing where a Judaean should settle upon returning from exile, within the ancient borders from Beer-Sheba to Jerusalem, the classical territory apportioned to the tribe of Judah" ("The Province of Yehud: the Vision and the Reality," *The Jerusalem Cathedra Studies in the History, Archeology, Geography and Ethnography of the Land of Israel* [1081] 17).

[191] Nehemiah 11 forms a chiasmus with Ezra 2 (as Nehemiah 12 is the conclusion of Ezra 1): it completes the settling down that begins in Ezra 2:1. The וישבו of Ezra 2:1 is only partly accomplished in Ezra 2:70 but more fully achieved in Neh 11:3, as the threefold repetition of ישבו in Neh 11:3–4 emphasizes.

[192] Note "These are the priests and the Levites who came up with Zerubbabel the son of Shealtiel and Jeshua: Seraiah, Jeremiah, Ezra, Amariah, Malluch, Hattush . . ." (Neh 12:1).

[193] See Myers, *Ezra, Nehemiah*, 196, for a good discussion of some major problems.

Joiakim (Neh 12:12–21) but not for the earlier time. Lacking one for the earlier era, he simply copied material from the available list.[194] This is not implausible. From a literary perspective it is important to note the book's concern with spanning the era with such lists, however awkward this proves to be. The lists demonstrate that Ezra-Nehemiah is committed to describing the links in terms of numerous people who hold the events together, even if this means tampering with priestly lists.

All these lists, recounting past figures and linking them in the present, establish the harmonious whole which is the restored community. Together they set the stage for the communal celebration of the completed task. The united community, a community whose many members Ezra-Nehemiah's extensive lists diligently honor, is now ready to meet the new day with unmitigated joy.

C. Dedication of the House of God (Neh 12:27–13:3)

In this brief, concluding section, diverse elements in the book and in the community combine in a resounding celebration. The two-pronged processional, with Ezra and Nehemiah moving in opposite directions before they meet again and the groups combine, symbolizes the diversity and unity in the book. All earlier movements and people, like so many instruments, are now heard in the symphonic climax: "And the joy of Jerusalem was heard afar off" (Neh 12:43).

Structure

1. Dedication ceremony (Neh 12:27–42)
    a. Assembly (12:27–29)
    b. Purification of priests, Levites, people, gates and wall (12:30)
    c. Procession: circumambulation (12:31–42)
        1) List of marchers to the right (with Ezra) (12:31–37)
        2) List of marchers to the left (with Nehemiah) (12:38–39)
        3) The joined circle in the house of God (12:40–42)
2. Celebration "on that day" (12:43–13:3)
    a. Sacrifices with joy (12:43)
    b. Appointment of personnel for tithing (12:44–47)
    c. Reading and implementation of the book of Moses (13:1–3)

A large cast, much scenery, and stereophonic sound (as Clines aptly puts it),[195] characterize the dedication celebration. The festivities are initiated by an unspecified group of people. The indefinite plural subject could refer to

---

[194] Rudolph, *Esra und Nehemia*, 196. See Fensham's cautionary remarks, *The Books of Ezra and Nehemiah*, 252.
[195] *Ezra, Nehemiah, Esther*, 230.

the people as a whole (as Neh 12:43 implies) or to a chosen few (as Neh 12:26 could imply).[196] Nehemiah's own report, typically focusing on his role, begins only later (probably in Neh 12:31), after the assembly itself, and the mass purification, have already been set in motion. His role is circumscribed. This section is brief but, as befits a climax and a conclusion, expresses nevertheless the three themes.

The People

The action in this section begins — and ends — with a plural subject (with Israel as a whole clearly intended in Neh 12:43–13:3). From beginning to end, the dedication ceremony evokes the spontaneous rejoicing of the people, with leaders submerged amidst the clutter and the noise. The people are clearly the subject of the unit.

The previous section specified communal expansion beyond the city limits (Neh 11:24–35). Now comes the thronging to Jerusalem from the surrounding area.[197] Clines suggests that the author "has delayed this climax not so much for dramatic reasons as to convey a rounded impression of the Jewish community enclosed (symbolically if not actually) by the wall."[198] This is only partly true. Ezra-Nehemiah envisions an enclosed community, but the final chapters deliberately expand the boundaries of the community beyond these walls. Within the walls dwell the specially dedicated ones — priests, Levites, and a tenth of Judah and Benjamin. They are the inhabitants of the holy city. Others dwell beyond. All of the people, including those from the surrounding communities, gather together for the dedication.

A clue to the significance of this event, and to the heightened status of all members of the community, is the rite of preparatory purification: "And the priests and the Levites purified themselves; and they purified the people and the gates and the wall" (Neh 12:30). This report about purification is extremely important, even though obscure in some respects. Priests and Levites have been purified before (e.g., Ezra 6:20) in preparation for Passover. Nothing was said at that time about the purification of the rest of the people. Neither the temple nor the Passover required more than priestly purification. In Neh 12:30, however, the people, gates, and wall, like the priests and Levites, are purified.[199] The purification of all the people is especially important. It demonstrates that they are brought into the same ritual status as priests and Levites. They become a holy people. This amplifies the point

[196] Most commentaries remain surprisingly silent on this question.

[197] An indefinite "they" sought out the Levites to come to Jerusalem — shades of Ezra's seeking of Levites, now adopted, presumably, by other members of the community, possibly the people as a whole.

[198] *Ezra, Nehemiah, Esther*, 228.

[199] The details of this process are not given. Speculations on the basis of other purification rites in other texts help but little. See R. de Vaux, *Ancient Israel* (2 vols.; New York: McGraw-Hill, 1965) 2. 464–465, and Myers, *Ezra, Nehemiah*, 202–203.

made by the Israelite pedigrees: the sanctity of the people, not merely of clergy, matters. For Ezra-Nehemiah, the people as a whole, not simply the cultic personnel, attain purity as they become a congregation of God (Neh 13:1) and enter together the newly dedicated house of God.

Nehemiah himself describes the procession which follows. Names of participants in the procession impress on the reader the multiplicity of persons involved, reiterating the book's emphasis on the people themselves, not their leaders. The route of the procession is not altogether clear, made less coherent by our limited knowledge of the landmarks.[200] The activities of the people are somewhat clearer. Typically, Nehemiah asserts his own role, claiming that he orchestrates the movements. He depicts a bifurcated procession, with Ezra and Nehemiah themselves in opposite groups. The opposed groups finally come together in the house of God (Neh 12:40–42). Ezra and Nehemiah, however, are not themselves the stars of the procession, surrounded by supernumeraries. On the contrary, they are literally and literarily lost in the crowd. The musicians, priests, Levites, and the rest of the people,[201] occupying the center of the account as well as the center of the stage, drown out the leaders amidst the noisy commotion. Nehemiah, surprisingly, brings up the rear (so too in the coda, Neh 13:4–31). The whole community gathers in the house of God.

Communal participation, heightened through the naming of names, includes not only the procession but sacrifices and Torah reading as well. Neh 12:43–13:3 places three actions by the people (including women and children) "on that day" (Neh 12:43, 44; 13:1) at the climax of the section. The people sacrifice and rejoice. Their joy is heard afar (Neh 12:43; note the five-fold repetition of the root שמח, "to rejoice"). The passage recalls the earlier rejoicing at the founding of the temple (Ezra 3:8–13). The present celebration, however, expresses "unalloyed joy" (to borrow Williamson's felicitous description),[202] free of the disappointed tears and the growing threat that marred the previous one.

The people as a whole are responsible for the appointment of supervisors over priestly and Levitical provisions, as an outgrowth of communal joy concerning priests and Levites (Neh 12:47). The people also take charge, upon hearing the Torah, and separate the foreign from their midst. They perceive themselves as a congregation of God (Neh 13:1) and behave accordingly.

---

[200] See, e.g., Williamson, *Ezra, Nehemiah*, 369 n. 37a and 373–376 for details.

[201] The references to Judah and Benjamin in a list of individuals (Neh 12:33) in the procession are deemed puzzling, all the more since they occur in a priestly and Levitical context without being familiar priestly and Levitical names. I suggest that they are here as the collective names for the Judean and Benjaminite settlers of Jerusalem, whose special role has been indicated by the pedigrees of Neh 11:4–9.

[202] Williamson, *Ezra, Nehemiah*, 376.

The threefold repetition of ביום ההוא, "in that day" (Neh 12:43, 44, 13:1) evokes eschatological possibilities. Neh 12:43 is particularly suggestive. As Simon J. DeVries, who attributes it to Nehemiah, observes, the expression "on that day" in Neh 12:43,

> functions less as an epitomizing statement than as a sequential introduction to the final Godward act that gives the entire narrative its ultimate meaning. This day is seen as something memorable, not in itself, but as containing the festive event to which the entire work of Nehemiah has been proceeding.[203]

The climactic nature of this episode is well stated.[204] The entire narrative indeed points to "that day," not as Nehemiah's work, however, but as the community's. Hence Nehemiah is mentioned in the threefold account of activities "on that day" only in conjunction with others (Neh 12:47). His role is limited. Success has been achieved by the activities and efforts of many who have actively participated by going up and building, from Cyrus onwards. The achievement is communal. Therefore the people as a whole, women and children included (Neh 12:43), celebrate and sacrifice. Members of the community also supervise tithing on that day and implement what is written in the Torah. DeVries captures another pertinent dimension of this dedication. He comments in a footnote to "on that day" in Neh 12:43: "The phrase nevertheless plainly signals one of Yahweh's mighty acts, though now in strictly cultic and institutional terms. It is no longer Yahweh who acts *bayyôm hahû*, but the people who serve him."[205] The active role of the people reaches a new height. Ezra-Nehemiah, from its very beginning, demonstrates how humans implement divine word in the earthly realm. The focus has shifted indeed from the mighty acts of God (in Nehemiah 9) to the responsive acts of the people of God (Neh 13:1). The word has reached its fulfillment.

The House of God

The assembly of cultic personnel (Neh 12:27–29) first signals in this section that the dedication is not of mere protective walls but of a religious edifice such as the house of God. The purifications of the wall, gates, and

---

[203] *Yesterday, Today and Tomorrow: Time and History in the Old Testament* (London: S.P.C.K., 1975) 115. DeVries is less impressed by the force of the other two references to "on that day" (Neh 12:44, 13:1), considering them as typical secondary expansions for the purpose of linking disparate materials (ibid., 76).

[204] Ackroyd also speaks of the climax: "The context of this is in reality the completion of the wall in 6.15, but the narrator has placed the celebration of dedication as the climax of Nehemiah's work, properly seeing that all else may be regarded as subordinate to this one moment of his achievement" (*I & II Chronicles, Ezra, Nehemiah*, 311).

[205] *Yesterday, Today and Tomorrow*, 115.

people in Neh 12:30 reiterate more emphatically the cultic aspect of the wall and the celebration. As Myers observes in this connection:

> More was involved than an ordinary dedication, as may be surmised from the ritual purification of the participants (vs. 30); this was a ritual performed to assure the removal of any possible impurity and perhaps to invest the wall itself with a kind of sanctity or power to be what it was supposed to be.[206]

Other purifications of space and objects in the Hebrew Bible are illuminating. Although there are some examples of purification of secular domiciles (Lev 14:48 ff.), the more typical purifications are of sacred items. The altar is purified in Ezek 43:26. The house of Yahweh is purified in Hezekiah's time in 2 Chr 29:15–19. In Chronicles, as in Nehemiah 12, the purification precedes fanfare by Levites with musical instruments and sacrifices. The difference between the accounts highlights Ezra-Nehemiah's focus on the people as a whole. In 2 Chr 29:15, the priests sanctify themselves before undertaking purification of the house of God. In Neh 12:30, priests and Levites purify not only themselves, the wall, and the gates, but the people as well, hence broadening the realm of the sacred. The wall in Ezra-Nehemiah encloses a sacred space, one that is dedicated to God and requires special purification upon entering. Only after the purification can the procession begin. The purified people now enter the house of God, whose perimeters have also been duly purified.

The purification of the gates, which is unique to Neh 12:30 in the Hebrew Bible, is comprehensible in light of the social and religious significance of city gates and in light of the transformation implicit in Ezra-Nehemiah.[207] As Mircea Eliade points out, gates are the threshold between two modes of being, the religious and the profane, as well as their meeting place; "hence their great religious importance, for they are symbols and at the same time vehicles of *passage* from the one space to the other."[208] The wall in Ezra-Nehemiah now encloses a uniquely sacred realm, i.e., a holy city. The world beyond is of a different sort. The sanctity of the passage between the two realms therefore becomes of vital importance, since it marks the boundary of the house of God.[209]

The sanctity of all the space within the wall is expressed in the report about the procession. Neh 12:40 in particular implies that the city itself is now the house of God. Earlier verses depict the two parading lines, with priests, Levites, and laity, marching on the outside or the top of the wall,

---

[206] *Ezra, Nehemiah,* 203.

[207] See F. S. Frick, *The City in Ancient Israel* (SBLDS 36; Missoula, MT: Scholars Press, 1977) 125–127.

[208] *The Sacred and the Profane* (New York: Harcourt and Brace, 1959) 25.

[209] Note Williamson: "The purification of the wall and gates is an unparalleled idea, but may reflect an increased awareness of the sanctity of Jerusalem, 'the holy city' (cf. 11:1)" (*Ezra, Nehemiah,* 373).

entering at last through the gates.[210] Neh 12:40 specifies that both companies finally stood in the house of God.

Scholars, uneasy with the implication of this verse, postulate either that at this point the laity must have separated from the clergy or that the assembly takes place in front of the temple or the house of God rather than *in* it. Some, like Clines, resort to both solutions. He comments thus on Neh 12:40–43:

> The two processions join forces in the temple court, the first having entered it by the Water Gate (v. 37) and the second by the Gate of the Guard (v. 39; probably the Muster Gate of 3:31). The two choirs apparently took up their position in the temple, but Nehemiah, the lay leaders and the instrumentalists *must have* stood outside (cf. on 6:11).[211]

They must have, according to Clines, because laity are not permitted to enter such holy sphere. Clines cites the fear of profanation in Neh 6:11 to buttress his interpretation.[212] He also speaks of the temple *court,* creating some distance and diffusing thereby the force of Neh 12:40 which simply states that they stood *in* the house of God, בבית האלהים. Fensham shows a similar equivocation, commenting: "With the dedication ceremony in the temple the laity is separated from the clergy. We may derive this from vv. 40 and 41."[213] But Ezra-Nehemiah does not indicate separation. The two processions, laity and all, stand in the house of God. They can do so from the cultic perspective because they have been purified; they can do so practically because the house of God refers to the wide space within the wall. It is because the wall is the real boundary of the house of God that the initial building of the wall began with sanctification by the high priest (Neh 3:1). The processions which walked on the wall, entered the city through its gates. Having entered, the purified people have now entered the dedicated house of God, a house whose boundaries have expanded to include the city as a whole.[214] The circle has come to its fullness. The community has truly arrived.

---

[210] There is a debate whether the procession takes place on the wall itself or outside. Williamson, among others, identifies several points at which the procession is probably outside. See *Ezra, Nehemiah*, 374.

[211] *Ezra, Nehemiah, Esther*, 233 (emphasis added).

[212] In Neh 6:11 Shemaiah's invites Nehemiah to enter the temple: נעד אל בית האלהים אל תוך ההיכל/ונסגרה דלתות ההיכל. Nehemiah refuses, claiming that such an act by one like himself would be sacrilegious.

[213] *Books of Ezra and Nehemiah*, 257.

[214] Such expansion of sacred space is hardly unique to Ezra Nehemiah. It can be seen in the prophets and the Psalms, especially when one observes how the terms "mountain," "city," "Zion," "house," and "temple," are used. J. D. Levenson addresses this movement in his discussion of Zion: "It may have been noticed that in this discussion we have moved easily from talk of Zion to talk of Jerusalem and even of the land of Israel in its entirety. This is not sloppiness, but rather another characteristic of the cosmic mountain, for, as Eliade puts it, "every temple or palace, and by extension, every sacred town and royal residence, is assimilated to a 'sacred mountain' and thus becomes a 'centre.' [Eliade, *Patterns*, 375]" (*Sinai and Zion* [New York: Winston Press, 1985] 135.)

The Documents

The Torah which opened the ceremonies in Neh 8:1 also closes the dedication ceremonies in Neh 13:1–3. The document envelopes the celebration from beginning to end. As Ezra-Nehemiah concludes, the book of Moses is read again in public (Neh 13:1–3). The written text is then implemented, interpreted to apply to the present time.[215] The finale in that great day depicts a community that has purified itself from all dross on the basis of what is written. It is thus a congregation of God (13:1)—a parallel to the house of God (note also the use of "congregation" in Neh 8:2). The final sentence reiterates the significance of Torah: "When the people heard the law [תורה], they separated from Israel all those of foreign descent" (Neh 13:3).

The restoration has been completed and dedicated on that day. A holy seed now dwells in a holy city, fervently following the Torah to which it had committed itself anew. Johnson asks concerning this idealized picture of community: did Ezra-Nehemiah believe "that the actual Jewish community of Neh 12:44–13:3 was so perfectly the realization of the theocratic ideal that it was for him no longer an eschatological hope?"[216] Ezra-Nehemiah does indeed depict the restored community as a realization of the theocratic ideal. Calling it "perfect," however, is an overstatement. For Ezra-Nehemiah, the restored community will have setbacks. There is no "once and for all" resolution. Ezra-Nehemiah operates not in terms of a linear development but rather with ups and downs within an ever widening circle, a circle bound by walls, but a boundary within which the dimensions of what is holy expand. Transformation occurs not through miraculous intervention by God in history but through the arduous task of building, sorting, separating, and also combining (see Ezra 6:21)—a tedious but fruitful process. The restoration follows blueprints in the process of building: royal edicts and God's Torah. God is present as a voice, flowing through human searching of the Torah. Tenacity, building and rebuilding by a faithful community, generation after generation: this is Ezra-Nehemiah's distinctive vision of restoration.

D. Coda (13:4–13:31)

A solo voice, that of Nehemiah, sounds the last note, invoking God's remembrance. This is his account of the reforms which he instituted, punctuated by calls to God for remembrance on their account (Neh 13:14, 22, 29,

---

[215] See Clines, "Nehemiah 10 as an Example," for an insightful analysis of the process of interpretation in Ezra-Nehemiah. Clines's observations apply to Neh 13:1–3 as well.

[216] *Purpose of Biblical Genealogies*, 75. Johnson continues: "Or, quite the opposite, did he intend to show that the ideal of the theocracy had not been attained even during the reigns of David and his descendants and was not to be attained in the missions of Ezra and Nehemiah but would reach its fulfillment only in the future realization of the prophetic promises?" (ibid., 75). Rudolph proposes the first of these two options (*Chronikbücher*, xxiii).

31). The calls crescendo toward a brief summary and the final "Remember me, O my God, for good" (Neh 13:31).

Structure

1. Nehemiah's reforms for the sake of the house of God (Neh 13:4-14)
   a. Cleansing the chamber of the house of of God (13:4-9)
   b. Levitical tithing and care of house of God (13:10-13)
   c. Call for remembrance (13:14)
2. Nehemiah's Sabbath regulations (13:15-22)
   a. Actions against traders (13:15-21)
   b. Appointment of cultic guardians for the city (13:22a)
   c. Call for remembrance for these (13:22b)
3. Nehemiah's purifications of community (13:23-29)
   a. Reaction to marital and linguistic contamination (13:23-28)
   b. Call for remembrance (13:29)
4. A final, summarizing call for remembrance with reasons (13:30-31)

The very end of the book is a coda.[217] This coda in Ezra-Nehemiah trails like an afterthought, looping back to a time before the climax of the celebration.[218] It is anchored in the preceding event as the beginning of the section shows: "Now before this . . ." (Neh 13:4).[219] The section functions as an appendix to the book, summarizing earlier material, but narrated this time from the perspective of Nehemiah, who is granted the last word. Ezra-Nehemiah's threefold concern with the centrality of the community, the house of God, and the documents is more implicit than explicit.

[217] A coda, literally meaning "tail," is "a concluding musical section that is formally distinct from the main structure" (*Webster's Seventh New Collegiate Dictionary* [1969], s.v. "coda").

[218] For an alternative structure, see Williamson, *Ezra, Nehemiah*, 380 and 393-394. Williamson divides the units into Neh 12:44-13:14 and 13:15-31. According to Williamson, the formula "In that day" (Neh 12:44; 13:1) is tightly linked to "Before this, however," of 13:4, and separable from "in those days" of 13:15. In addition, the call for remembrance in 13:14 indicates the end of the unit. Some of the same elements suggest, in my judgment, that the major break is therefore with Neh 13:4 which set the stage for the recurring "in those days" (13:15, 23) and for calls for remembrance (13:14, 22, 29, 31). Oddly enough, Williamson himself includes some similar observations at a later point (which appear to conflict with his structure): "The editor thus aimed to show that the outcome of the dedication was support for the cult and maintenance of its purity. . . in a sense, therefore, he regarded the whole of 13:4-31 as pluperfect, 12:26-13:3 forming an abiding climax of his work" (383-384). This is indeed the structure I propose.

[219] Like the list of Nehemiah 7:6-72, which closes the middle section of the book but loops back in time and recapitulates what happened in former times (Neh 7:5), so too this final part recapitulates what happened at the earlier time.

The emphasis on the people is largely indirect. It appears in the juxtaposition of the material about Nehemiah's self-proclaimed reforms. The reforms consist of purifying the cult, restoring effective tithing, Sabbath observances, and an attack on mixed marriages. Provisions for tithing have been undertaken in Neh 12:44–13:3, but with a difference, however. Neh 12:44–13:3 describes what the *people* themselves have done: they gladly provided for the cultic personnel and separated from foreigners. In Neh 13:10–13 Nehemiah himself energetically imposes these measures, acknowledging no overt support from the community.

An even more striking parallel exists between Nehemiah 13 and Nehemiah 10.[220] Clines presumes throughout his discussion of these two chapters that, historically speaking, the material in Nehemiah 13 precedes Nehemiah 10 and precipitates the pledge of Nehemiah 10. In Clines's assessment, Nehemiah 13 describes Nehemiah's initial measures, his direct intervention to resolve problems he encountered; Nehemiah 10 is a later, more measured, response in order to cope with these same problems on a long-term basis.[221] Clines interprets the present sequence of the chapters (which, according to him, reverses the historical one) as the book's attempt to provide a proper conclusion to the work of Ezra. Chapter 10 is therefore appended to Nehemiah 9. However, the absence of Ezra in MT Nehemiah 9 makes Clines's hypothesis less than convincing. Furthermore, Nehemiah 13 would upset any such conclusion, since it could imply that Ezra's resolutions did not in fact take root and Nehemiah had to do these things all over again. Clines does not discuss the impact of Nehemiah 13 in its present location.

Jepsen, who is responsible for one of the most thorough studies of Nehemiah 10, also wrestles with the similarities between the two chapters. He observes the implicit conflict between the two claims, that of Nehemiah 10 and that of Nehemiah 13: the pledge declares that the reforms were freely instigated by the community as a whole; Nehemiah is silent about any such previous reforms or obligations.[222] Nehemiah's silence and the incongruity between the two accounts—Nehemiah 10 and Nehemiah's own—impels Jepsen to disengage Nehemiah 10 from Nehemiah himself. What is pertinent for our present purpose is the effect of the juxtaposition of Nehemiah 10 and 13. The arrangement in Ezra-Nehemiah ascribes the reforms to the community as a whole, making Nehemiah's activities essentially the administering

---

[220] See Jepsen, "Nehemia 10," and Myers, *Ezra, Nehemiah,* 87–106.

[221] See Clines, *Ezra, Nehemiah, Esther,* 245.

[222] "Wenn nun Nehemia im Anschluss an solche Reformen das Volk feierlich darauf verpflichtet hätte, auch in Zukunft den Gesetzen gehorsam zu sein, dann wäre es doch wohl merkwürdig, wenn er von einer solchen Verpflichtung, die gewissermassen der Abschluss seiner Wirksamkeit war, nichts mehr berichtet hat. . . ." (Jepsen, "Nehemia 10," 99.) Jepsen also adds: "Nehemia erwähnt, dass er für die Durchführung des Zehnten für die Leviten gesorgt habe, ebenso für Holz und Erslinge. Aber dass er die Gemeinde zu einer weitergehenden Versorgung bestimmt habe, ist nicht angedeutet" (ibid., 101).

of communally ordained regulations. In doing so, Ezra-Nehemiah subsumes the would-be leader to the community and reiterates the centrality of the people.

The house of God is stressed in the reforms themselves, which largely pertain directly to the house of God. The reforms describe sanctification of space (esp. Neh 13:4-9), time (Neh 13:15-21), and people (Neh 13:23-28). There is the obvious concern with a contaminated precinct within the house of God and with the need to purify the place (Neh 13:4-9). There is the proper provision of tithing. The Sabbath, also, reflects a concern for the house of God.[223] Proper observance is to encompass the whole city. The appointment of the Levites to guard the city gates (Neh 13:22) bespeaks the expansion of the sanctity of the city as a whole. Not only are Levites appointed; they are also purified. Clines writes,

> The Levite gatekeepers hitherto had been responsible for the temple gates only, but now the keeping of the city gates on the sabbath (they are not replacing the regular gatekeepers) is made a religious duty, requiring like other divine service (cf. 12:30; Ezr. 6:20) ritual purification.[224]

Clines supposes that these measures were later rescinded, once the later, long-term provisions of Nehemiah 10 had been devised. Ezra-Nehemiah, in its present arrangement, does not repeal the measures but leaves them standing at the book's conclusion. We must not underestimate the significance of this canonical arrangement. In Ezra-Nehemiah, the holy city corresponds to the house of God. For this reason, cultic personnel, usually responsible for the temple gates only, now stand at the city gates, performing their religious duty. As Williamson observes,

> The use of the Levites for this role is intelligible, and there may even have been an early precedent for it; see my *comment* on 7:1-2. Their normal duties related to the temple; now with the increasing regard for the sanctity of the whole of the city (cf. Isa 52:1; Joel 4:17 [3:17]), and with their new role being associated with the holiness of the Sabbath, this task was probably regarded as only an extension of what they were already doing. The command that they should first "purify themselves" supports this understanding as well as being explained by it.[225]

The emphasis on documents flows from the sequence of the last few chapters. Despite Nehemiah's silence about the origin of his reforms, the book of Ezra-Nehemiah is so structured that his reforms appear to be the result of that earlier document. What Nehemiah implements are the commitments specified in the written pledge. In this sense the book concludes with the governor responding to and executing the written religious and social commitments of the community as a whole.

---

[223] See Levenson, *Sinai and Zion*, 145.

[224] *Ezra, Nehemiah, Esther*, 245.

[225] *Ezra, Nehemiah*, 396.

By appending Nehemiah's reforms to the conclusion of the book, Ezra-Nehemiah casts shadows on the finale as a whole. This protects the reader from confusing the "ideal community" (as Clines calls 12:44–13:3)[226] with an idyllic or idealized community. As Williamson observes, the biblical author of Ezra-Nehemiah does not stop with a "triumphant and climactic account. Rather, he deliberately presses forward to speak of at first sight comparatively trivial daily arrangments and then of subsequent setbacks, for by these tokens too is true progress to be measured."[227] The recurrence of problems and the necessity of repeated resolutions permeate the book. They preclude an innocent illusion of a happy "ever-after." Problems have to be addressed anew in each generation. Sacred documents guide the community in the resolution of these problems. Remembrance by God and community attends those who set their heart and hand to implement these documents and thereby care for the house of God.

Ezra-Nehemiah's account of the return and restoration has come to its conclusion. Going up to build the house of God in Jerusalem required the concerted efforts of hundreds of people whose names are preserved in Ezra-Nehemiah and myriads of others whose names are forgotten but whose contribution is nevertheless remembered. The great and the small, laity as well as clergy, joined hands in this building, which was both architectural and spiritual. Their efforts spanned generations, including different streams of population. Certain individuals had risen periodically to the top in the process, but their chief tasks were finally those of "civil servants." Like Ezra, they took charge only when the community invited them (Neh 8:1); like Nehemiah, they were finally the executors of public pledge.

The book closes with a community not so much restored to some earlier, familiar state, but rather living up to a prophetic vision in which sanctity pervades the people and city as a whole. The words of the Torah take root in the daily life of the people who recite and practice them. Unmitigated joy engulfs the celebrating community. The words of Jeremiah have reached their culmination.

---

[226] *Ezra, Nehemiah, Esther,* 234.
[227] *Ezra, Nehemiah,* 377.

4
CHARACTERS

What is character but the determination of incident?
What is incident but the illustration of character?
Henry James[1]

I. Characterization in Biblical Literature

The inextricability of character and event, in the Bible as in other literature, elucidates why a literary analysis of characters is another angle from which to perceive a book's intention. Characters, whether historical or fictional, are often mouthpieces for the author.[2] Either as spokespersons for the book, or as the coalescing of events, they convey, directly or indirectly, the book's overall intention. The inevitable intertwining of characters and events also explains why the previous discussion of structure and themes necessarily included some attention to characters. The present chapter is thus not a wholly new evaluation of characters in Ezra-Nehemiah, but represents a changed focus with two basic goals: first, to identify and examine the specific literary techniques that most fully account for the book's characterization; second, to sketch the characters of Ezra-Nehemiah in light of these techniques and discern from them the book's intention.

Ezra-Nehemiah has three main characters. The people as a whole constitute the main character. As we have seen, the book articulates the centrality of the community through narrative structure and thematic development. In addition, certain significant individuals emerge, the most prominent of whom are Ezra and Nehemiah. Not only does the amount of space allotted to each support this claim,[3] but so does in particular the use of the so-called "memoirs" which allow Ezra and Nehemiah to speak for themselves.[4] At first glance, the prominence of these individuals appears to

---

[1] From "The Art of Fiction," *The Portable Henry James* (ed. M. D. Zabel; New York: Viking, 1967; original publ. 1884) 401. See Bar-Efrat, *The Art of Narration in the Bible*, 100, for a discussion of the reciprocity of characters and events in the Bible.

[2] See Bar-Efrat, *The Art of Narration in the Bible*, 72.

[3] Representational proportions are among the literary criteria specified by Sternberg; see, e.g., *Poetics of Biblical Narrative*, 39.

[4] Ezra stands out in Ezra 7–10, and some portions of Nehemiah 8. Nehemiah dominates

conflict with my assertion that Ezra-Nehemiah shifts the focus from the heroic individual to the community as a whole. But the following literary analysis of characterization will, instead, show how the book utilizes Ezra and Nehemiah to articulate its views, especially the emphasis on the centrality of the community.[5]

Deciphering when and how a character is a genuine vehicle for Ezra-Nehemiah requires attention to the multiple ways in which characterization is accomplished in literature in general and in the Bible in particular. According to one standard model, characterization in narrative takes three basic forms: 1) direct definition; 2) indirect presentation; 3) reinforcement by analogy.[6] All three basic ways are prominent in the Hebrew Bible in general[7] and Ezra-Nehemiah in particular.

Direct definition is "akin to generalization and conceptualization,"[8] and can be specified either by the narrator or by a character within the work. Bar-Efrat points out that direct definitions by the narrator are relatively scarce in the Bible, occurring mostly as epithets. Epithets in biblical narrative, therefore, invariably prove crucial to the plot.[9] Note, for example, the importance of Ehud's epithets ("left-handed man") and Eglon's ("a very fat man") in Judg 3:15–17.[10]

Indirect presentation is characterization which does not mention a trait directly but exemplifies it instead through action, speech, or external appearance.[11] Indirect presentation is the most prevalent mode in biblical narrative, requiring readers to be attentive to nuanced details.

Nehemiah 1–7 and appears in other sections as well (e.g., Nehemiah 13). Other important individuals are Zerubbabel, Jeshua and Artaxerxes. None of them, however, receives comparable attention. As the discussion of Ezra 1–6 has shown (Chapter Three above), Zerubbabel and Jeshua are clearly circumscribed in terms of importance. Zerubbabel in particular is not accorded the centrality that he has in other sources, such as 1 Esdras (see Chapter Five below).

[5] The historicity of Ezra and Nehemiah, the actual nature of their activities, and the order of their appearance on the scene have all been debated. Scholars tend to grant authenticity to the Nehemiah memoirs and hence to the figure of Nehemiah (dating his activities in approximately 445–433 B.C.E.). The historicity of Ezra and of a genuine Ezra memoirs has been doubted more frequently. Torrey calls Ezra a figment of the Chronicler's imagination (*Ezra Studies*, ix). Other scholars grant authenticity to various portions of the Ezra material or, at the very least, posit a historical Ezra, while acknowledging that an accurate description of his activities cannot be recovered. For good summaries of these issues, see Childs, *Introduction to the Old Testament*, 627–630, and Klein, "Ezra and Nehemiah in Recent Studies," esp. pp. 361–372.

[6] Rimmon-Kenan, *Narrative Fiction: Contemporary Poetics*, 60–70.

[7] See Berlin, *Poetics and Interpretation*, 33–42, and Bar-Efrat, *The Art of Narration in the Bible*, 73.

[8] Rimmon-Kenan, *Narrative Fiction: Contemporary Poetics*, 60.

[9] *The Art of Narration in the Bible*, 75–88, esp. p. 79.

[10] See Sternberg's treatment of Judg 3:15–17 in *Poetics of Biblical Narrative*, 331–337.

[11] Rimmon-Kenan, *Narrative Fiction: Contemporary Poetics*, 61–67; also Bar-Efrat, *The Art of Narration in the Bible*, 89.

Reinforcement by analogy, as the third basic way of characterization, is the most indirect manner of making a point. "When two characters are presented in similar circumstances, the similarity or contrast between their behaviour emphasizes traits characteristic of both."[12] Biblical narrative frequently uses reinforcement by analogy to convey its meanings. Note, for example, the heightening of David's ignominy through the contrast with the devoted Uriah the Hittite in 2 Sam 11:6–25.

All of these modes filter through some kind of perspective, which Rimmon-Kenan labels "focalization" and most critics call "point of view."[13] Focalization or point of view provides a decisive clue for the intention of a work because a narrative typically makes its evaluation by its mode of presentation. As Berlin states,

> a character is not perceived by the reader directly, but rather mediated or filtered through the telling of the (implied) author, the narrator, or another character. For the reader is shown only what the author wishes to show. Never can the reader step behind the story to know a character other than in the way the narrative presents him.[14]

As we shall see, Ezra-Nehemiah, like other biblical books, employs all of these narrative strategies to convey its intention. But it is Ezra-Nehemiah's sophisticated use of "points of view" that differentiates it from other biblical literature and constitutes, therefore, an important key for a literary analysis of characters in the book.

Ezra-Nehemiah brings a new dimension to biblical characterization with its striking interplay of points of view, alternating between memoirs and third person perspective. The memoirs are generally considered unique to Ezra-Nehemiah in biblical narrative.[15] These memoirs present characters from within, occasionally giving glimpses of the interior thoughts.[16] They allow Ezra and Nehemiah to speak directly to the reader, as it were, telling their stories in their own words, giving the illusion that the reader, in fact, does step behind the narrative to know a character directly. In contrast to an older style of historical criticism that too readily equated memoirs with historically reliable account, I want to follow the lead of more recent literary theory that recognizes the use of such a source as a specific narrative strategy. As Sternberg notes, with the memoirs Ezra-Nehemiah sharply breaks with the biblical narrative tradition where the narrator typically remains

---

[12] Rimmon-Kenan, *Narrative Fiction: Contemporary Poetics*, 70. This mode is roughly comparable to what Bar-Efrat associates with "secondary figures," his third mode of indirect presentation (*The Art of Narration in the Bible*, 107–110).

[13] *Narrative Fiction: Contemporary Poetics*, 71–85.

[14] *Poetics and Interpretation*, 43.

[15] The Ezra memoirs comprise Ezra 7:27–9:15, and the Nehemiah memoirs comprise most of Neh 1:1–7:5 and Neh 13:4–31.

[16] See Rimmon-Kenan, *Narrative Fiction: Contemporary Poetics*, 74–77, for distinctions between within/without and internal/external focalizations.

anonymous and distinct from the characters.[17] The memoirs are a literary form that obliterates the distance, granting a new role to the "I," speaking in his voice. Ezra-Nehemiah's attention to the narrating "I" is so rare in biblical narrative that Sternberg calls the memoirs the exceptions that "only prove the rule of narration, by which self-reflexive language is conspicuous for its absence."[18] In addition to these memoirs, the book incorporates the more typical, anonymous, omniscient, third person perspective, expressed either by the book's overall narrator or by means of juxtaposition of the material. The third person narrative reflects back upon the memoirs.

Transitions between the two points of view—first- and third-person accounts—are far more pronounced in Ezra-Nehemiah than in other biblical narratives, making an overt claim upon the interpreter's attention.[19] They are virtually impossible to ignore. Their prominence signals importance and compels the reader to inquire about their implications.[20]

Most scholarly attention to the shift between first- and third-person report in the book has concentrated on the Ezra material, revolving largely around question of sources and authenticity.[21] Mowinckel, however, contends (correctly, in my judgment) that literary, rather than historical, considerations account for these shifts. According to Mowinckel, the turn between first- and third-person report is deliberate.[22] It is a literary device used by the author of the *Esrageschichte* to dramatize and animate the material in the interest of edifying the community and not in the interest of writing history.[23]

----

[17] *The Poetics of Biblical Narrative*, 73. Sternberg writes: "The otherwise assorted books conform to a single model of narration, whereby the narrating persona wields powers not just different from but closed to his historical maker, whoever he may be. It is exactly here that Ezra (in part) and Nehemiah, both late works from the Persian period, break with the tradition. If taken as apocryphal memoirs . . . then the writer is the first to keep his frontsman on his own level, bestowing on the memoirist no supernatural powers of vision. And if these accounts are taken as real memoirs composed as well as narrated by Ezra and Nehemiah themselves, like Xenophon's *Anabasis*, then the departure from the biblical model even sharpens" (ibid., 73).

[18] Ibid., 66. See also Japhet, "Biblical Historiography in the Persian Period," 182–183.

[19] See Berlin, *Poetics and Interpretation*, 43–82, for a good discussion of alternations in points of view in the Bible.

[20] Kapelrud's conclusion that the first- and third-person narrative go back to the same hand (*Question of Authorship in the Ezra-Narrative*, 95) increases rather than decreases the imperative of interpreting the purpose of the shift.

[21] For a summary of representative views, see Mowinckel, " 'Ich' und 'Er' in der Ezra-geschichte," esp. pp. 213–216.

[22] "Wir können somit feststellen, daß der Wechsel von I. und 3. Person in in der jüdischen wie in anderen altorientalischen Literaturen eine *bewußt benutzte Stilform* war. Hinter dem Wechsel liegt grundsätzlich nicht Willkür, sondern bewußte literarische Absicht" (ibid., 223).

[23] Ibid., 223 and 231. Mowinckel writes, "Der Verfasser der EG [Esrageschichte] ist gar nicht an der Geschichte als solcher interessiert. Er ist an der Geschichte nur insofern interessiert, als sie erbaulich ist—oder gemacht werden kann. Er schreibt, um einen modernen Ausdruck zu benutzen, 'Kirchengeschichte für das gläubige Volk' " (ibid., 231).

Mowinckel does not develop the ramifications of these literary concerns at work beyond their use as rhetorical devices with aesthetic significance. I wish to press his observation further, exploring additional implications. As Sternberg points out, aesthetics, history, and ideology are rarely apart in biblical narrative.[24] One must therefore inquire in what sense alternations between points of view serve to edify.

Uspensky's definitive study of points of view, *A Poetics of Composition*,[25] is particularly useful at this juncture. Uspensky lists four levels at which points of view operate: ideological, phraseological, spatial and temporal, and psychological. Two levels are pertinent to our discussion: first, the psychological level, pertaining to the angle from which events are *described;* second, the ideological level, pertaining to the angle from which they are *evaluated*. Delineating the "psychological level," Uspensky observes:

> When an author constructs his narration, he usually has two options open to him: he may structure the events and characters of the narrative through the deliberately subjective viewpoint of some particular individual's (or individuals') consciousness, or he may describe the events as objectively as possible. In other words, he may use the *données* of the perceptions of one consciousness or several, or he may use the facts as they are known to him. Different combinations of these two techniques are possible; the author may alternate between them or may combine them in various ways.[26]

Ezra-Nehemiah uses both techniques more dramatically than do other biblical books. The memoirs offer what Uspensky calls "subjective" viewpoint, sustaining the perspective of the character within the book. The interspersed third person narrative offers an "objective" one, that of the book's overall narrator. Aesthetically and psychologically, the juxtaposition of the perspectives allows the reader to encounter multi-dimensional characters, naturalistically recreated. This in itself is remarkable. It indicates that the book curtails the role of the omniscient narrator, relying on other, realistically accounted sources, for portrayal of characters. A narrating individual is granted a more direct role in the story while the omniscient narrator operates now even more obliquely. The relation of this literary style to Ezra-Nehemiah's overall mode of indirection, wherein God operates behind the scene, is worth noting.[27] The diversity of overt points of view in the book, however, also compels the reader to compare, integrate, and adjudicate among them. One therefore moves to the ideological level.

---

[24] *Poetics of Biblical Narrative*, 46.

[25] Much of what Rimmon-Kenan and Berlin say on this subject is based on Uspensky's observations. See Berlin, *Poetics and Interpretation*, 55–57, and Rimmon-Kenan, *Narrative Fiction: Contemporary Poetics*, 77–85, for a concise summary.

[26] *A Poetics of Composition*, 81; see also Berlin, *Poetics and Interpretation*, 56.

[27] See my comments about indirection in Ezra-Nehemiah in the discussion of Ezra 1:1–4 in Chapter Three.

Uspensky describes the ideological level as essentially the most basic aspect of points of view, while at the same time the "least accessible to formalization, for its analysis relies, to a degree, on intuitive understanding."[28] The ideological level seeks to ascertain "whose point of view does the author assume when he evaluates and perceives ideologically the world which he describes."[29] The book's point of view,

> either concealed or openly acknowledged, may belong to the author himself; or it may be the normative system of the narrator, as distinct from that of the author (and perhaps in conflict with the author's norm); or it may belong to one of the characters.[30]

It is crucial, in interpreting any book, to ascertain which perspective among competing visions actually reflects the book's own point of view, the view "according to which the events of the narrative are evaluated or judged — i.e., were certain actions approved or disapproved."[31]

Certain norms in biblical literature allow the reader to evaluate a book's perspective. Berlin points out that in the Bible, "the ideological viewpoint is that of the narrator. It is he, according to his conceptual framework, who evaluates. Occasionally the ideological views of characters are present, but in general these are subordinated to that of the [omniscient] narrator."[32] Ezra-Nehemiah, with the memoirs, reproduces the views of characters more extensively and more directly than do other biblical narratives. Subordination is at most implicit. It must be detected by identifying the speakers (psychological level) and adjudicating among them (ideological level).

In the Bible, the omniscient narrator or implied author for the book as a whole is always reliable.[33] It is thus axiomatic that, in biblical narrative, the omniscient narrator's version of reality takes precedence over the character's version and has absolute weight and authority.[34] Presentations by a character within the book are subject to further scrutiny, their credibility depending

---

[28] *A Poetics of Composition*, 8.

[29] Ibid., 8.

[30] Ibid., 8.

[31] Berlin, *Poetics and Interpretation*, 55.

[32] Ibid., 55–56. For the extensive uses of shifts in points of view in the Bible, see also pp. 43–82. By "narrator" Berlin refers to omniscient narrator who, in biblical narrative, is also the implied author of the book as a whole. An implied author, of course, is not to be confused with a real author or connected with the "authorial fallacy." Implied author, like implied reader, is a literary construct not an objective reality external to the book. See Rimmon-Kenan, *Narrative Fiction: Contemporary Poetics*, 86–105, esp. pp. 86–89 for clarification. The implied author of Nehemiah's memoirs is perforce Nehemiah, regardless of real authorship. The implied reader of his call for remembrance, for example, is the God who is therein invoked. The real reader is of course altogether different.

[33] As Berlin points out, "It is generally accepted that biblical narrative is narrated in the third person by an omniscient (and reliable) narrator" (*Poetics and Interpretation*, 43).

[34] Ibid., 80.

on congruence with the omniscient narrator's perspective. Biblical narrators, however, are typically reticent, expressing themselves obliquely through indirect presentation, the compositional nature of the work, and reinforcement by analogy.[35] The book's point of view is thus woven into the fabric of the text and needs to be unraveled with care.

Frequently a character's point of view corresponds to the narrator's and represents the narrator. The text indicates this by direct confirmation or through repetition which reiterates the same view clearly from the "mouth" of the omniscient and reliable narrator. When no direct confirmation has been made, one must be careful to ascertain the position of the book since, as Uspensky points out, "the narrator's perception may be at variance with the perception of a character."[36] An important tool for conveying disagreements with a character is the "nonconcurrence of points of view,"[37] or what Berlin calls "dissonance." In such instances "the point of view manifested on the level of ideology may be nonconcurrent with points of view manifested on other levels."[38] Irony is one of the results of such disharmony.[39] Repetitions help identify dissonance. "Change in repeated information can be significant."[40] It either corroborates or challenges a previous statement by a character, resulting in either confirmation or dissonance.[41]

The characterization of Ezra and Nehemiah relies heavily on the interactions between the omniscient narrator's point of view and that of the characters. The memoirs express the view of the characters themselves, whereas the third person perspective reflects the book's point of view. Through confirmation, silence, or dissonance between the two, Ezra-Nehemiah comments on the characters and the events, advancing its own authoritative evaluation.

The most important effect of shifts in points of view in Ezra-Nehemiah, aside from the presumed aesthetic value which Mowinckel suggests, is the corroboration of Ezra's perceptions by the omniscient narrator. The book

---

[35] Sternberg develops a theory concerning the ideological basis for the Bible's predilection for indirect modes of presentation. See *Poetics of Biblical Narrative*, esp. pp. 46–57.

[36] *Poetics of Composition*, 111.

[37] Ibid., 102.

[38] Ibid., 102. Here note also R. Polzin's interpretation of shifts in perspectives in *Moses and the Deuteronomist* (New York: Seabury, 1980). Sternberg's chapter, "The Play of Perspectives" (*Poetics of Biblical Narrative*, 153–185), is also pertinent to this discussion.

[39] "Irony occurs when we speak from one point of view, but make an evaluation from another point of view; thus for irony the nonconcurrence of point of view on the different levels is a necessary requirement" (Uspensky, *Poetics of Composition*, 103).

[40] Ibid., 76; see also Sternberg, *Poetics of Biblical Narrative*, 365–440, on repetition.

[41] Berlin offers Judges 4 as an example in which the narrator never confirms the character, i.e., Sisera's perception or point of view; "in fact, he subtly undermines it, either by his silence or by his dissonant narration" (Berlin, *Poetics and Interpretation*, 71). Other examples of dissonance are on pp. 72–73, including the story of David dancing before the ark, and Eli in Shiloh.

demonstrates congruence between Ezra's words and the omniscient narrator's, thereby establishing Ezra as a reliable recorder of events.

The omniscient narrator, for example, corroborates Ezra's assessment of reality by repeated references to divine support for Ezra. In Ezra 7:6, the narrator, in one of the few instances of direct definition in Ezra-Nehemiah, states concerning Ezra that "the king granted him all that he asked, for the hand of the LORD his God was upon him." The narrator reiterates such divine favor by repeating the expression: "for the good hand of his God was upon him" (Ezra 7:9). Ezra himself, in his memoirs, attributes the success of his mission to the hand of the Lord, using once again the same expression (Ezra 7:28; 8:18). These citations confirm not only the fact that divine favor has been bestowed upon Ezra, but also Ezra's correct perception of that reality.

One finds still another example of the narrator's corroboration in the report of Ezra's impact upon the community in the mixed marriage incident. Ezra himself describes the public's reaction to his confession by mentioning that his mourning attracted God-fearing members of the community (Ezra 9:4). Ezra 10:1 shifts to the omniscient narrator's report, who not only corroborates Ezra's description but also underscores it, indicating that it was a "very large congregation" (קהל רב מאד) which assembled around Ezra. Such confirmations establish Ezra as a reliable narrator whose point of view coincides with that of the omniscient narrator and hence a vehicle for the book's point of view.

It is otherwise with Nehemiah. No narrator witnesses Nehemiah's activities or confirms them; no independent source attests to Nehemiah's greatness but Nehemiah himself. The narrator is either silent or, by indirect means of juxtaposition of the material, analogy, and sequential arrangement, creates some dissonance between Nehemiah's words and the rest of the narrative. Tension between the "I" of the memoirs and the third person perspective occurs when Nehemiah claims credit for certain actions while the third person narrator speaks of how "they," presumably the community as a whole, accomplished the deed. Three examples tell the tale. First, Nehemiah 3 describes the building of the wall at the prompting of Nehemiah. The narrator takes much time and space to alert us to the broad involvement by many. Nehemiah, however, essentially ignores this communal effort, stating in Neh 6:1: "I had built the wall." The list which preceded him in chapter 3 (which, incidentally, does not mention Nehemiah) undercuts Nehemiah's self-assertion by specifying who in fact did the work.

Second, Neh 13:1–3 reports how the people separated themselves from foreigners: "On that day they read from the book of Moses in the hearing of the people. . . . When the people heard the law, they separated from Israel all those of foreign descent" (Neh 13:1–3). In Neh 13:30, however, Nehemiah claims credit for purging the priesthood from foreign influence.

Finally, the location of Nehemiah 13 exemplifies the dissonance between Nehemiah and the narrator's account. In Nehemiah 13, Nehemiah describes the reforms which he, single-handedly it would seem, instigated. Nehemiah 10, however, reproduces the community's written pledge to implement largely the same reforms. Nehemiah's silence about any such previous reforms creates a certain dissonance between the accounts. Clines, among other scholars, responds to the implicit tension by claiming that the chapters are dislocated. According to Clines, Nehemiah 10 properly belongs *after* Nehemiah 13, since it describes long-term measures instigated by Nehemiah as a result of the confrontations depicted in Nehemiah 13.[42] Had Nehemiah 10 been positioned after Nehemiah 13, the book would be implying an obvious causality: the pledge (now in Nehemiah 10) would most naturally appear to be the direct influence of Nehemiah. The present juxtaposition in the book, however, reverses this relationship. It depicts the reforms as the freely assumed commitment by the whole community, including Nehemiah. Nehemiah's own activities, in the present form of the book, come only *after* the pledge had been undertaken. Rather than initiating such reforms, Nehemiah consequently becomes their executor. He is the arm of the community, not its head. Clines may be right about the historical reality behind the events. But Ezra-Nehemiah structures these events to express its own ideology, one in which the activities of a self-appointed leader ultimately flow from the community's written pledge. The book, thereby, casts doubts upon Nehemiah's own claims for his unique single-handed achievement, granting him his achievement only as a communally sanctioned act.

Careful attention to the interplay between points of view—that of the memoirs and that of the omniscient narrator—allows the reader to evaluate these characters and hence the book's ideology. This is therefore not only necessary for understanding Ezra and Nehemiah as characters but crucial for interpreting Ezra-Nehemiah as a whole.

We are now in a position to sum up the answer to the first question posed in this chapter: what accounts for Ezra-Nehemiah's characterization and what does that entail? The most prominent literary device in Ezra-Nehemiah is an innovative use of shifts in points of view. The book employs this technique to identify Ezra as a reliable narrator, one who embodies the book's ideology. At the same time, the book uses this literary device to deflate Nehemiah. Other typical literary techniques, such as direct and indirect presentation and reinforcement by analogy, serve to confirm this basic distinction between Ezra and Nehemiah. They also allow us to specify what is commendable about these characters and what is suspect. Now we must turn to the book's portraits of these two men in order to highlight the particular embodiments of these techniques.

---

[42] *Ezra, Nehemiah, Esther,* 199.

II. The Portrait of Ezra

Ezra is heralded by the omniscient narrator (Ezra 7:1–10) with the longest introduction in the book. The very length of the introduction signifies his importance, as does the technique of characterization which combines pedigree, epithets, and direct definitions to emphasize Ezra's unique role in the book. Here the normally unobtrusive omniscient narrator, who rarely resorts to privileged information in Ezra-Nehemiah, steps forth and vouches directly for Ezra and his mission. No one in Ezra-Nehemiah receives comparable introduction.

Ezra is a priest with the most touted pedigree in the book. Impeccable credentials link him directly with Aaron, and form the longest pedigree in the book (longer here than the parallel in 1 Esdr 8:1–2). Having demonstrated Ezra's priestly background, the narrator defines Ezra as "a scribe skilled in the law of Moses which the LORD the God of Israel had given; and the king granted him all that he asked, for the hand of the LORD his God was upon him" (Ezra 7:6). The epithets and direct definition are important, especially in Ezra-Nehemiah which is short on titles of any sort.[43] As Sternberg shows, biblical epithets do not appear for the sake of realism, but supply decisive clues for the development of the story, functioning on occasion as proleptic portraits. They are always crucial for the development of the story.[44] In Ezra-Nehemiah they define Ezra's own agenda and identity in relation not to the cult but to the Torah. Ezra is a divinely approved scribe of the Torah; his "master" is the book of the Torah. The narrator's reference to divine favor is particularly enlightening. No other individual receives precisely this kind of confirmation by the narrator. (Nehemiah claims to have such favor [see Neh 2:8], but the narrator does not confirm that directly.)

The narrator also defines Ezra's goals: "For Ezra had set his heart to study the law of the LORD, and to do it, and to teach his statutes and ordinances in Israel" (Ezra 7:10). The narrator establishes Ezra's motives, placing study, practice, and teaching of the Torah at the center of Ezra's mission. It is important to notice that the narrator's description penetrates Ezra's innermost thoughts and wishes, moving beyond empirically observed phenomena. Such reports are extremely rare in Ezra-Nehemiah. The narrator does rely on similarly privileged information in the very beginning of the book, testifying that the spirit of Yahweh was at work (Ezra 1:1 and Ezra 1:5). Elsewhere the narrator usually confines himself to what is normally accessible to mortal eye. It is significant therefore, that the narrator resorts to a clearly omniscient perspective to confirm Ezra. Given literary conventions, such direct definitions in which the narrator clearly displays his omniscience

---

[43] Zerubbabel and Jeshua have none. Persian kings are identified as such, but only rarely are other persons so identified. Sheshbazzar the prince (Ezra 1:8) and Eliashib the high priest (Neh 3:1) are notable exceptions.

[44] *Poetics of Biblical Narrative*, 328–341.

are fully authoritative evaluations, leaving no room to doubt the nature of the described events or characters. They also point the way to future developments. As Fensham correctly observes, commenting on Ezra 7:10, "Ezra's actions in the rest of the book must be interpreted in the light of this verse."[45]

The narrator's confirmation of Ezra gives way to the king's letter (Ezra 7:11–26), which extols, confirms, and heaps privileges upon the thus far silent figure of Ezra. Artaxerxes' letter reiterates Ezra's priestly and scribal qualifications (see esp. Ezra 7:12 and 21), investing Ezra with authority, powers, and funds that defy credibility.[46] The extravagance of the king's generosity toward Ezra, combined with the narrator's praise, create great expectations concerning Ezra. One anticipates a grand figure to step onto the stage and perform marvelous deeds. Instead, the book presents a rather unassuming person, who confesses that he is ashamed to ask for an escort (Ezra 8:22), who is not always aware of community affairs (Ezra 9:1), and who does not readily use the enormous powers that have been bestowed upon him, but lets others take the initiative and make decisions. There emerges, in particular, a sharp contrast between what Ezra is entitled to do (according to the lengthy introduction and royal edict) and what he does, in fact, with this bounty in the rest of the narrative.

Batten, observing this contrast,[47] concludes that the edict is a fraud and Ezra ineffectual: "Ezra is here clothed with all of the power of the Pers. king in the whole of Syria, yet he was unable to effect a single divorce except by a pathetic appeal to the people."[48] Adin Steinsaltz too suggests ineffectual leadership, depicting Ezra as an idealist, implying, however, a failed idealist.[49]

A literary rather than historical reading of the material points in another direction. The narrator's confirmation of the edict and of Ezra's royal favor

---

[45] Books of Ezra and Nehemiah, 101.

[46] Batten expresses the inevitable doubts and problems that such an edict raises in the minds of scholars: "It is difficult to believe that the Pers. king would bestow such immense grants upon Ezra, including c. $140,000 in cash; indeed, it is impossible that Ezra, whose purpose was the proper institution of the temple ritual, should need any such sum. It is absolutely out of the question that such enormous powers were conferred upon a Jewish pr., making him really the supreme authority in the whole Syrian province, with power to impose even the death penalty. The decree is even inconsistent with itself in this respect, for a part of it authorises the Pers. officers to pay Ezra money, and then he is clothed with power that would have enabled him to displace them if he saw fit" (Ezra and Nehemiah, 307).

[47] Batten continues: "Moreover, a large part of the decree is flatly at variance with the work of Ezra, which is described with more fulness than any other event in this period. There is not a hint in the whole story that this pr. ever received as much as a kid from any foreigner whatever. He says himself that he would not ask even a guard from the Pers. king. There is no hint of any tremendous sacrifices such as we should have heard of if the leader had received such liberal donations" (ibid., 307–308).

[48] Ibid., 307–308.

[49] A. Steinsaltz, "Ezra, The Ideological Leader," Biblical Images (New York: Basic Books, 1984) 205–214.

excludes derogating Ezra's actions to inability. It implies, instead, a deliberate restraint in the use of these prerogatives. The narrator's definition of Ezra's goals, i.e., to study, do, and teach the Torah, impels the reader to interpret Ezra's behavior (hence his restraint) in light of these goals. The study, practice, and teaching of Torah appear to preclude certain use of vested power. To paraphrase Batten, one is led to conclude that Ezra, "clothed with all the power of the Persian king," was *unwilling* (presumably because of his goals) to effect a single divorce "except by a pathetic appeal to the people."

Ezra's purpose is to teach Torah. Ezra's chosen method involves persuasion, example, and appeal, rather than coercion. The enormity of the powers in his possession heightens the magnitude of Ezra's restraint, stressing thereby his abnegation of such means. Even if the effectiveness of teaching by example might be questioned in real life, Ezra-Nehemiah's answer is quite clear: Ezra is successful. He influences the community, first, to follow his example and, second, to continue to follow the Torah even without him. As a true teacher, he makes himself ultimately dispensable. The survival of his teachings and the community's ability to persevere without his supervision testify to his success. His achievement is intimately linked to what he does and does not do.

Every episode where Ezra appears exemplifies his manner of teaching. At the core of Ezra's activities is the transfer of power and knowledge from himself to the community as a whole. He does so by example, delegation of power, joint decision making, reading of the Torah, and finally departing, leaving the community and the Torah in each other's care. In other words, Ezra succeeded in teaching God's "statutes and ordinances in Israel" (Ezra 7:10b).

The Ezra memoirs (Ezra 7:27–9:15) grant Ezra the opportunity to speak for himself, allowing the reader to see the world through Ezra's eyes. Ezra's first words typify him. His thanksgiving (Ezra 7:27–28) acknowledges, first, that God has acted on behalf of the house of God and, second, that Ezra's good fortune is the product of this. Here as elsewhere Ezra does not lose sight of his own instrumentality. Ezra addresses God as the God of "our fathers" (Ezra 7:27), introducing thereby Ezra's preeminent identification with the community. The "we" in Ezra's memoirs precedes the "I" (in a sharp contrast to Nehemiah).

Ezra's first reported action likewise typifies him. He gathers his compatriots to go up with him (Ezra 8:1–14). The list of names which heads Ezra's own report shows that Ezra immediately associates himself with others and credits them as an integral part of his accomplishments. Ezra is invariably surrounded by coworkers.

Yet Ezra, whom the king endowed with overwhelming privileges, is too timid to seek his own safety by asking for an escort, and relies, instead, exclusively on God (Ezra 8:21–23). This detail, like much else in the characterization of Ezra, will later provide a telling contrast to Nehemiah. On the other hand, when the returnees lack Levites in their midst, Ezra takes charge and does not rely on divine intervention alone. He promptly commissions a delegation to go and obtain Levites, names the members of the delegation, and credits them with success (Ezra 8:15–20). Having enlarged the company with Levites, Ezra immediately transfers responsibility to them and to the priests. Ezra once again does not see himself as sufficient unto himself but includes others. He submits the wealth of the community in trust into the hands of others, declaring the gifts and the cult personnel as holy (Ezra 8:28). As is customary for Ezra, he does not hoard sanctity and authority, but delegates them to others. Furthermore, Ezra issues instruction that the possessions—vessels and gifts— be transferred to the proper authorities in Jerusalem (Ezra 8:29), extending delegation even further.

Delegation of responsibility is likewise expressed by the plural subject of Ezra 8:36: "They also delivered the king's commissions. . . ." The king's commissions are presumably copies of Artaxerxes' letter, granting Ezra much power and authority (Ezra 7:12–26). It is apparently not Ezra alone, perhaps even not Ezra at all but others, who delivered these letters. The result is support from the king's satraps and the governors of the province Beyond the River who "aided the people and the house of God" (Ezra 8:36b).

Ezra-Nehemiah steadily portrays Ezra as a person who elicits cooperation, delegates tasks and powers, and then repeatedly recedes from the limelight, reappearing only by popular demand. He is brought back into action by a report about mixed marriages (Ezra 9:1). It is striking that Ezra has to be told about the mixed marriages in his community and does not see the situation on his own. A contrast with Nehemiah, who does see for himself, is at hand. Readers, ancient as well as modern, have been embarrassed by the fact that Ezra has to be told such things and does not—like Nehemiah, perhaps—observe them himself; they offer at times ingenious solutions.[50] Ezra's behavior here is quite consistent, however, with his actions elsewhere and need not surprise us. He is a self-effacing community servant who does not impose himself, and does not meddle. This is a striking, even humorous, contrast to Nehemiah.

Ezra, shocked by the news, goes into mourning and prayer. The prayer (Ezra 9:6–15) is an example of his subtle, nonautocratic manner of operation. As Williamson observes, "Ezra's handling of the problem of mixed marriages is noteworthy in that, quite unlike Nehemiah (cf. Neh 13:23–27), he used no direct coercion, but rather he encouraged the people to see the problem for themselves and to formulate their own response."[51] Ezra scorns no one, attacks no one. He does not threaten with penalties (which he is clearly

---

[50] Rudolph, too, comments on the astonishing fact that Ezra had to be told. He suggests the possibility of an earlier cooperation between Ezra and Shecaniah (*Esra und Nehemia*, 93). See also Fensham, *Books of Ezra and Nehemiah*, 123–124.

[51] *Ezra, Nehemiah*, 133.

authorized to impose on the basis of Ezra 7:12–26) nor does he command.[52]
He subjects only himself to repentance, fasting, and mourning. His example
stirs the community's conscience and prompts the people to act. Batten
observes that "the writer apparently meant that Ezra's tears were contagious."[53] One may expand and say that, throughout the book, Ezra's behavior
in general seems contagious. His power is the power of influence rather than
coercion, relying on example, embodying the difference between genuine
power and force.[54]

After Ezra's first-person report (Ezra 7:27–9:15), the third-person
narrator resumes in Ezra 10:1. The very movement from first to third person
replicates the dynamics of Ezra's role. It also serves to give the reader another
perspective from which to perceive Ezra. The narrator corroborates Ezra's
report, then continues to give account of subsequent developments. As the
text stands, Ezra proposes no resolution. Initiative for the specific action to
be followed comes from another member of the community who recognizes
Ezra's leadership and asks him to assume it (Ezra 10:4). Ezra consents.
Characteristically, he immediately includes others, prompting the whole
community to take an oath. Leadership and responsibility are thereby
extended and Ezra, temporarily, withdraws.[55]

Ezra's conduct in the subsequent resolution of the mixed marriages
problem illustrates his characteristic style. He remains in the background
while commands are issued to convene an assembly.[56] He assumes the role
he had been asked to take only after the people have assembled.[57] At long

---

[52] Williamson notes the following concerning Ezra's prayer: "Reflection on this outline [of the
prayer] reveals first that it comprises confession only, with no supplication in the imperative or
jussive whatsoever. . . . This not only distinguishes the passage from the penitential psalms of
lament . . . , but even from such passages as Neh 1:5–11" (*Ezra, Nehemiah,* 128–129).

[53] *Ezra and Nehemiah,* 340.

[54] Note also Rudolph on Ezra's emphasis on voluntary action (*Esra und Nehemia,* 89). Hannah
Arendt and Gandhi in our century amplified the differences between power and violence in
theory and in practice. See, for example, Arendt, *On Violence* (New York: Harcourt, Brace &
World, 1970), esp. pp. 1–5. Like Gandhi, Ezra in Ezra 9 avoids coercing others. The only pain
he is willing to inflict, the only deprivations he imposes, are upon himself. And, as was so often
the case with the more recent example of Gandhi, his people respond.

[55] The reference to Ezra's going to the room of Jehohanan (Ezra 10:6) functions in several
ways: it links Ezra with the current leading priest. It also shows that Ezra is welcome in that
chamber, which sets up a contrast with Nehemiah in Neh 6:11.

[56] Batten writes concerning Ezra's response to the mixed marriages: "The authority for the
edict, and which undertook to punish heavily those who disobeyed it, was not that of Ezra, but
of the oligarchy, 'the leaders and elders,' v. 8. . . . Ezra shows fervent zeal, a passion for the law,
an eloquence in prayer, but not a shred of authority to enforce his ideas" (*Ezra and Nehemiah,*
342). Batten is right that Ezra does not enforce his ideas, even though the readers know that
he *has* the authority to do so (Ezra 7). Instead, Ezra implements his ideas by different means
than enforcement. His passion, zeal, eloquent prayer, and the power of persuasive example seem
to suffice.

[57] Edicts and commands are issued in the plural, without naming Ezra as subject (Ezra

last Ezra directly issues instructions: the members of the community are to thank God and separate from foreign women. The community's response is revealing: a resounding "Yes" coupled with a subsequent "But," which is not really an equivocation but a counterproposal to ease the pressure. Ezra appears to be willing to negotiate and modify his instructions. In contrast to Nehemiah whose directives are immediately enforced without murmur, Ezra's directives elicit negotiations and a compromise to which he assents. The dialogical nature of Ezra's leadership, the give and take which he evokes and implements, could not have been illustrated more vividly. Here is a leader who listens to his community, who shuns dictatorial measures (even though he clearly has authority to use them), who works through committees, who hears the needs of his people, and who devises *with them* a procedure that will be most responsive to their needs, without thereby compromising his own rigorous standards. The negotiations result in a committee of which Ezra is a part. Ezra disappears from view once the committee completes its job, remaining unobtrusive until summoned again by the community.[58]

A new figure emerges in our story, and emerges brightly: Nehemiah, whose voice constantly proclaims his own importance. The boisterous voice of Nehemiah, who never has anything good to say about his predecessors (see Neh 5:15, for example, where Nehemiah criticizes previous governors), threatens to lull the reader into forgetfulness that there ever was an Ezra. But if Nehemiah's words ring too shrilly in our ears at times it is because, in a large measure, the echoes of the Ezra story are still with us as an oblique commentary on Nehemiah's rise to power and his activities.

And if the reader has forgotten about Ezra in the intervening chapters and (given the book's chronology) in the intervening years, clearly the community itself has *not* forgotten him. On the great day of assembly (Nehemiah 8), the people gather as one and tell Ezra to read from the Torah. The initiative here, as in Ezra 10:2, comes from others to whom Ezra responds. Ezra reemerges only by popular demand.

The long delay between Ezra's commission and arrival (Ezra 7) and the public reading of the Torah (Nehemiah 8) suggests the following: It is only after his people ask him to do so, not simply when the Persian king appoints him, that Ezra formally brings the Torah to his people.[59] Once again, Ezra

---

10:7–8). It has been suggested that Ezra's portrait seeks to avoid presenting him as a priest who usurps another's priestly role. After all, another priest heads the cult in Ezra's time (Neh 12:26 mentions Joiakim). K. Galling ("Bagoas und Esra," *Studien zum Geschichte Israels im persischen Zeitalter* [Tübingen: Mohr, 1964] 149–184), offers historical and political explanations; Ezra was careful not to inflame passions or create tensions.

[58] Note the expression, "and the sons of the captivity did so" (Ezra 10:16), which further stresses communal involvement.

[59] The delay is expressed both temporally and literarily. Years have presumably elapsed; Ezra

does not pursue a leadership role; the people ask him to assume it. Once again, he does not hoard power but immediately shares it.

Ezra's propensity to share power, authority, and visibility quickly manifests itself once more in the reading of the Torah. Ezra, and Ezra alone, has been asked by the people to bring the Torah (Ezra 8:1). Ezra, however, shares this role with priests, Levites and, eventually, with Nehemiah as well (Neh 8:9). Thus when Ezra stands on the wooden pulpit which "they" made, he is flanked by partners whose names are recorded.[60] The reading begins with Ezra, as the singular verb ויקרא, "and he read," in Neh 8:3 indicates. But, as is consistently the case with Ezra's portrait, this quickly turns into a communal activity, as the plural ויקראו, "and they read," in Neh 8:8 suggests. The intervening verses accomplish the shift from the singular to the plural (linguistically and existentially).[61]

The characteristic portrayal of Ezra as one who does not seize or monopolize power and leadership, as one who does not demand attention but is sought out, is further amplified in the next episode: "On the second day the heads of fathers' houses of all the people, with the priests and the Levites, came together to Ezra the scribe in order to study the words of the law" (Neh 8:13). According to the narrator, Ezra has made no demands. He merely introduced the Torah to his people (at their request) and exhorted them to rejoice in it and in the holiness of the day (Neh 8:9–10). But immediately afterwards, the heads of the community voluntarily seek Ezra in order to learn the words of the Torah. The text is revealing: "And they found it written in the law . . ." (Neh 8:14). Ezra apparently does not "tell them" but enables them to find God's commandments in Moses' Torah. He acts as a midwife between the community and the Torah and does not keep himself between the two any longer than is necessary. As soon as his task is complete, and the community can find for itself God's commandments in the Torah, Ezra fades away. Neh 8:14–16 indicates that Ezra has accomplished his task: Israel is able to approach the Torah, to know it, and carry it out; the assembled readers find out that Israel should dwell in booths and they go out and do so.

Ezra, who has made himself dispensable, as true teachers do, now vanishes. He no longer appears as a major actor. Neh 12:26 names him as one

---

7 speaks of the seventh year of Artaxerxes; Neh 2:1 specifies the twentieth year of Artaxerxes. Roughly eleven chapters have intervened.

[60] Some of these names have been mentioned earlier as part of Ezra's entourage; some will appear later; some are not otherwise known. Batten writes: "The list of names is regarded by Mey. as quite worthless (*Ent.* 179⁴). Torrey regards these men as laymen (*ES*²⁶⁸). There must originally have been but twelve, six on each side" (*Ezra and Nehemiah*, 355). In terms of historicity the list may be useless. But its narrative significance is clear: it extends leadership by having Ezra share his pulpit with others on this momentous occasion.

[61] Batten writes, "The plural verb is evidently a mistake, for Ezra alone was the lector" (ibid., 356). Not so in our interpretation. 1 Esdras parallels retain the implication that Ezra is reading while the others assist in making it comprehensible.

of the landmark figures of the era. Last seen, he marches in the procession in a direction opposite Nehemiah (Neh 12:36). His name, however, is glaringly absent from some of the most important events that follow the public reading of the Torah. The great prayer of Neh 9:6–37, which the LXX attributes to Ezra, remains in the MT loosely attached to no particular speaker or, at best, to the people as a whole (Neh 9:4 and 9:5).[62] The silence concerning Ezra at this point is apt. Ezra's effectiveness as a leader and teacher has made further emphasis on him no longer necessary. He taught his people well. He initiated a process for transmission and continuity. Having done so, he steps aside and lets others carry on.

His success is demonstrated by the fact that the people do indeed carry on. One notes that some of the names in Neh 8:4 and 8:7 recur in 9:4 and 9:5. Some of the leaders now are the ones who held leadership roles with Ezra. The power and knowledge that have been shared have also been effectively transferred.

Ezra's absence is consistent with the way Ezra has been portrayed throughout. His fading into the shadows is striking to us because we expect great leaders to remain in the limelight, because they usually try to, and because Nehemiah always does so. But Ezra and his leadership are in direct controversy with such a model, embodying another mode,[63] one that shifts the limelight from the outstanding leader to the community. This is an important aspect of Ezra-Nehemiah's emphasis on the prosaic as over against the poetic or epic mode.

Scholars occasionally point to similarities between Ezra's confession in Ezra 9 and Nehemiah 9, suggesting that Ezra is implicitly the author of the latter, even if his name is omitted.[64] But since Ezra-Nehemiah disengages Ezra from the narrative, such similarities become another reflection of Ezra's effectiveness. They demonstrate that even without his immediate presence,

---

[62] Batten argues that Ezra's name in the LXX "is a late interpolation, and contradicts vv[1-5]" (ibid., 352). His choice of the MT for this reading is significant since Batten often prefers other readings, not being bound by any special prior commitment to a preference for the MT. See also p. 365.

[63] R. Negah in her article "Why is Ezra's Name Absent from the List of Signatories of the Convenant?" (*Beth Mikra* 80 [1979] 79–80), puzzles over Ezra's role and finds a clue in the rabbinic silence over this matter. She concludes that Ezra must be the author of the covenant and therefore need not sign it—as was the case with Moses (Exod 19:8). She also concludes that the rabbis most likely recognized such an implicit role for Ezra and therefore were not perturbed by the absence of his name. I suggest, instead, that the rabbinic lack of concern stems from rabbinic preference for leaders who do not center their teachings too firmly upon themselves. The rabbis were especially wary of emphasis on personalities and sought to move away from it. Note the silence over Moses in the Haggadah. Indeed, theirs is largely a view of life which moves away from the "great men" theory of history, which is why Ezra becomes so significant.

[64] Note, for example, Fensham, *Books of Ezra and Nehemiah*, 222–223.

Ezra's teachings are perpetuated. His words live on in the mouths of others. The community, and presumably the next generation, follow in his footsteps, having learned the teachings he uttered (Ezra 9) and the Torah he taught (Nehemiah 8). Others now act on these things and pass them on. Ezra succeeded in teaching his people to *know* the Torah and to *do* it (cf. Ezra 7:10). Nehemiah 10 is another example of the ways Ezra's impact is per-petuated and does not fall apart when he leaves the scene—a fate most leaders suffer (note Nehemiah's mounting troubles during his absence). Ezra's teachings survive and flourish. The community perseveres in its com-mitment to follow the teachings of the Torah and binds itself to it in a written oath. The mantle has been passed on, not to a single individual but to a group.

The direct definition, prominent in the introduction of Ezra, and the indirect presentation, constituting the rest of the Ezra narrative, combine to depict Ezra as the model character and the most important individual in the book. He is portrayed constantly as the "self-effacing teacher of Torah."[65] His leadership takes the form of dialogue and equips others to do without him. He influences others by example, delegates responsibilities, works with committees, trains future leadership and then steps aside, leaving Torah and community to each other. Every one of these characteristics not only defines Ezra positively but also contrasts him with Nehemiah.

III. The Portrait of Nehemiah

Whereas Ezra is the exemplar, Nehemiah is the foil. Nehemiah bursts on the scene with hardly an introduction, bristling with energy and concern, constantly struggling with opponents. His portrayal is complex and the book's attitude toward him may be best described as ambivalent. On the one hand he is built up—largely through the quantity of material explicitly or implic-itly attributed to him. On the other hand, there is an undercutting which prompts Kellermann to speak of the "degradation" of Nehemiah.[66]

The absence of pedigree and the sudden introduction establish an immediate contrast with Ezra's venerable credentials. Nehemiah comes from no place—no family is mentioned beyond his being "son of Hacaliah"—a silence significant in a book so attentive to pedigrees.[67]

Nehemiah, like Ezra, is initially presented as a pious person. In time of crisis he first turns to God; only afterwards does he turn to the king. In this

---

[65] Whedbee, "Ezra and Nehemiah: A Tale of Torah and City, of Piety and Politics," 1.

[66] Kellermann, *Nehemia*, 92. Kellermann lists numerous parallels and contrasts between Ezra and Nehemiah which serve to elevate Ezra over Nehemiah (ibid., 95).

[67] It has been contended that Nehemiah was of Davidic descent (see Kellermann, *Nehemia*, 156–159). Even if this were the case, the point is that he has no such credentials in Ezra-Nehemiah. Ezra-Nehemiah presents him as one of no particular familial importance. For a good discussion of whether Nehemiah was a eunuch, see E. M. Yamauchi, "Was Nehemiah the Cupbearer a Eunuch?" *ZAW* 92 (1980) 132–141. Yamauchi reviews and discredits the arguments in favor of such of a view.

he somewhat resembles Ezra who thanks God for his good fortune. But the similarity also ends here. The *contrast* to Ezra is thorough and persistent. Whereas Ezra is always asked by others and never asks for anything, especially for himself, Nehemiah is always demanding—of God and of men. His first appearance is cluttered with demands—and these continue.[68] He asks God's support (Neh 1:5–11; note the repetition of the imperative, "let thy ear be attentive," תהי נא אזנך קשבת, in 1:6 and 1:11) and the king's authorization (Neh 2:5). Requests typify him. His most ardent request—that he be remembered—punctuates the book (Neh 1:8, 5:19, 13:14, 22, 31). All of Nehemiah's requests keep him at the center. Even when concern for his people motivates him to journey to Jerusalem, his own vested interests are not neglected.[69]

Nehemiah's prayer sets the tone for much of Nehemiah's posture: he casts himself in the line of the worthies—the true servant of God. In sharp contrast to Ezra, who throws himself upon God's mercies as one of the undeserving community, Nehemiah speaks from the perspective of one who belongs to the circle of those who love God and keep God's commandments and is therefore deserving of God's attention and support (see Neh 1:5–11, esp. v 11). The premise of his prayer is the righteousness of the one who now approaches God. Nehemiah's confidence is both endearing and irritating, as bravado often is. His success is evident: the city wall is rebuilt; he is remembered. Less clear is the magnitude of the obstacles, especially in view of his claimed royal support. It remains plausible that Nehemiah exaggerates these, much as he exaggerates his own importance.

Nehemiah rarely waits for an invitation. He invariably intervenes, with zeal and heavy handedness. Having asked about the state of affairs in the land (Neh 1:2), he acts on the received news without having been invited to intervene. Having captured the king's ear, he asks permission to rebuild the city. When granted his wish, he asks for yet another thing, viz., written permission (Neh 2:7). Having assessed the situation in Jerusalem, he urges the Judeans to rebuild (Neh 2:17). One wonders if irony is intended when Nehemiah points out the obvious to those who have been living in peace with the reality of the shattered walls. He declares to those who dwell in Jerusalem: "You see the trouble we are in, how Jerusalem lies in ruins with its gates burned" (Neh 2:17). But obviously they have not been troubled, since they live in the midst of this situation, seemingly unperturbed.[70]

---

[68] There are generic differences between the two prayers. These account for some aspects of the contrast. But this does not thereby excuse the differences. It only heightens them. Ezra's chosen words are presented as thanksgiving and confession; Nehemiah's as petitions of various sorts. The genres thus characterize them.

[69] Notice how Nehemiah asks for wood for his own house as well (Neh 2:8).

[70] Rashi, reading שבר as meaning "to break," says that Nehemiah, in his nocturnal journey, increased the breaches in the wall. Such reading of the verb is not farfetched. After all, the usually ascribed rendering of שבר in Neh 2:13 as "inspect" is unique in the Bible (note also the

Nehemiah in his memoirs portrays himself as a liberator in all areas of life — social, military, economic, and cultic. His zeal is reminiscent of one who will help the elderly person across the street, whether that elderly person wants this or not. It is not at all clear that his subjects — and other people are consistently cast by him in that role of "subjects" (i.e., inferiors to be manipulated) — appreciate being "liberated." His direct intervention on behalf of the perceived oppressed (whether they wish it or not) is apparent in Neh 13:4, 13:10, 13:15, 13:23, 13:28. Some of the negative consequences of his liberation emerge in Nehemiah chapter 5. In most cases he seems to be up against other established authorities among the Judeans. He is invariably in conflict (note the repetition of אריב/אריבה, "I remonstrated," in Neh 13:11, 17, 25). Whereas Ezra is typically surrounded by coworkers and elicits cooperation, Nehemiah is surrounded, instead, by adversaries.

Wordplay in Nehemiah's memoirs, especially Nehemiah 2, reveals much about his frame of mind. There is a striking repetition of the words טוב and רע, "good" and "evil." They echo throughout the Nehemiah story and are most frequent in the early sections (esp. Neh 2:1–10).[71] One notes also the play in the name of his chief opponent, Tobiah. These indicate Nehemiah's polarized views of reality. Nehemiah sees the world in terms of good or evil, friend or foe, in contrast to an Ezra who interacts amicably with others.

Nehemiah's belligerent posture toward the world is evident in his military escort (Neh 2:9). Nehemiah avails himself to such a military escort. His announcement "Now the king had sent with me officers of the army and horsemen [וחיל ופרשים]" (Neh 2:9b), finds its polar opposite in Ezra's timid confession "I was ashamed to ask the king for a band of soldiers and

---

LXX which translates שבר as συντρίβων, "mourn"). The root normally means "to break." According to Rashi, Nehemiah's purpose was to increase the damage and thereby elicit, the next day, the community's consent to rebuild. See Rashi commentary on Neh 2:12–13. Such a mode of exacting consent is interesting, and it is even more interesting that Rashi considers Nehemiah capable of such tactics.

[71] Wordplay of good and evil, טוב and רע, dominates Neh 2:1–10. The passage moves from "evil" which concentrates in its beginning towards a series of "good," closing with a reversal which nevertheless ends on a note of "good."

ולא הייתי רע לפניו (Neh 2:1)

מדוע פניך רעים ואתה אינך חולה אין זה כי אם רע לב ואירא הרבה מאד (2:2)

... מדוע לא ירעו פני ... (2:3)

These are contrasted with emphasis on the good:

... אם על המלך טוב ואם ייטב עבדך לפניך ... (2:5)

... וייטב לפני המלך (2:6)

... אם על המלך טוב ... (2:7)

... כיד אלהי הטובה עלי ... (2:8)

and finally,

וישמע סנבלט החרני וטוביה העבד העמני וירע

להם רעה גדלה אשר בא אדם לבקש טובה לבני ישראל (2:10)

horsemen [חיל ופרשים]" (Ezra 8:22a). There is a touch of irony in that such an escort proves unnecessary in either case. But Ezra's reliance on God and his acceptance of vulnerability in this sphere provide a telling contrast to Nehemiah who thereby emerges as "overdressed" for the occasion.[72]

Ezra's primary community is that of the children of the exile,[73] a community of which he is an integral part. The locus of Nehemiah's attention, his sphere of activities, is the Judeans, to whom he is largely an outsider barging in. In contrast to Ezra, Nehemiah does not really seek to work with local leadership, but imposes his plans on them.

It is thus characteristic of Nehemiah that his first reported act upon arrival is one of exclusion of the local community. This is precisely the opposite of what Ezra does. An analogy between the two men is indicated by the reference to a three day interval between their arrival and initial activities in Jerusalem. The repetition of the "three days" (Ezra 8:32 and Neh 2:11) alerts the reader to possible parallels. The similarity, however, serves to accentuate the contrast in what follows: Ezra's first activity is a public transfer of gifts and authority in broad daylight; Nehemiah's is a secret (note the double emphasis on not having told anyone of his plans, Neh 2:12, 16), lone inspection of the city walls at night. Public, communal, diurnal activity is contrasted with a secretive, solo, nocturnal one. Since Ezra has been favored by the narrator, his mode is clearly praised by means of this comparsion whereas Nehemiah's is obliquely criticized. Ezra establishes links and continuity by publicly transferring wealth and power into the hands of the local leaders, even though the reader knows that he is authorized to keep power to himself. Nehemiah does the reverse.

It is rather striking that Nehemiah's name does *not* appear in the list of Nehemiah 3 among those who actually—physically—built the wall, even though the high priest also participates in that task. Indication of Nehemiah's

---

[72] Fensham, attempting to defend Nehemiah, writes: "Some scholars want to see in these verses [Ezra 8:22] an apologetic tendency against Nehemiah, because he travelled with a military escort (Neh 2:9). It is often regarded as a subtle hint of the superiority of Ezra over Nehemiah [Myers, 71]. But we can explain this difference of approach as follows. Ezra the priest went to Jerusalem on a religious mission. In such a case a military escort would have seemed strange, because the religious group would then have shown no faith in their God. Nehemiah went as a political official, a governor, to Jerusalem. In such a case, the king would protect his official with a military escort" (*Books of Ezra and Nehemiah*, 117).

Aside from the circularity of Fensham's argument, it must be remembered that a large contingent of men, women, and children, carrying a vast amount of gold and silver, as the returnees did, would be an easy prey for attack and merits protection. The trust in God is clearly the important ingredient in Ezra's refusal to ask for such protection. The risks awaiting Nehemiah do not justify greater precaution. He did not have to have one (as one knows in retrospect). More significantly, the book could have omitted such details. As things stand, the parallels accentuate a contrast.

[73] The term gola recurs throughout the Ezra narrative. See Vogt, *Studie zur nachexilischen Gemeinde*, 21–42.

actual doings, beyond the initial call to action in 2:17, awaits chapter 4. Perhaps the exhortation itself, in 2:17, is our hint of things to come; he says: לכו ונבנה, literally, "[you] go and let us build," rather than נלך ונבנה, "let us go and let us build."

Hostilities seem to bring out the best in Nehemiah and rally him to action. Nehemiah lives defensively, combatting presumed attacks, armed for battles which never quite take place. Note the elaborate defense precautions (Neh 4:2–17) and Nehemiah's arrival with a military escort to Jerusalem. One could argue that Nehemiah's preparedness for battle and his willingness to show force serve to discourage attacks. This argument would be convincing were it not for the fact that Ezra, who leaves himself defenseless, is not molested either (Ezra 8:21–23). The contrast renders Nehemiah somewhat like Don Quixote who charges against windmills, dressed up in full armor for battles that never materialize.

Nehemiah 5, describing the cry of the oppressed people, is a tantalizing chapter in its present location. At first glance, Nehemiah appears to be engaged in fence mending on several levels. Breaches in the wall are paralleled by breaches in the social structure; both require attention. On the one hand, this invites us to see Nehemiah as one who is concerned with building of community as much as with building of walls. Social gaps are deemed as dangerous as architectural ones; neither is to be neglected by our hero. On the other hand, coming directly at the heels of massive war efforts by the populace, it implies a relation between the two events. A connection between building and oppression, which has a long standing precedence in the Bible, is implicit here as well.[74] The social-economic oppression appears to be the other side of the extravagant war efforts of building. Nehemiah thus appears to be responsible. His grand scheme, intended to solve a problem which did not bother the people, has now resulted in hardships which he seeks to remedy and for which he expects gratitude. The painful irony of the vicious cycle of such reform measures is not without parallels in our culture.

But upon closer inspection, Nehemiah is implicated even more in Nehemiah 5. His first response to the people's outcry is to quarrel with the leaders because they exact interest from their brothers (Neh 5:7). But from Neh 5:10 one learns that Nehemiah himself is guilty of the same practice! His righteous anger rapidly becomes self righteousness when he concedes that he too practiced this usury. Let us listen to his language: "You are exacting interest each from his brother," says Nehemiah. He continues, "And I held a great assembly against them" (Neh 5:7b). And again, "The thing that you are doing is not good (Neh 5:9a)"—"you" rather than "we." Ironically, Nehemiah

---

[74] See, for example, 1 Sam 8:7–18 and Exodus 1; see also the Gilgamesh Epic. Batten writes concerning chapter 5, "The placing of this c. so that it breaks the story of the rebuilding of the wall indicates that the compiler regarded these hard conditions as due to the work on the walls" (*Ezra and Nehemiah*, 237).

himself has been doing the same thing to the people, as the next verse confesses: "And I and my brethren and my young men also charged interests of silver and grain from them" (וגם אני אחי ונערי נשים בהם כסף ודגן [Neh 5:10]).[75]

It is uncertain how to read the third person singular ויאמר, "and he said," in Neh 5:9. The implicit speaker appears to be Nehemiah, so indicates the Qere (and the commentaries follow). But the third-person introduces Nehemiah's words. It is this remark by the narrator which discloses the embarrassing information, i.e. that Nehemiah is as guilty as those whom he attacks. His own words (which he withheld from us, but the narrator's "he said" supplies) condemn him.

Further criticism is implicit in the juxtaposition of Neh 5:1-13 and its account of social ills with Neh 5:14-19 and its description of Nehemiah's sumptuous table, kept by Nehemiah at his own expense. Ostensibly this is an additional example of Nehemiah's generosity, compounding his remission of debts. But the present arrangement undermines this impression.[76] Nehemiah's generosity toward the oppressed whose debts he willingly annuls in Neh 5:10-13 loses much of its magnanimity by the display of wealth which directly follows in Neh 5:14-18. Nehemiah, who can well afford to entertain as lavishly as he describes in Neh 5:17-18, can surely also afford to forego the interest that he and his comrades have been collecting up to now (by his own admission, Neh 5:10). By placing the two episodes side by side, the book turns Nehemiah's generosity and restoration of justice to a mocking gesture reminiscent of Marie Antoinette's "Let them eat cake!"

Nehemiah's amassing of power reaches a surprising apex in Neh 5:14 (see too וימלך in Neh 5:7). If Ezra astonishes us by not using authority that we know he has, Nehemiah astonishes us by claiming authority we do not know he has. Having been privy to Nehemiah's conversations with the king, we are unprepared for the statement that the king *commanded* him to be the people's governor. One senses a sleight of hand not unlike that in the Bathsheba-Nathan scene in 1 Kings 1.[77]

---

[75] My translation. Nehemiah's culpability is clearer in the MT than in most English translations, which obscure and tone down this verse (note, e.g., the RSV).

[76] Batten's comment on 5:17 is illuminating. Having described the various persons invited to Nehemiah's table, Batten writes, "The text adds: *and the rulers*. But it is difficult to see what place they have here. Their presence would not be accounted a good deed on his part. Feeding the poor is meritorious, but feeding the rich is a different matter. We may best follow G [LXX] and om. [omit] this word. Further the text inserts *and*, making two classes sitting at the governor's table, the Judaeans and *those who had come in from the nations*. This again obscures the point of merit" (*Ezra and Nehemiah*, 246). The merit in the received text is indeed obscured, as Batten notes. Such obfuscation is probably intentional, reflecting the book's misgivings about Nehemiah's merit. It places a credibility gap between how Nehemiah perceives himself and how the reader is asked to perceive him.

[77] The withholding of information by the narrator is one of the literary techniques that create

We readers know that three things have been requested and granted by the king to Nehemiah: 1) a leave of absence; 2) written orders for safe passage; 3) written orders for timber for Nehemiah's construction projects (Neh 2:8). Even if standard rhetoric of the time implies a strong claim on Nehemiah's part, i.e., even if such building activity and its permission automatically signal certain high office and commission which the reader and/or the king recognize, what transpires can in no way be described as a *commandment* from the king. Yet Nehemiah uses the verb צוה in Neh 5:14. Here we have another ironic reversal between Ezra and Nehemiah. Ezra *is* commanded to take charge and rule the people, but does not; Nehemiah is not so commanded over the people but takes this role upon himself. Ezra, who was sent for a supervisory role, never claims such authority; Nehemiah, who had to wrest permission to go, claims to have been commanded to govern. The reader, surprised that Nehemiah had been appointed governor, wonders whether Artaxerxes himself would also be similarly surprised.

Ambiguity increases when one realizes the absence of an antecedent for the verb "command."[78] This equivocation, or rather the missing subject of Nehemiah 5:14, may be an accurate reflection of the reported reality; no one has been specifically mentioned as one who commanded Nehemiah to be governor. As such, it is an indirect commentary on Nehemiah by the text. This mode of narration reinforces the portrait of Nehemiah as a self-made man. It also reiterates the contrast between Ezra, who surprises by what he does not do with his official powers, and Nehemiah, who surprises by what he does without them.

Nehemiah characteristically does more than he is asked to do and in areas where he has no clear role. He was authorized to build the wall and gates of Jerusalem. But his own words tell us that he expanded his activities. He repeatedly asks to be remembered precisely for these other tasks (e.g., Neh 13:31).

Nehemiah, unlike Ezra, does not engage in the give and take of negotiation. In Neh 6:2–8 and 6:19 Nehemiah rebuffs conciliatory overtures by others. In Neh 2:12–16 he specifically excludes from decision making those who are to be affected by it ("and I had not yet told the Jews, the priests, the nobles, and the officials, and the rest that were to do the work" [2:16b]). Nehemiah's only confidence is in himself and in the God who is presumably always on his side. It is this God who is purported to be the real reader of

---

dissonance. See Berlin, *Poetics and Interpretation,* 71, and Bar-Efrat, *The Art of Narration in the Bible,* 73–74.

    [78] Rudolph, commenting on Neh 2:1–10, says the following about Nehemiah's appointment as governor: "Daraus ergibt sich, daß seine Ernennung zum Statthalter (5:14) nicht sofort, sondern erst etwas später erfolgte, sonst hätte er hier davon gesprochen. (Die Meinung Hölschers, daß die Frage 6a [Neh 2:6] nur ein Scherz gewesen und das Schlußsätzchen von 6 ein späteres Mißverständis sei, ist so unwahrscheinlich wie möglich" (*Esra und Nehemia,* 107).

Nehemiah's work, as the "remember me, O my God" formulas state (e.g., Neh 13:14).

Nehemiah ends as he began, with the emphasis on himself: "Remember me, O my God, for good" (Neh 13:31). His final reforms have been anticipated by the narrator who reports that the people themselves had organized cultic provisions (Neh 12:44 and 47), were observant of purities (Neh 12:45), and separated themselves (Neh 13:3). The community's commitment to these activities had been stated and sealed in Nehemiah 10. When Nehemiah declares that it was he who accomplished all these things (Neh 13:29–31), one suspects exaggeration. Nehemiah, for example, states, "I also found out that the portions of the Levites had not been given to them.... So I remonstrated with the officials and said, 'Why is the house of God forsaken?' [נעזב]' "(Neh 13:10–11). But the people have previously pledged not to forsake (נעזב) the house of God (Neh 10:40), and the reader has already been informed that giving such daily portions was in effect in Zerubbabel's time (Neh 12:47). Consequently, Nehemiah, at most, is merely enforcing the community's pledge and prior practices.

Thus, even though Ezra-Nehemiah allows Nehemiah to have the last word, the reader is aware that Nehemiah's self-adulation is not wholly justified. The narrator, who preceded Nehemiah, undermines Nehemiah's self-glorification and undermines our trust. While Nehemiah repeatedly declares how uniquely beneficial he has been, the narrator casts doubts on these assertions by placing other information in strategic points, deflating Nehemiah's claims to uniqueness and grandeur. Nehemiah's "I did this . . ." is contrasted with the narrator's "they."

Ezra-Nehemiah presents Nehemiah's final accomplishments as executing what others in the community have agreed upon. Far from being the master of circumstances, as he claims, he is tamed into the role of a civil servant, carrying out the community's prior decisions. This twist on Nehemiah's role and portrait could have been avoided had the memoirs of Chapter 13 preceded Nehemiah 10. Such arrangement would have confirmed Nehemiah's influence and impact by suggesting that he precipitated reforms which the community then consented to undertake. The present arrangement, however, reverses the relation and turns Nehemiah's claim into a hollow boast.

Ezra-Nehemiah's portrait of Nehemiah is more ambivalent than some of the later traditions about him. It reflects a controversy and definite unease with the man. Morton Smith points out that with Nehemiah we have an image from the Persian Greek world, i.e., the tyrant,[79] coming into Jewish tradition. Ezra-Nehemiah incorporates it in some measure. This incorporation, however, is not wholehearted, as I have shown. It serves to undermine

---

[79] *Palestinian Parties and Politics That Shaped the Old Testament* (New York: Columbia University Press, 1971), 137.

and deflate. The book is not as enamored with Nehemiah as Nehemiah
himself is. The ambivalence is indicated, as I have shown, by juxtapositions
with Ezra, by shifts in points of view, and in the use of various narrative
techniques.

Ezra-Nehemiah's ambivalence stands out when we compare Nehemiah
with other portraits of heroic figures. Zerubbabel in 1 Esdras is sufficiently
similar for a useful comparison. Zerubbabel in 1 Esdras is a heroic figure
unencumbered with ambivalence. His glorification is clear and unambiguous. There is congruity between what the narrator states and what the
hero — and Zerubbabel is clearly the hero — does and says. The overall effect
creates a steady admiration for the man and his accomplishments (see
Chapter Five below).

Nehemiah in Josephus is likewise unambiguous. In quick but decisive
strokes, Josephus depicts a man moving from success to success.[80] Even
though he is never called governor (whereas Zerubbabel is), Nehemiah's
merits and achievements are clear. He receives the king's permission to build
the wall and finish building the temple. He inspires the Jews to build, wards
off real antagonists (real in the sense that they have in fact killed many Jews
according to *Ant.* XI.174). He repopulates the city and dies at a great age.

Ezra-Nehemiah is more reserved. It is significant, however, that Ezra-
Nehemiah does not finally reject Nehemiah. It recognizes Nehemiah's
significance but defuses him by embedding him in a larger context where his
abilities are duly represented and memorialized but without his own exces-
sive veneration of these activities and accomplishments. Ezra-Nehemiah's
deflation of the figure of Nehemiah is not aimed exclusively at Nehemiah; it
is part and parcel of the larger concern of the book, namely, the subordination of the so-called heroes to the needs and primary significance of the
community as a whole. Ezra emerges as a wholly exemplary leader because
he expresses such subordination. Nehemiah's claims to be above it, reinterpreted through the final shape of the book, are shown to be spurious.[81]

IV. Conclusions

A study of the portraits of Ezra and Nehemiah is finally a study in
contrasts. But it is a contrast of a "matched . air."[82] Ezra-Nehemiah

---

[80] *Ant.* XI.159–183. The section about Nehemiah is considerably shorter than those about
either Zerubbabel or Ezra. It is approximately one third of the one on Zerubbabel and about
one third shorter than that of Ezra.

[81] A similar shift from the "great man" view of history to the emphasis on the acitivities and
abilities of the larger community is accomplished in the rendition of the other outstanding
individuals in Ezra-Nehemiah: Zerubbabel and ˌeshua.

[82] Childs comments on the fact that in the linking of the two figures, their individuality is
retained: "Significantly, no attempt was made otherwise to alter the sources which dealt with
each man individually" (*Introduction to the Old Testament*, 635). The sharp contrast between
the activities and persons of the two men belies the independence of the sources or the shaping

deliberately pairs the two men, linking their activities and persons even at the cost of awkward phraseology and possible historical modifications. Such pairing is characteristic of Ezra-Nehemiah as a whole. One sees a similar pairing in the story of Zerubbabel and Jeshua, who are more consistently balanced in Ezra-Nehemiah than in 1 Esdras. One sees this also in the linking of Haggai and Zechariah. This last pair has become so entrenched in the tradition *as a pair* that one often forgets that Haggai and Zechariah themselves never acknowledge each other's activities in the prophetic books which bear their names. Pairing of significant figures — dual leadership — is a persistent thread throughout Ezra-Nehemiah.[83] This may be a conscious substitution for the diarchy envisioned in Haggai and Zechariah.[84] If so, it represents a radically altered vision. The two men do not lead their community in the manner of Zechariah's Joshua and Zerubbabel, for example. They are not an elite, exclusively named from among an abstraction labelled "the people." On the contrary, as the ubiquitous lists in the book make clear, the ultimate prominence in the book rests with the people themselves. Moreover, Ezra-Nehemiah's characterization of these individuals serves to underscore the centrality of the community as a whole.

I have delineated the portraits of Ezra and Nehemiah by grouping segments strewn throughout the book to form a coherent and continuous picture of each man. Like historical reconstruction, so too character reconstruction entails rearranging the text, abstracting from it. It is important to bear in mind, therefore, that Ezra-Nehemiah itself does not present these characters in a continuous fashion. Their words and activities are dispersed throughout different sections of the book, presenting them more as collages than typical portraits. Their characterizations are neither continuous nor do they provide continuity for the narrative. Instead, the people themselves provide continuity and constitute the central subject of the book, as the repetition of lists emphatically shows.

The portraits have been assembled in order to show how Ezra and Nehemiah compare and how they advance the book's ideology. We have seen that Ezra is pictured as a self-effacing teacher of Torah who diligently includes others as coworkers, delegates authority, and teaches his people to function well without him. He demonstrates and embodies the shift from the person to the book of the Torah and to the community. Nehemiah, on the other hand, persistently asserts himself, amasses power, issues unilateral directives, and places himself as the indispensable center. Parallels force a

---

of the tradition. The contrast is established as much through the differences as through the parallels.

[83] See P. R. Ackroyd, *The Age of the Chronicler.* Supplement to *Colloquium: The Australian and New Zealand Theological Review* (Auckland, 1970) 25–26.

[84] See Petersen, *Haggai and Zechariah 1–8,* 233–234.

comparison between Ezra and Nehemiah; similarities create analogies between them, accentuating the differences and contrasts. Kellermann is right that, in Ezra-Nehemiah, Nehemiah is somewhat diminished—or perhaps ridiculed—by these means. But Kellermann overlooks the fact that Ezra-Nehemiah finally affirms this somewhat diminished Nehemiah.

This affirmation is crucial to Ezra-Nehemiah's perception of community and restoration. Diversity is incorporated. Nehemiah participates with Ezra in the ceremony of the reading of the Torah, and they speak together (Neh 8:9). Both Ezra and Nehemiah march in the encircling procession in the grand finale (Neh 12:36–40). The fact that they march in opposite directions dramatizes the book's view of these men and their relationship. They are opposites. Nevertheless, it is also revealing that the two processions in which they march finally join together in the house of God (Neh 12:40). Both men, both movements, opposite though they be, are necessary to complete the circle.

Such incorporation of diversity, of opposites, also accounts for the fact that these two figures are never subordinated to each other. They are poised in the balance as contemporaries whose activities combine. Neither is the other's apprentice (cf. Elijah and Elisha), nor do they, finally, replace one another. Such pairing without hierarchy is relatively rare in the Bible. It is common to find characters who act as foil to the main one and who, as secondary characters, accentuate both portraits by means of contrast (e.g., David and Uriah, Jacob and Esau). Ezra-Nehemiah contrasts these two characters, but acknowledges that both provide for continuity. Both are finally embraced. Their contrasts are also complementary. As in some M. C. Escher drawings, such complementary figures delineate each other's boundaries and combine to form the full picture.

The self-glorifying entrepreneur is as necessary as the self-effacing teacher of Torah. Their distinctive efforts and gifts are eventually brought together. But the book's emphasis on the priority of Ezra, both temporally and ideologically, articulates the book's conviction that it is Ezra who embodies the ideal to be emulated. Such an ideal diverts attention from a heroic person to a community living in accordance with the book of Torah. Ezra the leader exits, leaving people and Torah in each other's care. His success is precisely that he can afford to do so.

5

THE RELATION OF EZRA-NEHEMIAH
TO 1 ESDRAS

I. The Perimeters of 1 Esdras

1 Esdras and Ezra-Nehemiah are two early interpretations of the return and reconstruction. The particular emphases of Ezra-Nehemiah are highlighted more vividly when the two accounts are set side by side. This chapter reviews the structure and themes of 1 Esdras as a basis for comparing the books in order to illuminate the distinctive tendencies of each. This will be done in two steps. The first part discusses the perimeters of 1 Esdras; the second part examines the structure and themes.

As is well known, 1 Esdras (also known as 3 Ezra or Εσδρας α) has been preserved in the Greek versions, where it usually precedes Ezra-Nehemiah.[1] Nearly all parts of 1 Esdras correspond to parts of Chronicles and Ezra-Nehemiah; the most obvious exception to this is the story of the three guardsmen (1 Esdr 3:1–5:6), which is without parallel. Pohlmann describes the approximate relationship among the books as follows:[2]

    1 Esdr 1:1–20   = 2 Chr 35:1–19
    1 Esdr 1:21–22 without parallel
    1 Esdr 1.23–55   = 2 Chr 35:20–36:21
    1 Esdr 2:1–3a   = 2 Chr 36:22–23 = Ezra 1:1–3a
    1 Esdr 2:3b–11   = Ezra 1:3b–11
    1 Esdr 2:12–26   = Ezra 4:7–24
    1 Esdr 3:1–5:6 without parallel
    1 Esdr 5:7–71   = Ezra 2:1–4:5
    1 Esdr 6:1–9:36 = Ezra 5:1–10:44
    1 Esdr 9:37–55   = Neh 7:72–8:13a

One sees at a glance that the major differences, in terms of arrangement, are as follows: Ezra-Nehemiah includes Neh 1:1–7:71 and Neh 8:13b–13:31,

---

[1] See Swete, *Introduction to the Old Testament in Greek*, 201–210, and also Jellicoe, *Septuagint and Modern Study*, 290–294.

[2] *Studien zum dritten Esra*, 14. Pohlmann's versification for 1 Esdras appears to follow Rahlf's edition of the text.

which are not included in 1 Esdras. 1 Esdras, on the other hand, includes 1 Esdr 1:21–22 and 3:1–5:6 as well as 2 Chronicles 35–36, which are not included in Ezra-Nehemiah. The two books assign a different location for the Artaxerxes correspondence (1 Esdr 2:15–25; Ezra 4:7–24).

The presence of such variant yet closely related traditions about the return and restoration has engendered various explanations concerning their relationship in terms of dependence, priority, unity, etc. No consensus exists. Opinions remain sharply divided between two main theories, which Pohlmann conveniently labels the "Compilation Hypothesis" and the "Fragment Hypothesis." The former hypothesis assumes that 1 Esdras was compiled from Chronicles-Ezra-Nehemiah (viewed as the work of the Chronicler). The latter hypothesis considers 1 Esdras to be a fragment out of the original work of the Chronicler which comprised Chronicles-1 Esdras; it views Ezra-Nehemiah as a later rearrangement of that material (with added Nehemiah traditions).

The upholders of the Compilation Hypothesis maintain that 1 Esdras presupposes the canonical books of Chronicles and Ezra-Nehemiah. They assume that 1 Esdras has been transmitted largely as its author intended it, although some (e.g., Rudolph) slightly modify the ending. Proponents of this view recognize the fact that Josephus follows 1 Esdras and not Ezra-Nehemiah but conclude that he did so for convenience sake and his own apologetic reasons, not because he did not know Ezra-Nehemiah.[3] They also consider the omission of the Nehemiah material to be deliberate.

It should be added, even though Pohlmann does not make this point, that the advocates of the Compilation Hypothesis also assume that Chronicles and Ezra-Nehemiah have a common author. There is, however, no necessary correlation between the two assumptions. All that the Compilation Hypothesis requires, and claims to demonstrate, is that both Chronicles and Ezra-Nehemiah existed prior to 1 Esdras. Continuity between Chronicles and Ezra-Nehemiah has not been established by advocates of this hypothesis; it is simply presupposed.

The most significant evidence for the Compilation Hypothesis is contained in the works of P. Edmund Bayer and Bernhard Walde.[4] Each of them amassed examples that show the dependence of 1 Esdras on Ezra-Nehemiah and hence the priority of Ezra-Nehemiah. Their evidence has been accepted by many scholars as decisive proof for the dependence of 1 Esdras on Ezra-Nehemiah. The noncanonical status of 1 Esdras may have contributed indirectly to the widespread willingness to grant priority to Ezra-Nehemiah.

---

[3] Ibid., 15–19. Some of the major proponents of the Compilation Hypothesis are L. Bertholdt, E. Bayer, B. Walde, and W. Rudolph.

[4] Bayer, *Das Dritte Buch Esdras und sein Verhältnis zu den Büchern Esra-Nehemia* (Biblische Studien 16/1; Freiburg im Breisgau: Herder, 1911); Walde, *Die Esdrasbücher der Septuaginta* (Biblische Studien 18/4; Freiburg im Breisgau: Herder, 1913).

Advocates of the Fragment Hypothesis hold that 1 Esdras has not been transmitted in its original state. What has been preserved as 1 Esdras is but a fragment of the Chronicler's work. According to this view, 1 Esdras is an old translation of a Semitic *Vorlage*, representing the original sequence of the Chronicler's account of Ezra. Its beginning and end have been broken off when the separation from Chronicles took place. Josephus used 1 Esdras because he did not know MT Ezra-Nehemiah, the latter being a later rearrangement of 1 Esdras.[5]

C. C. Torrey was one of the most important early advocates of the Fragment Hypothesis. Torrey, following Howorth, claimed to have produced in his *Ezra Studies* "the proof of the fact that 'First Esdras' is a rescued fragment of the old Greek translation of Chronicles-Ezra-Nehemiah, not an apocryphal writing."[6] As such it is older than Ezra-Nehemiah which only came into its present form in the second century C.E.[7]

A form of this Fragment Hypothesis has been gaining new credibility in recent years largely due to Pohlmann's careful and effective argumentation of the case. Pohlmann essentially resurrects many of Torrey's views, arguing, however, with greater finesse and much less extravagance. His careful analysis and balanced presentation have added new weight to this theory. Pohlmann sets out to do two things: to refute the Compilation Hypothesis and to bring positive evidence to the effect that 1 Esdras is a fragment. As Williamson demonstrates,[8] however, Pohlmann does not reach his objectives. Pohlmann's thought provoking and careful analysis fails, finally, to demonstrate with great force that 1 Esdras is a fragment of the original, continuous work of the Chronicler. Nor does Pohlmann show positively that Josephus did not know Ezra-Nehemiah. Pohlmann nevertheless continues to merit close attention first, because of his impact on current scholarship,[9] and second, because his work clarifies the issues by articulating the main lines of argument of both the Compilation and the Fragment Hypotheses.

Further support for Pohlmann's position seems to have emerged from Klein's text critical work.[10] Klein's meticulous study of the text of Ezra-Nehemiah and 1 Esdras claims that on numerous occasions the text of 1 Esdras preserves a more ancient reading than MT Ezra-Nehemiah. This

---

[5] Pohlmann, *Studien zum dritten Esra*, 19–26. Some major proponents of the Fragment Hypothesis are J. D. Michaelis, A. Treuenfels, H. H. Howorth, J. Marquart, C. C. Torrey, G. Hölscher, and Pohlmann himself.

[6] *Ezra Studies*, xi.

[7] Ibid., 30.

[8] Williamson essentially dismantles Pohlmann's impressive edifice stone by stone. See *Israel in the Books of Chronicles*, 21–35.

[9] See, for example, Klein, "Ezra and Nehemiah in Recent Studies," 268–270.

[10] "Old Readings in 1 Esdras."

could imply that 1 Esdras is older than Ezra-Nehemiah.[11] Klein's textual work forms the basis for a new hypothesis by Cross concerning Chronicles, 1 Esdras and Ezra-Nehemiah. Cross differentiates three editions of the Chronicler's work, labelling them Chr_1, Chr_2, Chr_3. Cross writes, "Chr_3 is the final edition, made up of 1 Chronicles 1–9 + 1 Chr 10:1–2 Chr 36:23 + Hebrew Ezra-Nehemiah. Chr_2 includes 1 Chronicles 10–2 Chronicles 34 + *Vorlage* of 1 Esdras."[12] Cross, in an important sense, offers an attractive compromise between the Fragment Hypothesis and the Compilation Hypothesis by connecting both Ezra-Nehemiah and 1 Esdras with Chronicles, whereas the other hypotheses presume an either/or relation (i.e., either Ezra-Nehemiah or 1 Esdras continues Chronicles).

My article "The Chronicler and the Composition of 1 Esdras"[13] proposes another hypothesis, claiming that neither Ezra-Nehemiah nor 1 Esdras forms a continuous work with Chronicles. I argue, instead, that 1 Esdras is a distinct composition by the Chronicler, i.e., by the persons, circle, or school responsible for the book of Chronicles.[14] This "author," who used Samuel and Kings as his major source for preexilic Israel in Chronicles, used Ezra-Nehemiah as his major source for postexilic Israel in 1 Esdras. As such, 1 Esdras is indeed compiled from Ezra-Nehemiah, but by the Chronicler. It is not, however, a fragment out of the larger unity; it is, rather, a discrete book by the Chronicler, reflecting Chronicles' point of view.

My theory assumes the antiquity of the text of 1 Esdras while asserting the slight priority of Ezra-Nehemiah. I take Klein's textual work to indicate that 1 Esdras preserves ancient, variant, traditions without thereby being necessarily older than Ezra-Nehemiah. Two aspects of Klein's work lead to this conclusion (which differs from Klein's). First, there is the textual

---

[11] Klein concludes: "From a relative point of view, therefore, 1 Esdras often preserves an older form of Ezra than is present in Ezra MT and G, and so it must be older than Ezra G" (ibid., 107).

[12] "A Reconstruction of the Judean Restoration," 11. Cross suggests 450 B.C.E. as the approximate date for the older version, and 400 B.C.E. (or slightly later) for the final edition, i.e., Chr_3 (ibid., 12).

[13] "The Chronicler and the Composition of 1 Esdras" *CBQ* 48 (1986) 39–61.

[14] The Chronicler is perceived here largely in accordance with the following description by Ackroyd: "In many ways the use of the term 'school of the Chronicler' would be more appropriate. . . . References to the Chronicler in what follows, therefore, presuppose an awareness that we are more likely to be dealing with a particular type of theological tradition to which various men have contributed over a period of time but with a community of thought linking them together. If there are inconsistencies within the work—and such may well be observed in all Old Testament traditions—this may be explained by such a process of composition, though I believe in fact that such inconsistencies are less evident in this work than in other Old Testament works comparable with it, except in so far as the use of sources not totally rewritten for their present context sometimes leaves unresolved roughness" ("History and Theology in the Writings of the Chronicler," 503). Unlike Ackroyd, however, I do not attribute portions of Ezra-Nehemiah to the Chronicler.

evidence from Qumran concerning Chronicles and Samuel. The Qumran manuscripts show that Chronicles at times preserves a different and more ancient version of Samuel than MT Samuel.[15] Scholars do not conclude from this that Chronicles is older than MT Samuel. 1 Esdras, I suggest, reflects a similar phenomenon. It preserves variant, at times more ancient, sources without thereby being older than Ezra-Nehemiah. As Chronicles incorporates ancient but variant traditions in its reconstruction of preexilic Israel, so too 1 Esdras incorporates variant and ancient sources in its account of postexilic Israel. Second, Klein's list of variants suggests a deliberate balance in 1 Esdras' list of returnees between Ezra 2 and Nehemiah 7.[16] This observation contributes to the conclusion that 1 Esdras is aware of Ezra-Nehemiah and renders it in accordance with 1 Esdras' own ideology.

The present chapter focuses on 1 Esdras as it has been transmitted in the LXX in order to compare it with Ezra-Nehemiah.[17] As the discussion of the ideology of Chronicles helped bring into focus Ezra-Nehemiah's own, different tendencies, so too a comparison with 1 Esdras helps highlight Ezra-Nehemiah's distinctive emphases. Such comparison is all the more necessary on account of the debates over the relationship between the two books. These debates invariably resolve in favor of considering one book as the rearrangement of the other and, usually, in the dismissal of the other book as insignificant. In this chapter the question of priority is bracketed. The books are compared and contrasted as two works that use related sources, combined in a distinctive manner to articulate a particular story. The unique story of 1 Esdras is sought in order to highlight Ezra-Nehemiah's distinctive account.

II. The Structure and Themes of 1 Esdras

1 Esdras is the story of the destruction and restoration of the Davidic leadership, the temple, and cult. As such 1 Esdras is far from being an arbitrarily (or accidentally) snipped fragment from a larger book, i.e., Chronicles.

---

[15] F. M. Cross, *The Ancient Library at Qumran and Modern Biblical Studies* (Garden City, NY: Doubleday, 1958) 140–142. See also R. W. Klein, *Textual Criticism and the Old Testament* (Philadelphia: Fortress, 1974), esp. pp. 42–50.

[16] Klein observes that 1 Esdras' list of returnees follows Ezra 2 on nineteen occasions and Nehemiah 7 on another nineteen. Not all of these cases can be explained in terms of preserving the older or better reading ("Old Readings in 1 Esdras," esp. p. 100). The symmetry suggests that 1 Esdras, faced with two similar lists, attempted to represent both in some fashion. Walde had suggested that 1 Esdras attempts to synthesize Ezra-Nehemiah, but Pohlmann dismisses this explanation as an anachronistic misconcenption of how ancient texts were composed (*Studien zum dritten Esra*, 55). Klein's findings give indirect support to Walde.

[17] The text for this analysis is that of R. Hanhart, *Esdrae liber I* (Septuaginta: Vetus Testamentum graecum 8/1; Göttingen: Vandenhoeck & Ruprecht, 1974). The English quotations follow J. M. Myers, *I and II Esdras* (AB 42; Garden City, NY: Doubleday, 1974) for convenience. His text is not Hanhart, but follows the same versification, and there are no significant differences among these texts for the purpose of this analysis.

It is, rather, a carefully structured book with three major parts. The first part describes an ideal state of affairs: Jerusalem under a faithful Davidic monarch, supervising the flourishing cult. The second part depicts the destruction, or reversal, of that state of affairs: disobedience by king and people leads to three waves of deportation of people and holy vessels. The third part depicts the return to a variation of the original situation. Three waves of return restore the Davidic heir to power, the cult to its proper form, and the holy vessels to the temple. The book ends as it begins: with the celebrating community at the temple.

This pattern replicates Chronicles in reverse, with a positive rather than negative emphasis. As Mosis[18] observes, the narrative of Chronicles opens and closes with disaster. Between the two episodes of destruction lies Israel's golden age: the monarchy under David and Solomon, with God's temple prospering in Jerusalem. The fall under Saul is followed by a rise under David and Solomon, then followed by another fall as a result of disobedience to God. The book concludes with an open-ended note of hope.

1 Esdras reverses this pattern. The book begins and ends with a celebration at the temple. A Davidic ruler is restored to the helm. The temple and cult are in good working order. The ruler issues at the conclusion, as Josiah did at the beginning, special instructions to the Levites (1 Esdr 9:49–52). A series of violations had propelled destruction. A series of renewal efforts accomplishes reconstruction, taking place under three Persian kings (1 Esdr 7:4).

The basic structure of 1 Esdras can be described as follows:

A. Ideal state of affairs : The period of Josiah (1 Esdr 1:1–22)
B. Destruction (1:23–55)
C. Return and restoration (2:1–9:55)
   1. First return under Cyrus and Sheshbazzar (2:1–2:25)
   2. Second return under Darius and Zerubbabel (3:1–7:15)
   3. Third return under Artaxerxes and Ezra (8:1–9:55)

1 Esdras's basic themes emerge when we examine the flow of this text, paying special attention to those places where 1 Esdras and Ezra-Nehemiah differ.

A. Ideal State of Affairs: The Period of Josiah
(1 Esdr 1:1–22)

Structure

   1. Josiah's model Passover (1:1–20)
   2. Summary of Josiah's works (1:21–22)

---

[18] *Untersuchungen zur Theologie,* 17–43.

Happy throngs at the temple in Jerusalem open 1 Esdras and close it. The great events in between are understood best in terms of the activities of famous men and their followers on behalf of the temple. The book's opening lines emphasize the temple's glory and the heritage of David and Solomon. The deeds of the monarch are specified first: "And Josiah celebrated in Jerusalem the passover to his Lord . . ." (1 Esdr 1:1a). The repetition of David's and Solomon's names (1 Esdr 1:3, 4) provides a clear backdrop for the book's intended emphasis. Josiah is only later identified as king (1 Esdr 1:16).[19] What the opening lines stress is not only this particular monarch but the lines of traditions which he, as king, represents, namely, the Davidic dynasty. Thus Josiah instructs the Levites, "so now serve the Lord your God, minister to his people Israel, and prepare [the Passover] according to your families and tribes in conformity with the decree of David, king of Israel and the grandeur of Solomon his son" (1 Esdr 1:4b).

A detailed description of the cultic festivities follows. The very specificity of the depicted rituals reminds one how silent Ezra-Nehemiah is on such matters, how sparse are *its* cultic details beyond enumerating how many animals were sacrificed (usually in symbolically eloquent numbers). The feast is declared unique in recent history, clearly implying a high water mark (1 Esdr 1:18).

A summary of Josiah's activities and impact, which has no parallel in MT Chronicles, closes the section. It states a theory of retribution that explains many of the ensuing events. It also points out the importance of the ruler for the people's welfare by stating: "The works of Josiah succeeded before his Lord because of the piety with which his heart was filled . . ." (1 Esdr 1:21a). The passage continues, indicating that the people at that time, however, were sinning against the Lord "beyond every nation and kingdom" (1 Esdr 1:22). According to 1 Esdras, the good deeds of King Josiah can counterbalance the wicked deeds of his people and stem the tide of destruction, at least temporarily.

This opening section is densely packed with themes and symbols that are important to 1 Esdras: the continuity of the Davidic dynasty, the temple and the cult, and retribution. It heralds, as most introductions do, the book's main areas of interest.

---

[19] Pohlmann considers this beginning abrupt. He writes, "Woher sollte der Leser wissen, welche Person hier mit Josia gemeint ist, zu welcher Zeit dieser Mann lebte, und wann nun eigentlich das von ihm veranstaltete Passahfest stattfand!" (*Studien zum dritten Esra*, 33). In response to Pohlmann one can point out that the beginning narrative of Chronicles (1 Chr 10:1ff.) is no less abrupt. Here too one does not have a date, an identification of Saul as king, etc. One is thrown into the midst of a battle in Chronicles as one is thrown into the midst of a feast in 1 Esdras. The preceding genealogies in Chronicles do not illuminate the events in 1 Chronicles 10.

B. Destruction (1 Esdr 1:23–55)

Structure

1. Josiah's disobedience and death (1:23–31)
2. Three waves of deportation of people and holy vessels (1:32–55)
   a. First deportation (1:32–40)
   b. Second deportation (1:41–43)
   c. Third deportation (1:44–55)

Shadows begin to fall when Josiah disregards the words of Jeremiah the prophet. As in Chronicles, retribution follows response to the prophetic message. Josiah, in an episode unique to 1 Esdras, ignores the prophetic message and brings his downfall. The downfall of the nation as a whole ensues. Destruction and death come in the wake of royal abuses. One king after another did what was evil, and the nation followed their lead. As a result, God's anger is unleashed, bringing destruction of the nation. The holy vessels are removed three times (1 Esdr 1:39, 43, 51).

The plunge into destruction is both sharp and temporary. A seventy-year sabbatical follows, intended to expunge sin from land and people and to execute retribution. It is astounding how one of Israel's most traumatic and formative events is confined in 1 Esdras. This is accomplished not only by means of the definite seventy-year specification but also by means of a structure that absorbs rather than focuses on the destruction. The dominant scenes in 1 Esdras are those of renewal. The seventy years of doom and exile are contained in seven verses (1 Esdr 1:48–55) that are tightly appended to another section. One-and-a-half of these seven verses report God's warnings by the prophets (1 Esdr 1:48–49a), while another one-and-a-half speak of promise and restoration (1 Esdr 1:54b–55). The destruction is by no means an end, but only a temporary respite. What appears elsewhere as an unparalleled catastrophe is circumscribed in 1 Esdras from the start and safeguarded from the despairing finality. Restoration is promised in specific terms.

Continuity is an important theme for 1 Esdras, as it is for Chronicles.[20] Calling the exile a Sabbath, as does 1 Esdr 1:55 (following 2 Chr 36:21), considerably minimizes the trauma. 1 Esdras turns the exile into a temporary disruption which is quickly absorbed into the rhythm of retribution.

C. Return and Restoration (1 Esdr 2:1–9:55)

Three waves of pillaging the temple and deportation of persons and holy vessels are followed by three waves of return of persons and vessels. Restoration occurs with the help of three Persian kings and three Jewish leaders.

---

[20] Japhet explains Chronicles' silence about the Exodus as an aspect of Chronicles' emphasis on the continual habitation on the land. See *Ideology of the Book of Chronicles,* 111, for example.

Each wave reflects the same general pattern: an exchange between the Persian king and the Jewish leader, transfer of letters and holy vessels/gifts, return, rebuilding or refurbishing of temple. Tension and conflicts arise. They are resolved and celebration ensues. To that extent 1 Esdras is similar to Ezra-Nehemiah. But sharp contrasts emerge in the ways these events are embedded in the overall story and in the emphases within each of these waves of return.

1. First Return Under Cyrus and Sheshbazzar (1 Esdr 2:1–25)

Structure

    a. Decree and response (2:1–14)
       1) Decree (2:1–6)
       2) Response (2:7–8)
       3) Holy vessels returned by Sheshbazzar (2:9–14)
    b. Conflict: Artaxerxes' correspondence (2:15–24)
       1) Letter of accusations against building temple (2:15–20)
       2) Response (2:21–24)
    c. Results: stoppage of building (2:25)

As in Ezra-Nehemiah, God and Cyrus initiate the first return. 1 Esdras reports that, following Cyrus's decree (1 Esdr 2:3–6), a contingent of "the chiefs of the families of the tribes of Judah and Benjamin, with the priests and Levites, indeed all whose spirit the Lord had inspired arose to go up to build the house of the Lord in Jerusalem" (1 Esdr 2:7). In contrast to Ezra-Nehemiah, however, 1 Esdras does not proceed to name and enumerate the returnees. Only the list of vessels is specified (1 Esdr 2:9–13). Ackroyd has shown that holy vessels constitute a theme of continuity for the Chronicler.[21] The emphasis on these vessels is also strong in 1 Esdras, stronger than in Ezra-Nehemiah. The brief summary of returning people in 1 Esdr 2:7 and 2:14, juxtaposed with the longer itemized list of vessels, is one indication of the different perspectives of the two books. The large contingent of named persons dominates Ezra-Nehemiah's account of the first return; 1 Esdras, however, lets the itemized vessels dominate his account and names only Sheshbazzar, who is titled "the governor of Judah" (1 Esdr 2:11).

Nothing is reported directly by the narrator concerning the activities of these earliest returnees. We learn about them indirectly, from Artaxerxes' correspondence. Ezra-Nehemiah and 1 Esdras incorporate the Artaxerxes letters into different places in their narratives in accordance with their respective interests. 1 Esdras places them early, directly after the report of the first return and before the list of returnees headed by Zerubbabel and

---

[21] "The Temple Vessels—A Continuity Theme."

Jeshua. These thus constitute the first event of the return. In Ezra-Nehemiah this correspondence comes in Ezra 4:7–24, after the large wave of named returnees (Ezra 2), and after the foundations of the temple had been laid. A few details also differentiate the content of this correspondence. The most obvious detail concerns the temple. Ezra 4:7–24 does not mention the temple; the opposition concerns the city and walls. The temple is prominent, however, in 1 Esdras's version of the letters. The Samaritan informants report to Artaxerxes that the Jews "have begun to rebuild the rebellious and evil city, to restore its marketplaces and walls and, to lay the foundations of a temple" (1 Esdr 2:17; see also 2:18). As in Ezra-Nehemiah, the king responds by issuing orders to restrain the builders (2:24), and the work stops.

Despite similarities between 1 Esdras and Ezra-Nehemiah in this scenario, the overall effect is quite different. In 1 Esdras, given the Artaxerxes correspondence, the return under Cyrus marks an era in which nothing much has happened beyond a modest return of people and a significant return of holy vessels. Thus far nothing more has been accomplished in Jerusalem itself. The building of the temple has been aborted before anything of substance could emerge. The section closes with a picture of a partly failed mission, of an anonymous community at a standstill, without any success to its credit, waiting for something to happen.

2. Second Return Under Darius and Zerubbabel (1 Esdr 3:1–7:15)

Structure

    a. Introduction of the main characters: story of the bodyguards (3:1–4:41)
       1) Setting: the royal banquet (3:1–3)
       2) Wager in a nutshell (3:4–15)
       3) Bodyguards' and Zerubbabel's speeches (3:16–4:40)
          i) Address of first on wine (3:16–23)
          ii) Address of second on king (4:1–12)
          iii) Address of Zerubbabel on women and truth (4:13–40)
       4) Conclusion: Popular acclaim of Zerubbabel (4:41)
    b. Dialogue of Zerubbabel and Darius (4:42–60)
       1) Initial dialogue (4:42–46)
       2) Darius's decrees (4:47–57)
       3) Zerubbabel's song of praise (4:58–60)
    c. Preparations for return (4:61–5:45)
       1) Zerubbabel's enlisting of Babylonian Jews (4:61–63)
       2) List of returnees (5:1–45)
          i) Setting of return and major characters (5:1–3)
          ii) Names of major figures (5:4–6)
          iii) List of leaders (5:7–8)

It is at a bleak moment—when all efforts have ceased, possibly have been given up—that Zerubbabel, the hero of 1 Esdras, steps onto the stage. The great length of this unit indicates that this is the central focus of the book. For 1 Esdras the decisive era is Zerubbabel's. The story of the three guardsmen introduces Zerubbabel, with much pomp and circumstance, as a youth able to win the hearts and minds of the king and all his magnates with his wisdom and rhetoric. His speeches inspire what amounts to a standing ovation (1 Esdr 4:41). These details set Zerubbabel up as a figure comparable to David. As a result of Zerubbabel's wisdom and charm, the king graciously offers to fulfill all of his wishes, above and beyond the initial terms of the contest. Zerubbabel asks the king to ensure the building of Jerusalem and the temple and to restore the vessels (1 Esdr 4:43–45).

Illustrative comparisons with Ezra-Nehemiah are at hand. The exchange between King Darius and Zerubbabel (1 Esdr 4:42–57) contrasts with the one between Nehemiah and Artaxerxes (Neh 2:1–9).[22] In both cases a celebrating king addresses a favorite foreigner. But Nehemiah must extract a grant from Artaxerxes with fear and trembling. Dark and light play in Nehemiah's encounter with the king. Only bright sweetness, however, suffuses the dialogue between Zerubbabel and Darius. Zerubbabel's requests are granted with gusto. Darius lavishes upon Zerubbabel much more than

---

[22] For a comparison of Nehemiah and Zerubbabel, see Kellermann, *Nehemia*, 130–132.

was asked: protection for the people, exemption from taxation, provisions for
the temple, freedom to build the city, funds for the Levites, and more (1 Esdr
4:47). Royal prerogatives such as Darius in Ezra-Nehemiah gives to the
community (Ezra 6:6–12) and Artaxerxes to Nehemiah (Neh 2:5, 8) are
combined in Darius's grant to Zerubbabel in 1 Esdras—and exceeded.
Zerubbabel, like the pious Ezra, bursts into a song of praise to God in
response to Darius's decrees (1 Esdr 4:58–60). He then hurries to Babylon
and stirs up the rest of the Jews with his news.

Only now, as the aftermath of Zerubbabel's special activities, does the
great and successful return from Babylon takes place. Only due to an intervention by Zerubbabel, and not simply as a spontaneous response by the
people to a royal decree (and God's), does the great human wave start its
journey to Jerusalem. Heading the list of this return are:

> the priests, the sons of Phinehas, the sons of Aaron were Jeshua, the son
> of Jozadak, the son of Seraiah, and Joiakim, the son of Zerubbabel, the son
> of Salathiel, of the family of David, the line of Perez, of the tribe of Judah
> who uttered wise words before Darius . . . (1 Esdr 5:5–6a).

These are the first pedigrees in 1 Esdras. Neither is standardized; they
are approximately equal in length. The Davidic descent of Zerubbabel is
established without the ambiguities that plague Ezra-Nehemiah. It is not
surprising that 1 Esdras mentions Davidic descent at this strategic place:
Zerubbabel leads the return as a successful Davidic heir.

After this heading, 1 Esdras lists the twelve men (cf. Ezra 2:2 and Neh
7:7).[23] 1 Esdras refers to this group, which begins with Zerubbabel and
Jeshua, as leaders of the Jews (1 Esdr 5:8b), something Ezra-Nehemiah does
not do. The narrative describes the building of the altar, the laying of the
foundations, and celebration followed by interference from hostile neighbors.
These events largely follow the same form as in Ezra-Nehemiah (but without
the Artaxerxes correspondence).

The interference from neighbors leads to a two-year delay. But the work
resumes after another official investigation of records. The inquiries are
largely the same in Ezra-Nehemiah and 1 Esdras, with two differences, both
of which magnify Zerubbabel's role in 1 Esdras. First, in the report to Darius
(1 Esdr 6:7–21; cf. Ezra 5:6–17), the Jews claim that the holy vessels had been
handed by Cyrus to Zerubbabel and Sheshbazzar (1 Esdr 6:17). The
venerable symbol of continuity is thereby attached in 1 Esdras to Zerubbabel. Second, whereas Ezra-Nehemiah speaks of granting royal permission
to the elders and their unnamed governor, 1 Esdras specifies that Darius's
orders were to "permit Zerubbabel, the servant of the Lord and governor of
Judah, and the elders of the Jews to reconstruct that house of the Lord on its

---

[23] For details see Klein's thorough study, "Old Readings in 1 Esdras." Klein concludes that
the text of 1 Esdras preserves in places older traditions than does the MT (ibid., 107).

[former] site" (1 Esdr 6:26). Moreover, 1 Esdr 6:28 mentions additional provisions given to Zerubbabel the governor. Thus one sees that not only is Zerubbabel mentioned, but honorific titles, unparalleled in Ezra-Nehemiah, are also attached to him. Zerubbabel no longer appears after these appellations. But, in contrast to Ezra-Nehemiah, he has been credited unequivocally as the instigator of the return, the foundation builder, and the one whom the king uniquely empowered to restore the temple.

The scene closes, as in Ezra-Nehemiah, with the Passover celebration. In 1 Esdras this forms an *inclusio* with the beginning of the book, when the temple was standing and Passover celebrated. The "good old days" are restored, primarily due to the charismatic power of Zerubbabel. As in the beginning of the book, the temple is standing with a Davidic heir at the helm. This Passover celebration portrays the priests and Levites (again) slaughtering the Passover lamb and providing it for their brothers (1 Esdr 7:6–14; cf. 1:12–13).

1 Esdr 7:4 indicates, as does Ezra 6:14, that completion is yet to come, under Artaxerxes. In 1 Esdras, however, that completion is less the climax and more the finishing touch. The work of Zerubbabel marks the high point. Ezra will merely complete it.

Although many of the details of these subsequent events remain closely parallel to Ezra-Nehemiah, the very nature of the return has been greatly transformed. The spontaneous response by the mass of people to Cyrus' edict and God's stirring, which opens and sustains Ezra-Nehemiah, has been radically modified. Here there is no successful response until Zerubbabel's promptings. The earlier activities ended virtually in failure. It took a bright and resourceful Zerubbabel to get things going again. The success that follows is the result of his unique role and special privileges.[24] This emphasis constitutes a major difference from Ezra-Nehemiah, which systematically minimizes the role of leaders.

3. Third Return Under Artaxerxes and Ezra (1 Esdr 8:1–9:55)

Structure

    a. Introduction of the main characters (8:1–27)
       1) Introduction of Ezra (8:1–7)
       2) Letter of Artaxerxes (8:8–24)
       3) Ezra's song of praise (8:25–27)
    b. The return (8:28–64)
       1) List of returnees (8:28–40)
       2) Appeal for cult personnel (8:41–48)

---

[24] Note that the privileges are bestowed upon "all those [who] were going up with him [Zerubbabel]" (1 Esdr 4:47; see also 1 Esdr 4:48).

1 Esdras's introduction of Ezra closely resembles the introduction in Ezra-Nehemiah, but, in contrast, does not constitute the longest introduction of a character in the book. Ezra is greatly overshadowed by Zerubbabel who, cloaked with grandeur, precedes him; Ezra appears as but a pale imitation. Long pedigrees for Zerubbabel and Jeshua have already been mentioned. Ezra's is not the first. Others' pedigrees may not be as long as Ezra's, but they are as respectable (note, e.g., the reference to Aaron and Phinehas in the pedigrees of both Jeshua and Ezra). In addition, Ezra's own pedigree is truncated in 1 Esdras, from seventeen to fourteen names. But the more significant difference is the absence of reference in 1 Esdras to divine favor. Ezra-Nehemiah affirms that God's hand was upon Ezra (Ezra 7:6), as Ezra himself indeed claims. No such imprimatur occurs in 1 Esdras. We have only Ezra's words that God's grace was with him. The narrator merely concedes that "the king accorded him honor, inasmuch as he found favor before him in all his requests" (1 Esdr 8:4).

    Parallels between Ezra and Zerubbabel abound in 1 Esdras. Like Zerubbabel, Ezra brings the holy vessels (1 Esdr 8:17), and like Zerubbabel, Ezra responds to the decree with a song of praise to God (cf. 1 Esdr 4:58–60 with 8:25–26). In this they are peers. But Zerubbabel excels in other matters. Ezra's royal privileges fall short of Zerubbabel's: Artaxerxes' letter to Ezra exempts clergy from tribute (1 Esdr 8:22); Darius declares, however, that the Levites be paid from royal funds (1 Esdr 4:55). Like Zerubbabel, Ezra then leads a return. But his caravan of about 1,490 is hardly impressive compared with Zerubbabel's 42,360 (1 Esdr 5:41).

Such details diminish Ezra's stature relative to Zerubbabel's. Yet, since he too is a leader, and since 1 Esdras elevates leaders, Ezra receives great honor in 1 Esdras. Although the characterization of Ezra as a responsive rather than assertive leader persists in 1 Esdras, occasional changes portray him as a more commanding figure than he is in Ezra-Nehemiah. The resolution of the problem of mixed marriages is a case in point. In 1 Esdr 8:89 the resolution is still voiced, as in Ezra-Nehemiah, by someone other than Ezra. But Jechoniah, who advocates it, credits Ezra with the proposal (1 Esdr 8:89–90).[25] Moreover, in Ezra-Nehemiah this resolution leads to the formation of a committee by the people as a whole, whereas in 1 Esdras Ezra himself selects a committee (1 Esdr 9:16). This attributes to Ezra a more autocratic role.

The reading of the Torah takes place in 1 Esdras in front of the temple gate, whereas the temple is not mentioned in the parallel in Ezra-Nehemiah. The scene corresponds at first glance to that of Ezra-Nehemiah. Ezra, for example, is summoned, as in Neh 8:1, by the people themselves. But two small details, coupled with the very different structure of the book, produce a different effect. First, Ezra is elevated. 1 Esdras refers to him as the high priest (1 Esdr 9:49). He is also elevated in a more literal sense. As in Neh 8:4, so too here, Ezra stands upon a wooden platform which he shares with an entourage (1 Esdr 9:42). But 1 Esdras, as if unable to resist elevating Ezra higher, adds: "he [Ezra] was seated in the most pre-eminent place before all of them" (1 Esdr 9:45b). Second, the governor receives greater authority. Whereas Ezra-Nehemiah reports that Nehemiah, Ezra, and all the others issued instructions to the community in unison (Neh 8:9), 1 Esdras singles out the governor as the one instructing Ezra and the Levites (1 Esdr 9:49). The parallel with 1 Esdr 1:3–6, in which Josiah instructs the Levites, strongly links the conclusion of the book with its beginning.

The book ends with the gathering of an inspired people at the temple. Their old institutions and traditions have been reinstated. Past religious symbols like the holy vessels have been duly transferred by the religious elite, as was the ark in 1 Esdr 1:1–4. The ruler instructs the Levites, who in turn instruct the people. Grand celebration follows. The restoration has reached its culmination.

Rendering Ατφαρατης as "governor," as does Myers (1 Esdr 9:49), suggests yet another, important, possible allusion. The last named governor in 1 Esdras was Zerubbabel. His youthfulness at the time of Darius, which 1 Esdras so strongly emphasizes, implies that he could surely be alive in the eighth year of Artaxerxes, when the reading of the Torah takes place in

---

[25] The suggested explanation for this variant reading is as follows: אדני is read in the MT as Lord, referring to God. But in 1 Esdras that possible reading is taken to refer to "my lord," namely Ezra.

1 Esdras (in contrast to Ezra-Nehemiah, where the implicit date is subsequent to Artaxerxes' twentieth year, mentioned in Neh 2:1). Zerubbabel, as the last-named governor, may thus be the implied subject in 1 Esdr 9:49. If so, then the parallels with 1 Esdr 1:1–20 are even stronger, ending the book with a descendant of David who supervises the restored cult in Jerusalem. Even if Zerubbabel is gone, his descendant presumably rules. 1 Esdras establishes the fact that Zerubbabel indeed has such a descendant (1 Esdr 5:5).

In Ezra-Nehemiah the parallel scene (Neh 8:1–13) is but the opening section of a series of events depicting the transfer of power and responsibility to the community. In that book a second gathering, in which the people take the initiative and learn to read the Torah for themselves, directly follows; Ezra then fades from view. No such transference of power occurs in 1 Esdras. The governor and the high priest are still in charge, preeminently above the people. The old order has been restored.

The last words in 1 Esdras are καὶ ἐπισυνήχθησαν, "Then they assembled" (1 Esdr 9:55). In Neh 8:13 the Hebrew parallel, וַיֵּאָסְפוּ, comes in the middle of a sentence. The gathering together which ends 1 Esdras, and which in Neh 8:13 marks the beginning of the next scene, has usually been taken to be an abrupt ending. It is abrupt when one knows that there is a parallel passage which, in another book, continues further. But in 1 Esdras it simply captures the final state of the community, one of an ingathering in front of the temple in order to celebrate. It is my contention that 1 Esdras is aware of Ezra-Nehemiah and adapts it to its own views. Rather than continue to the Succoth celebration, the book ends in such a manner that the two Passovers (1 Esdr 1:1–20 and 7:10–15) remain dominant. The ending is no more abrupt than that of Chronicles, which also concludes on a verb, quoting a part of a sentence which continues in Ezra-Nehemiah. In both instances the final word encapsulates the sense of the whole, expresing the communal task. "Going up" is of paramount importance at the conclusion of Chronicles. "Gathering together" of the people at the temple completes 1 Esdras's vision of the restoration.[26]

III. Conclusions

Both Ezra-Nehemiah and 1 Esdras describe the return and reconstruction of Israel in the postexilic era. Both refer to some of the same persons and events, often in an identical way. Yet Ezra-Nehemiah and 1 Esdras are, finally, fundamentally different. Large and small variations between them tilt the narratives in significantly different, even opposing, directions. Consequently, they essentially tell different stories. This is discernible from their

---

[26] See my article, "The Chronicler and the Composition of 1 Esdras," 56–59, for a discussion of the implications of these parallel endings in Chronicles and 1 Esdras.

structure, themes and portrayal of characters. The central themes of 1 Esdras are, as we have seen: the emphasis on the temple per se and the unique role of the hero Zerubbabel. The two go hand in hand, since in 1 Esdras Zerubbabel is directly responsible for building the temple. Zerubbabel is the most prominent person in 1 Esdras and the true center of the narrative. Like his famous ancestor David, he is young and wise. He brings liberation to his people. Other major events in 1 Esdras also center around leaders who are responsible for both success and failure. History, for 1 Esdras, is shaped by such great men.

When 1 Esdras and Ezra-Nehemiah differ, one usually discovers in 1 Esdras the heightening of the role of the Davidic leader coupled with an emphasis on the temple. The treatment of Zerubbabel most vividly expresses these tendencies. With Zerubbabel, 1 Esdras not only has a hero but also reinstates the Davidic house. Like Chronicles, 1 Esdras places the Davidic dynasty at the center and shows, in sharp contrast to Ezra-Nehemiah, that the return and restoration were led by David's descendant. The emphasis on David's house and on the heroic Zerubbabel is apparent in several ways.

First, the fact that 1 Esdras begins with Josiah's Passover means that the book opens with positive references to the splendor and piety of the Davidic and Solomonic era. The change from a more neutral expression in 2 Chr 35:5 to "the grandeur of Solomon" in 1 Esdr 1:5 heightens this emphasis.

Second, the omission of Nehemiah's memoirs eliminates the disparaging comment about Solomon (Neh 13:26), preserving him as the positive paradigm which the beginning of 1 Esdras introduces. Opinions about the absence of Nehemiah's memoirs from 1 Esdras divide between the Compilation Hypothesis, which assumes that 1 Esdras deliberately omits them, and the Fragment Hypothesis, which claims that 1 Esdras's *Vorlage* did not include them. I concur with the Compilation Hypothesis that the omission is deliberate.[27] Kellerman, who delineates parallels between Nehemiah and Zerubbabel, suggests that Zerubbabel is elevated in order to degrade Nehemiah; this elevation of Zerubbabel, like that of Ezra, is a symptom of the anti-Nehemiah sentiments.[28] I propose a somewhat less polemical explanation: Nehemiah is omitted primarily in order to highlight the role of the Davidic figure. The passing reference to Nehemiah in 1 Esdr 5:40 indicates an awareness of his authority. But Nehemiah is not of the house of David (nor a priest). 1 Esdras transfers important traditions about him to Zerubbabel. Consequently Zerubbabel is called "governor" in 1 Esdras — a

---

[27] A strong case for the familiarity of 1 Esdras with Ezra-Nehemiah has been made by Walde (*Esdrasbücher der Septuaginta*, 142–54). Pohlmann attempts to overturn Walde's conclusions (*Studien zum dritten Esra*, 51–71) and to offer positive evidence to the contrary (ibid., 74–126). His arguments, however, are challenged and mostly refuted by Williamson (*Israel in the Books of Chronicles*, 21–36, esp. pp. 30–35).

[28] Kellermann, *Nehemia*, 131–133.

title which Nehemiah (but not Zerubbabel) possesses in Ezra-Nehemiah. The omission of Nehemiah by 1 Esdras allows this book to sustain what important omissions in Chronicles do: a relatively uncluttered stage with the limelight steadily focused on the dominant events and figures, in this case the Davidic hero.[29]

A third, and most obvious, example of Davidic emphasis in 1 Esdras is the story of the three guardsmen (1 Esdr 3:1–5:6). This lengthy section dramatically differentiates Ezra-Nehemiah and 1 Esdras. The material is generally recognized, since Torrey, as an interpolation with a Semitic *Vorlage* (either Hebrew or Aramaic). There is no agreement about the level of redaction at which the story has been inserted, but it is usually assumed to be early.[30] It is, however, certain that this story, whatever its origin, was added to make a point. And the point of the story, as well as its function in the present context, are quite clear: this story glorifies Zerubbabel and magnifies his role.[31] I suggest that this early insertion expresses the book's central emphases on the hero and the house of David. It has been introduced into this text in order to supply that which the source, Ezra- Nehemiah, so clearly lacks.

This insertion, one must remember, is quite long, dominating the first half of the book. Zerubbabel, the hero of this story, is identified as a descendant of David (1 Esdr 5:5), who wins the favor of the Persian king. He asks for — and receives — permission to build the temple and have the holy vessels returned (1 Esdr 4:42–57). 1 Esdras, in contrast to Ezra-Nehemiah, portrays Zerubbabel as the decisive figure in the return and the rebuilding of the temple: he in fact initiates the *successful* wave of return and brings it to completion.

With this story, 1 Esdras eliminates much of the ambiguity that marks Ezra-Nehemiah. One no longer puzzles over who really led the return and laid the temple's foundations. 1 Esdras is clear: a descendant of David is the

---

[29] The omission of Nehemiah by 1 Esdras or the mere cursory reference to someone who is important in another book is not surprising when one contemplates omissions by the Chronicler. Chronicles, after all, glosses over several formative figures and events in order to highlight its central theses. Abraham is barely mentioned; the Exodus and Sinai are passed over; even Moses is overshadowed by David. If Chronicles could so diminish these events and figures, it is not astonishing that 1 Esdras would gloss over a far less decisive figure when this figure diverts it from its central preoccupation.

[30] Howorth and Marquart attribute the story to the author of 1 Esdras. Pohlmann holds that the story was inserted by the redactor of the Greek translation (*Studien zum dritten Esra*, 35–52). In der Smitten ("Zur Pagenerzählung im 3 Esra (3 Esr.III,1–V,6)," *VT* 22 [1972] 492–495), arguing against Pohlmann, suggests that the story was inserted by the compiler of 1 Esdras. I concur with In der Smitten.

[31] As In der Smitten writes, "Das motiv für die Aufnahme der Pagenerzählung in den Text des 3 Esr. ist in der entscheidenden Rolle zu erblicken, die der Übersetzer des 3 Esr. *Serubbabel* zumißt" (ibid., 494).

real power behind the return. He wrests permission from the king for this return; he goes to Babylon and stirs up the exiled, who joyfully respond to him (1 Esdr 4:61–63); he leads the return, delivers the holy vessels which are, as Ackroyd has shown, a symbol of continuity for the Chronicler;[32] he lays the foundations for the temple and sees to its completion. The priest Jeshua, who in Ezra-Nehemiah is as prominent as Zerubbabel, is completely over-shadowed in 1 Esdras by this long insertion. The insertion, with its elabora-tion on the role of Zerubbabel (and of Zerubbabel alone!) makes this Davidic descendant the dominant figure in the return and restoration.

A fourth example of the emphasis on the Davidic dynasty through the glorification of Zerubbabel is the location of the so called "Artaxerxes corre-spondence" (Ezra 4:7–24; 1 Esdr 2:15–25). The correspondence describes opposition to the returnees, depicting the success of the opponents who stop the rebuilding of the temple. As noted above, this correspondence is situated differently in Ezra-Nehemiah and 1 Esdras. In Ezra-Nehemiah it comes after Zerubbabel, Jeshua, and the returnees had already built the altar; in 1 Esdras it appears before Zerubbabel is ever mentioned. Neither arrangement makes good chronological sense.[33] The different positions within the narrative result in two different versions of the return and restoration. In Ezra-Nehemiah, on the one hand, we have cycles of success and failure, a slow and laborious movement forward punctuated by repeated setbacks. The massive early return shows no clear leadership. One is uncertain who is in charge. Sheshbazzar, Zerubbabel and Jeshua, and the eleven or twelve men in Ezra 2 are all possible leaders, but none is so identified. The efforts of the returnees are curtailed by opposition. When the temple is finally complete, the individuals who rose to some prominence vanish (Ezra 6).

1 Esdras, on the other hand, paints a different picture. The obstacles precede the appearance of Zerubbabel. Once he struts upon the scene, progress and success ensue with only a minor disruption. The Davidic heir smooths all obstacles in his path and leads the community to glory. This particular flow of events highlights the effectiveness of Zerubbabel, making him responsible for everything good that happens in the first part of the book. Failures and false starts belong to an earlier epoch, before the Davidic heir took his proper place.[34]

---

[32] "The Temple Vessels—A Continuity Theme."

[33] The arrangement in Ezra 4 implies the following order of Persian kings: Cyrus (Ezra 1:1), Ahasuerus (Ezra 4:6), Artaxerxes (Ezra 4:7), Darius (Ezra 4:24). The arrangement in 1 Esdras 2–3 implies the following order instead: Cyrus (1 Esdr 2:1), Artaxerxes (1 Esdr 2:15), Darius (1 Esdr 3:1). The correct chronological order of the kings is Cyrus, Darius, Artaxerxes. Interestingly, both books reflect this latter order when they speak of the completion of the temple and of a decree or consent by "Cyrus, Darius, Artaxerxes" (Ezra 6:14 = 1 Esdr 7:4). This leads to the conclusion that it is not ignorance about chronology that accounts for the arrange-ment in each of these books; ideological motives most likely dictate both versions.

[34] Mosis (*Untersuchungen zur Theologie*) develops three paradigm epochs in Chronicles

The heroic emphasis of 1 Esdras places this book in direct conflict with Ezra-Nehemiah's ideology. Precisely because the two works purport to describe the same era, their differences throw Ezra-Nehemiah's uniqueness into sharper relief. And to the extent that such accounts not merely describe but also prescribe, they divulge competing postexilic visions not only of the past but also of the present and future. I Esdras strives for restoration as a return to a perceived golden age, the halcyon days of David. Its structure practically obliterates the disjunction between pre- and postexilic reality. Ezra-Nehemiah, however, separates from much of the past. Instead, it envisions a restructuring of life which orients itself around the community, not the individual hero; the city, not merely the temple; the book, not only the cult.

---

which he construes as the structural devices of the book: "Saul," "David," "Solomon." He applies these to Ezra-Nehemiah in a manner which is unconvincing to me. These paradigms, however, apply well to 1 Esdras: a Saul-like beginning in exile; a Davidic era with Zerubbabel; a Solomonic era with Ezra.

6
CONCLUSIONS

The preceding chapters apply the tools of literary criticism to Ezra-Nehemiah, identifying the central emphases of the book by means of close attention to the literary techniques that shape the narrative: structure, characters, interplay of points of view, and repetitions. Such an approach, claims Alter, "leads not to a more 'imaginative' reading of biblical narrative but to a more precise one."[1]

A century and a half of interpretation have done much to obscure Ezra-Nehemiah's specific intention by appending it to Chronicles, dividing Ezra-Nehemiah into two books, and rearranging it to conform to a presumed historical reality. Taking the book in its entirety, the literary critic analyzes, instead, Ezra-Nehemiah's distinctive structure, its particular themes, and the specific mode of presentation. Such a strategy enables the reader to discover what Ezra-Nehemiah itself conveys by the manner with which it depicts the formative postexilic era.

The literary approach leads to the conclusion that Ezra-Nehemiah's basic story is relatively simple. Put in a nutshell, Ezra-Nehemiah describes how the people of God build the house of God in accordance with authoritative documents. The book's structure is as follows:

I. Potentiality (objective defined): decree to the community to build the house of God (Ezra 1:1–4)
II. Process of actualization: the community builds the house of God according to decree (Ezra 1:5–Neh 7:72)
III. Success (objective reached): the community celebrates the completion of the house of God according to Torah (Neh 8:1–13:31)

The book opens with the decree (Ezra 1:1–4) that sets the agenda for the rest of the narrative by exhorting the people of Israel to follow God's command: "Whoever is among you of all of his people, may his God be with him, and let him go up to Jerusalem, which is in Judah, and rebuild the house of the LORD, the God of Israel—he is the God who is in Jerusalem" (Ezra 1:3). Having set the objective, the book describes its actualization (Ezra 1:5–Neh 7:72). A proleptic summary reports that those whom God stirred

---

[1] *Art of Biblical Narrative*, 21.

rose up to go to Jerusalem and build the house of God (Ezra 1:5–6). The rest of the section describes how they did it. There were three different movements, each involving a specific group of people, entrusted with a specific portion of the house of God. The report, therefore, is divided into three major parts. The first (Ezra 1:7–6:22) describes the building of the altar and the temple during the reigns of Cyrus and Darius. The second (Ezra 7:1–10:44) describes the building of the community itself during Artaxerxes' reign. The third (Neh 1:1–7:5) depicts the restoration of the city wall during Artaxerxes' reign. By framing all of these movements with the repeated list of returnees (Ezra 2 and Nehemiah 7), Ezra-Nehemiah asserts their cohesiveness. All three are bound together. Only when joined do they fulfill the decree of Cyrus and God's command. Ezra 6:14 spells out thematically what the list expresses structurally, summing up that the building of the house of God spanned the reign of the three Persian kings. The house of God is finally finished when the wall is rebuilt. A grand celebration ensues. The three movements then flow together, as "all the people gathered as one man" (Neh 8:1) for a series of ceremonies rededicating themselves and the house of God (Neh 8:1–13:31). Within this story, Ezra-Nehemiah develops three significant themes: the centrality of the people, the expansion of the house of God to encompass the city, and the primacy of the written text as a vehicle of authority.

These conclusions have emerged from an investigation of Ezra-Nehemiah that focuses on literary markers rather than historical ones, on "discourse-oriented" analysis rather than "source-oriented" inquiry.[2] In this study, literary concerns have overshadowed historical ones in order to sustain a methodological consistency and provide an alternative vision for material that has received ample historical scrutiny. Yet, as Sternberg correctly observes, the relation between historical information and literary analysis is necessarily dialectical.[3] Source-oriented inquiry provides some important questions for discourse-oriented analysis and some of the building blocks for interpretation. A few examples illustrate the point. First, historical information, such as the proper historical order of the Persian kings or priests, allows the literary critic to notice when Ezra-Nehemiah departs from historical reality in order to express its own point of view. Rearrangements thus call attention to Ezra-Nehemiah's specific intention. Second, conclusions about literary process influence interpretation. When, for example, Japhet and Williamson establish that Ezra 1–6 is the latest stratum of Ezra-Nehemiah, the intention of that section can be seen in a different light. The repetition of the list in Ezra 2, for instance, suggests different possibilities than it otherwise might (see the discussion of the lists below). Third, when the historicity

---

[2] See Sternberg, *Poetics of Biblical Narrative*, 15, for definitions of the terms; see also Chapter One above.

[3] *Poetics of Biblical Narrative*, 15–23.

of a detail is either established or denied, the literary weight of that element is altered. If it could be proven that Ezra and Nehemiah were, in fact, contemporaries, the significance of the pairing in the book would have to be reevaluated. Although my gaze has been fixed on literary issues, such historical considerations have been taken into account whenever available and applicable.

The dialectical relation between the two approaches also means that the conclusions of a literary study contribute to subsequent historical and literary studies of the book and of the era. The literary analysis of Ezra-Nehemiah identifies the ideology of the book. Historical-critical studies have uncovered many of the important tensions in the background of the restoration.[4] The literary study of Ezra-Nehemiah illustrates how a community responded to that reality. Consequently, the specific ideology of Ezra-Nehemiah becomes a significant historical datum for a fresh analysis of actual tensions. The critic who seeks access to the events and dynamics of the post-exilic era can now utilize Ezra-Nehemiah's own articulation as an important control. Future Ezra-Nehemiah studies can fruitfully compare the issues and conflicts that Ezra-Nehemiah itself highlights — or evades — with those known from other sources.

Furthermore, when one remembers to what extent biblical literature has been decisively shaped in the postexilic era, the ideological underpinnings of such a community acquire importance that transcends the mere acquisition of information regarding the particular community. One can, in addition, begin to explore the specific relation between Ezra-Nehemiah's ideology and the formation of the canon. Although such a question goes beyond the scope of the present study, the conclusions of this work provide clues about possible lines of thought that have influenced such formative literary developments.

In particular, literary study of Ezra-Nehemiah also contributes to the resolution of long standing scholarly debates. The problems that besiege studies of Ezra-Nehemiah have been recently surveyed by Ackroyd, Childs, Japhet, Klein, Talmon and Williamson.[5] Ackroyd succinctly summarizes the main areas of discussion about Chronicles and Ezra-Nehemiah under three

---

[4] Conflicts between returning Judeans and the Judeans who never left, class tensions, priestly competition between Zadokites, Levites, etc., messianic or revolutionary aspirations, and a drive towards theocracy are some of the issues. See, e.g., P. R. Ackroyd, "Archeology, Politics and Religion: The Persian Period," *The Iliff Review* 39 (Spring, 1982) 5–23, Kellermann, *Nehemia*, M. Smith, *Palestinian Parties and Politics That Shaped the Old Testament*, C. Schultz, "The Political Tensions Reflected in Ezra-Nehemiah," *Scripture in Context*, ed. C. D. Evans, W. W. Hallo, J. B. White (Pittsburgh: Pickwick, 1980) 221–244, and Williamson, *Ezra, Nehemiah*.

[5] Ackroyd, "The Historical Literature," 305–310; Childs, *Introduction to the Old Testament as Scripture*, 626–630; Japhet, "Biblical Historiography in the Persian Period"; Klein, "Ezra and Nehemiah in Recent Studies"; Talmon, "Ezra and Nehemiah (Books and Men)"; Williamson, *Ezra, Nehemiah*, xxi–xlvii. See Chapter Two above.

headings: ". . . the unity of the group, the sources and their use, and the purpose or purposes of the books. Inevitably, the three are interrelated."[6] The conclusions of this study bear directly on each of these issues.

1. Unity

A dominant, perhaps *the* dominant, issue in studies of Ezra-Nehemiah has been the relation between Ezra-Nehemiah and Chronicles. The recurrent questions are: Is Ezra-Nehemiah the continuation of Chronicles, written by the Chronicler and accidently severed from Chronicles? Can Ezra-Nehemiah be understood as a separate book? What is the connection between "Ezra" and "Nehemiah"?

On the one hand, as noted earlier, the pervasive view for the past 150 years has been that Ezra-Nehemiah and Chronicles form a single book, authored by the Chronicler.[7] Despite the rigorous challenge to this view, especially by Japhet,[8] and Williamson,[9] a lively discussion concerning the relation of Ezra-Nehemiah to Chronicles persists in scholarly circles.[10]

On the other hand, Ezra-Nehemiah is still commonly divided into two distinct books, Ezra and Nehemiah, printed separately in nearly all modern translations of the Bible. Ezra-Nehemiah thus receives a peculiar treatment and appears to have indeterminate boundaries.

In response to such issues, Japhet and Williamson have described and demonstrated the ideology of Chronicles. The present study complements theirs with a systematic analysis of Ezra-Nehemiah's own ideology and an overview of 1 Esdras's structure and themes. Such information allows us to reenter, newly equipped, the arena of the historical and literary debates on the relation among these books.

Since the present study is based on the MT of Ezra-Nehemiah, it already presupposes, hence cannot also claim to prove, the unity of Ezra-Nehemiah and its separation from Chronicles. Nevertheless, the literary study contributes to the current discussion in two significant ways. First, a comprehensive study of Ezra-Nehemiah's own intention allows us to compare Chronicles and

---

[6] "The Historical Literature," 305.

[7] See Chapter Two above.

[8] *Ideology of the Book of Chronicles;* see also, Japhet, "The Supposed Common Authorship of Chronicles," 330–371.

[9] *Israel in the Books of Chronicles,* esp. pp. 1–70.

[10] Note, for example, the special "Chronicles, Ezra, Nehemiah Consultation" at the Annual Meeting of SBL in Atlanta, 1986, devoted to the question of the relation between Ezra-Nehemiah and Chronicles. The session included a discussion on "The Unity and Extent of the Chronicler's Work" with Ackroyd, Japhet, and B. Halpern representing different positions. Note also the recent debate between M. Haran and Williamson in *Bible Review* (Haran, "Explaining the Identical Lines at the End of Chronicles and the Beginning of Ezra," *Bible Review* 2 [Fall, 1986] 18–20; Williamson, "Did the Author of Chronicles Also Write the Books of Ezra and Nehemiah?" *Bible Review* 3 [Spring, 1987] 56–59).

Ezra-Nehemiah in a more precise fashion than has been hitherto possible. The comparison highlights the distinctive orientations of the books. With Ezra-Nehemiah's own ideology before us, the contrast between the two books becomes more stark. Ezra-Nehemiah's major themes are neither similar to nor compatible with those of Chronicles. Chronicles, like 1 Esdras, espouses "royal ideology," eulogizing the Davidic monarchy as the ideal center for the community. Chronicles, as we have seen,[11] also focuses on the temple, genealogies, retribution, the role of the prophets, and the unification of the twelve tribes. To the extent that the Torah plays a role, it does so as an instrument of the kings and priests (e.g., 2 Chr 31:3–4, 21).

These concerns are not simply absent from Ezra-Nehemiah but also contradicted by the book's three basic themes. Ezra-Nehemiah does not merely ignore David but actively defuses any heroic aspirations of individuals. The center is firmly occupied by the people as a whole. A "great men" theory of history has been replaced by a communal emphasis. The temple and its cult, so central to Chronicles, are reinterpreted in Ezra-Nehemiah, with the city as a whole becoming the house of God. This development redefines the place of the cult in community life. Sacrifices continue, but they appear to be overshadowed by attention to the book of Torah.

The importance of the book of Torah and of texts in Ezra-Nehemiah provides a striking contrast to Chronicles, wherein concerns with the text are peripheral. Even when the book of the Torah comes to the foreground in Chronicles, as it necessarily must with its discovery in the temple (2 Chronicles 34), Chronicles limits the role of the book beyond what is already given in its source, 2 Kings 22. In 2 Kings, Josiah's major reforms (2 Kgs 23:1–24) *follow* the discovery of the book of Torah (2 Kgs 22:8–20) and explicitly seek to fulfill the teachings of the Torah ("Moreover Josiah put away the mediums and the wizards . . . that he might establish the words of the law which were written in the book that Hilkiah the priest found in the house of the LORD . . ." 2 Kgs 23:24). In Chronicles, however, Josiah's major reforms (2 Chr 34:3–17) *precede* the discovery of the book (2 Chr 34:18–33). Josiah's piety, his seeking of God (". . . he began to seek the God of David his father;" 2 Chr 34:2), is not prompted by the book of the Torah.

Such differences between Chronicles and its source accentuate the significant contrast between Ezra-Nehemiah and Chronicles on this subject. In Ezra-Nehemiah, as we have seen, texts govern all the important events, whereas other forces propel Chronicles. Ezra-Nehemiah's major emphases are either ignored or contradicted by Chronicles. These differences undermine any probability that the two can be linked to a single author. The two books reflect competing ideologies in the postexilic era.

Second, structure also differentiates Ezra-Nehemiah from Chronicles. Literary analysis supports the separation of two books by identifying the

---

[11] See Chapter Two above.

distinctive structure that accounts for Ezra-Nehemiah's peculiarities, a structure that is independent from Chronicles'. In so doing, the study illustrates
coherence in Ezra-Nehemiah which renders a connection to Chronicles less
plausible.

The structure of Ezra-Nehemiah becomes a pivotal issue in addressing
the dual pull of scholarly debates: the drive to submerge Ezra-Nehemiah in
Chronicles or to dissect it into Ezra and Nehemiah. Yet little progress has
been made in clarifying such a structure. Although it is no longer fashionable
to recompose Ezra-Nehemiah into a presumed, pristine "original," as L. W.
Batten,[12] for example, had done, very few scholars explain or even describe
the present form of the book. Most commentators appear content simply to
follow the sequence of chapters in Ezra-Nehemiah with but an occasional
glance at what the overall design might be. They describe some of the major
units in terms of literary or historical categories, noting the confusing
peculiarities in the book (such as the dispersion of the Ezra material in the
Nehemiah memoirs) without reaching conclusions about the nature of the
present composition of the book.[13]

We have seen, however, that the lists, often considered one of Ezra-
Nehemiah's most exasperating features, constitute, in fact, an important
literary key to the structure and hence the meaning of Ezra-Nehemiah. The
lists shape the book, affirm its integrity, and help differentiate Ezra-
Nehemiah from Chronicles.

These points can be illustrated by noting the predominance of lists in
Ezra-Nehemiah and their use in the book. Approximately one quarter of the
book is made up of lists, mostly lists of people. The major ones are:

> Ezra 1:9–11: list of returned vessels
> Ezra 2:1–70: list of returned exiles
> Ezra 8:1–14: list of Ezra's companions
> Ezra 10:18–44: list of men who separated from foreign wives
> Neh 3: 1–32: list of builders of the wall
> Neh 7:6–72: repeated list of returned exiles
> Neh 10:2–29 : list of signatories to the pledge
> Neh 11:3–36: list of settlers and settlements
> Neh 12:1–26: list of cultic personnel
> Neh 12:32–42: list of parading members of the community

The prevalence of such lists has frequently been used to support the
unity of Ezra-Nehemiah with Chronicles. Curtis, for example, mentions fondness for lists and genealogies as the trademark of the Chronicler, who was

---

[12] *Ezra and Nehemiah.*

[13] A major exception to this tendency is found in Japhet's "Biblical Historiography in the
Persian Period," 178–179.

responsible for both Chronicles and Ezra-Nehemiah.[14] Such a claim can now be reexamined. We discover that Ezra-Nehemiah, in fact, has but a single, brief genealogy (Neh 12:10–11); the rest are lists and occasional pedigrees (i.e., a line of ascent from the present to the past, such as Ezra's lineage going back to Aaron in Ezra 7).[15] In this sense, Ezra-Nehemiah is already different from Chronicles, where the genealogies (תלדות) dominate, especially in 1–9.[16]

At the same time that the lists have been claimed as evidence for *unity* of Ezra-Nehemiah with Chronicles, the repetition of the list of returnees (Ezra 2 and Nehemiah 7) has influenced scholars to *divide* Ezra-Nehemiah itself into two books. Talmon sums up a representative view: "If indeed Ezra and Nehemiah at one time were two separate works written by different authors, this could help in explaining the duplication of some events and the literary units in both, such as the list of returning exiles (Ezra 2 = Nehemiah 7)."[17] In such interpretations, the repetition has been understood as a vestige of an earlier, separate, circulation of Ezra and Nehemiah, preserved by scribes too pious to omit either of these venerable documents.

These arguments lose much of their power precisely in light of books such as Chronicles. The bold modifications of Samuel-Kings in Chronicles should teach us that the ancients were quite willing to tamper with sacred traditions in order to express their distinctive views. The preservation of the two lists, therefore, must point to something else. Literary study of the book allows us to determine what that "something else" might be.

The repeated list of the returnees, like other lists in Ezra-Nehemiah, has been the subject of numerous traditional studies focusing on the text,[18] setting, and original purpose.[19] There appears to be a consensus that each of

---

[14] *Chronicles*, 4.

[15] See Wilson, *Genealogy and History in the Biblical World* for the taxanomy of genealogies.

[16] See also Johnson, *Purpose of Biblical Genealogies*, esp. pp. 69 and 80, on the internal differences between Ezra-Nehemiah's lists and pedigrees and Chronicles'.

[17] "Ezra and Nehemiah (Books and Men)," 318. Elsewhere historical and textual questions and implications preeminently occupy discussions of these lists. See, for example, Galling, "The 'Gola List' According to Ezra 2//Nehemiah 7," 149–158. and Klein, "Old Readings in 1 Esdras."

[18] Klein's meticulous study, "Old Readings in 1 Esdras," analyzes the text of the lists and their relation to each other (and to 1 Esdras).

[19] Torrey assumes that the lists are fictitious (*Ezra Studies*, 250). Rudolph thinks that the lists are genuine but composed of different records between the years 539–515 (*Esra und Nehemia*, 17). According to A. Alt, Zerubbabel compiled the list in order to legitimate land rights ("Die Rolle Samarias bei der Entstehung des Judentums," *Kleine Schriften zur Geschichte des Volkes Israel* [Munich: Beck, 1953] 2:316–318). For G. Hölscher, this is a tax list drawn by the Persians ("Die Bücher Esra und Nehemia," *Die heilige Schrift des Alten Testaments*, ed. E. Kautzsch [4th edition; Tübingen: Mohr, 1923] 504). Galling sees the controversy between Samaria and Judah as the background for the list. It is drawn to demonstrate the right and ability of the Judeans to rebuild the temple and resettle the land (cf. Tattenai's request for names in Ezra 5:10). The list makes clear both legal and ecclesiastical structure of the community ("The 'Gola List' According to Ezra 2//Nehemiah 7," 153–154).

the lists is composite.[20] Social, political, and economic concerns most likely lurked in the background and explain their origin.[21]

What has been lacking, in spite of the wealth of information, is an analysis that considers the significance of the repetition and of the lists' present function. Even though, as Williamson wisely observes, chapters like Ezra 2—and perforce also Nehemiah 7—"are among the most uninviting portions of the Bible to the modern reader,"[22] they are literarily important. Whatever the original sense, one must ponder the role of the repetition of the list in the book's final form. This concern is all the more relevant when we take into account recent studies of the redaction of Ezra-Nehemiah. According to Japhet and Williamson,[23] Ezra 1–6 constitutes the latest stratum of the book. The repetition of the list of returnees in Ezra 2 is therefore not simply the product of an unyielding respect for sources but a voluntary, and thus presumably deliberate, act of the author/compiler. Important as this issue is, no satisfactory explanation has been forthcoming from historical criticism.[24]

A literary study of the functions of repetition in narrative in general and in biblical literature in particular illustrates, as we have seen,[25] the multiple roles of the repeated lists in Ezra 2 and Nehemiah 7. The lists shape Ezra-Nehemiah and articulate its distinctive ideology. We have noted how the lists function as an *inclusio*, unifying the intervening chapters and forming a central unit from Ezra 2 to Nehemiah 7.

The section thus formed is the longest in the book. It is the heart of the book and its central event. We can discern three distinct subunits or stories

---

[20] Williamson, *Ezra, Nehemiah*, 28–29

[21] Schultz, for example, connects the list with the rejection of the adversaries' building participation: "Clearly the builders of a temple had a monopoly, and in the case of the Jerusalem temple it was composed of the returning exiles. No outside assistance was allowed or wanted. Even as in the Craftsmen's Charter, so in the Golah list ancestry is traced, frequently in terms of skill" ("The Political Tensions Reflected in Ezra-Nehemiah," 227). The returnees alone had a monopoly; others may not be included. Schultz bases his work on D. E. Weisberg's study of ancient guilds, *Guild Structure and Political Allegiance in Early Achaemenid Mesopotamia* (New Haven: Yale, 1967) 1–4, which attests to building monopolies and rights concerning sanctuaries.

[22] Williamson, *Ezra, Nehemiah*, 38.

[23] Japhet, "Biblical Historiography in the Persian Period," 128; Williamson, "The Composition of Ezra i–vi," *JTS* ns 34 (1983) 1–30. Japhet and Williamson draw different conclusions about the date of the book. Williamson places it very late; Japhet dates it around 400 or shortly thereafter. I concur with Japhet.

[24] Williamson comes close by at least raising the question from a canonical perspective (*Ezra, Nehemiah*, 269), but his answer is quite limited, relying solely on Gunneweg's. According to Gunneweg, the repetition reiterates the view that the purified community is the same as the community that had first returned and undertaken the building of the temple (Gunneweg, "Zur Interpretation der Bücher Esra-Nehemia," 156). This explanation is probable but insufficient (see below).

[25] See "E. Recapitulation: The List of Returnees (Neh 7:6–72)," in Chapter Three, above.

within this largest section. Each story contains a specific cast of characters and a clear task, with complication and resolution.[26] These three subsections, typically understood as mere succession despite some chronological disarray, are firmly clamped together in Ezra-Nehemiah by the repetition. In this fashion, the repetition of the list indicates that these diverse stories constitute a single major event: the building of God's house by the people of God in accordance with a decree. The repetition allows us to discern the shape of Ezra-Nehemiah, making what precedes into an introduction and what follows into a conclusion. It serves to identify Ezra-Nehemiah as an independent, self-contained book with a specific beginning, middle, and end which do not conform in either structure or intention to Chronicles.

Other lists in Ezra-Nehemiah likewise help define the shape of the book. It is important to recall in this connection the list of cultic personnel (Neh 12:1–26). That list provides closure, tying together the loose ends of the tapestry that has been woven throughout the book. As Ezra-Nehemiah comes to an end, Neh 12:1–26 explicitly goes back to Ezra 2:1, recapitulating lines of cultic personnel back to those who came up in the first wave of return.[27] This list, like the repetition of the list of returnees, unifies the intervening years into a single era and a single event. The list begins in the days of Zerubbabel and Jeshua (Neh 12:1; cf. Ezra 2:1) and concludes "in the days of Nehemiah the governor and of Ezra the priest the scribe" (Neh 12:26). This statement articulates, as did the repetition of the lists, the oneness of the intervening generations and activities.

As was noted in an earlier discussion,[28] the list of priests and Levites in Neh 12:1–26 poses many historical and textual problems that remain unresolved. From a literary perspective it is important to note the book's concern with recapitulating the era through such lists, however awkward this proves to be. This list differentiates Ezra-Nehemiah from Chronicles in two ways. First, as Williamson has shown, there are differences between Neh 12:1–26 and the priestly courses in 1 Chr 24:1–18.[29] These differences imply separate views of priestly structures in the two works. Second, and probably more significant, is the fact that this concluding recapitulation links the ending to the beginning of Ezra-Nehemiah itself, and not to some events in Chronicles. The scope of the list thus indicates that Ezra-Nehemiah is a self-standing book and not the continuation of Chronicles. Nehemiah 12 thereby confirms the structure of Ezra-Nehemiah which the repetition of the list

---

[26] See Chapter Three above.

[27] Note "These are the priests and the Levites who came up with Zerubbabel the son of Shealtiel and Jeshua: Seraiah, Jeremiah, Ezra, Amariah, Malluch, Hattush . . ." (Neh 12:1).

[28] See discussion of this passage in Chapter Three.

[29] Williamson writes that the study of the list in Nehemiah 12 ". . . should remove any lingering temptation to compare this list with the twenty-four priestly courses known from 1 Chr 24:7–18 and later times; neither names nor numbers are now even remotely similar. The added six names, however, mark a clear step in that direction" (*Ezra, Nehemiah*, 360–361).

of returnees defines and illustrates thereby the integrity of the book. By showing that this book's conclusion returns to its beginning, Neh 12:1–26 serves to sever Ezra-Nehemiah from a plausible relation to Chronicles.

The structure of Ezra-Nehemiah corroborates the implications of the book's central themes. Such literary observations buttress Japhet's and Williamson's ideological and linguistic arguments against the unity of Chronicles and Ezra-Nehemiah.

2. Sources

The discussion of the structure of Ezra-Nehemiah already included references to sources, such as the lists of returnees. Ezra-Nehemiah is particularly rich in sources. Source analysis has been one of the most fertile areas of Ezra-Nehemiah studies. Scholars have been able to identify a variety of documents within the book and bring information about the diverse genres to bear on the assessment of each source. There emerged a consensus about certain indubitable sources even when the authenticity or date of these sources remain controverted. The distinguishing characteristics of sources such as Nehemiah memoirs, Ezra memoirs, and the Aramaic letters have been throroughly explored and assessed.[30]

As in the case of the lists and structure, so too with respect to sources, the study of Ezra-Nehemiah typically falls short of explaining *why* such sources were combined as they have been. Even Williamson, who devotes a section in his introduction to "Composition,"[31] only describes the history of the sources, not the role of the sources in the final composition. The present study not only explicates why sources were retained in their seemingly authentic, documentary form but also accounts for the interaction among these sources. Ezra-Nehemiah is a book which values the written text as a source of authority. Documents carry the weight that speech assumes in other biblical narratives. The sources are Ezra-Nehemiah's multiple voices preserved and compiled in a dialogue of texts.

Sources, and the particular ways Ezra-Nehemiah employs them, also illustrate the book's concept of unity. As Williamson observes, albeit in a different context, "unity and uniformity should not be confused."[32] Ezra-Nehemiah's model of unity does not eradicate individual distinctions but preserves them as a plurality. The use to which Ezra-Nehemiah puts its sources reveals an innovative and paradigmatic shift away from homogeneity to a harmony of diversity.

---

[30] See Williamson, *Ezra, Nehemiah*, xxiii–xxxiii, for a recent survey of such studies.

[31] Williamson, *Ezra, Nehemiah*, xxxiii–xxxv.

[32] *Ezra, Nehemiah*, 212.

3. The purposes of the books

The purpose and ideology of Chronicles have been elucidated by Japhet and Williamson and supplemented by insights from Willi and Mosis.[33] Ezra-Nehemiah's intention has been obscured by persistent scholarly efforts to accommodate historical reconstructions. The literary approach provides another angle of vision from which to perceive the book. From this perspective, Ezra-Nehemiah's purpose can be identified: to exemplify the postexilic era as a time when Israel built the house of God in accordance with the divine word embodied in texts. Ezra-Nehemiah weds people, city, and book[34] and sets forth patterns and expectations for its own era and for subsequent generations. The book advocates a vision of reality in which community replaces heroes, the house of God is expanded, and the word of God is accessible to all through documents that the community must follow. The three themes develop Ezra-Nehemiah's ideology.

The first theme is the book's main concern with the people as a whole. The numerous lists, and particularly the repetition of the list of returnees, indicate that Ezra-Nehemiah is adamant about conveying the flow of history through the activities and participation of many people and not merely through those of leaders. The book insists that history be understood in this prosaic manner, as the arduous efforts of numerous, specified persons over long stretches of time, with starts and stops, gradually building upon each other's work, and shunning the sweeping gestures of trailblazing, epic heroes on their way to either tragic doom or glory. Ezra-Nehemiah articulates this notion in at least three ways. First, Ezra-Nehemiah places groups and numerous individuals in the foreground. Second, it narrates events in a manner that attributes real successes and accomplishments to these groups. Third, it portrays the book's outstanding individuals as persons who facilitate the accomplishments of the people rather than as leaders who deserve primary credit for the success itself. These aspects work together to underscore the fact that it is Israel's story that is narrated. The people as a whole return, complete the house of God, read and implement the Torah, are purified, and finally celebrate.

The list of returnees in Ezra 2 introduces the reader to the large community. A cast of about 42,000 people is immediately thrust into view, making it practically impossible to ignore the fact that this crowd constitutes the major focus of interest. And should the reader overlook this fact, the book reiterates the point by repeating the list in Nehemiah 7.

The people in Ezra-Nehemiah constitute an entity wherein individual and group identities are neither blended nor obliterated. The model is not

---

[33] Willi, *Die Chronik als Auslegung;* Mosis, *Untersuchen.*
[34] Whedbee, "Ezra and Nehemiah: A Tale of Torah and City, Politics and Piety."

the melting pot, but a symphony or tapestry. The people provide the continuous subject of the book, the thread that holds events together, its very fabric. The effect is a complex and colorful society whose divisions and diversity—as well as tensions—are neither glossed over nor erased. These diverse groups and individuals nevertheless form a whole, an Israel, and thereby a unity. In this respect there is congruence between Ezra-Nehemiah's subject matter and form: the diversity of documents and genres in the book, the rough seams and lack of homogeneity, mirror the nature of the community.

Every step of the way in Ezra-Nehemiah involves many named individuals, graphically illustrating that the return and reconstruction meant their active engagement. We know who returns and builds the altar and the temple: those persons named in Ezra 2. Yes, Zerubbabel and Jeshua are among them, but they did not begin the task nor complete it—the people did. We know who identifies the problem of mixed marriages and takes the initiative to rectify it: the community does. Ezra is its instrument, as we have seen. We also know who builds the wall. Of course there is Nehemiah, as he repeatedly reminds us; but there are the others whose names have been preserved (Neh 3:1–32) and who actually construct the wall, stone by stone, at great cost and sacrifice (Nehemiah 5). Such naming, and the repetition of the long list of names, prevent the reader from forgetting where credit is due.

The community that builds the house of God gathers as a whole once this objective has been reached. The people initiate and largely conduct the ensuing ceremonies. They ask Ezra to bring the Torah; they listen to it and implement it. They gather together again, first specifically around Ezra, later without him. They recite the history of Israel's encounters with God, then pledge themselves to the Torah and to the house of God—all this without the supervision of any particular leader (Neh 8:12–10:40). They also arrogate to themselves roles that have hitherto been royal (or even divine) prerogatives, such as taxation (Neh 10:33). This accomplished, the people cast lots to determine who shall dwell in the now holy city (Neh 11:1–2). As Ezra-Nehemiah moves toward its conclusion, the book recapitulates names of persons (Neh 12:1–26), mapping this decisive era through lists, before reaching the climactic moment of celebration. The finale depicts the purified people celebrating their achievements with much fanfare and boundless joy (Neh 12:30–13:3).

Even though Ezra-Nehemiah insists on the centrality of the people as a whole, it does not reduce individuals to mere cogs in a larger wheel. The emphasis on communal identity is balanced and complemented by intense particularism and individuality. Ezra-Nehemiah's use of "memoirs" is generally considered unique in the Bible. This literary device articulates the importance of the individual by permitting Ezra and Nehemiah to speak in their own voices, as it were, and to present their stories directly. Other characters as well are privileged to express themselves via letters (e.g., King Artaxerxes).

Ezra and Nehemiah are multidimensional characters in the full sense of the term. The shifts of perspective between first- and third-person reports depict them from within and without, a complex mode of representation that defies "flat" stereotyping. Their place—in the book and in history—is clearly established. Ultimately, however, these leading individuals are surrounded by and woven with the rest of the community. Ezra, the book's most favored individual, embodies the shift from the hero to the community. He is stead-fastly portrayed as one who facilitates the transition from the leader to the larger community. Ezra invariably includes others, names them, delegates responsibilities to them, and transfers powers to them. Nehemiah's self-proclaimed heroics, on the other hand, are put into perspective by an oblique commentary that shifts the credit from Nehemiah to others. Each task, each accomplishment in the book, involves numerous people. Most have been lost to memory except for their brief appearance in Ezra-Nehemiah. And even though they do not, like Nehemiah, clamor to be remembered, Ezra-Nehemiah grants them a memorial nonetheless.

Ezra-Nehemiah's purpose is highlighted by a comparison with 1 Esdras. The differences between the two books reiterate a diverse perception of what the postexilic era was—or should have been. Their particular structures and themes clarify a pervasive contrast. At the center of 1 Esdras stands the reinstated Davidic dynasty, represented most fully by the glorious figure of Zerubbabel. 1 Esdras repeatedly exalts the role of the Davidic dynasty and the temple by additions and omissions. The book frames its narrative with two festivals at the temple, underscores the grandeur of what has gone by, seeks a return to it, and magnifies the role of the hero in particular. 1 Esdras sings the praise of the hero by attaching an edifying tale to Zerubbabel, by placing him at the head of the return, by crediting him with the overwhelm-ing success of the restoration. 1 Esdras exudes triumphalism.

Ezra-Nehemiah moves in the opposite direction. In Ezra-Nehemiah, the community as a whole receives the limelight. The past is viewed largely through jaundiced eyes (note the recapitulation of Israel's pathetic history in Nehemiah 9). The heroic is systematically undercut. Success is not a return to glory but the sanctification of the mundane, "daily, prose-bound, routine."[35]

The major contrast between Ezra-Nehemiah and 1 Esdras can best be illustrated by a modern analogy, comparing the Washington Monument and the recent Vietnam War Memorial in Washington. These two monuments capture two modes of understanding and remembering a national event. The one is a monument to the great hero; the other is a wall that lists names of participants, most of whom are not otherwise known to the wide community, but whose lives shaped that national event. 1 Esdras's view of the restoration

---

[35] Rich, "For Memory" (see p. 1 above).

corresponds to the mentality of the Washington Monument. It commemo-
rates a great hero, Zerubbabel, who is singularly held responsible for the
events. Ezra-Nehemiah's perception, on the other hand, approximates the
spirit of the Vietnam Memorial, with its countless names. The shape of the
book and the prevalence of lists ensure that the reader is aware of the real
actors. References to "Israel" in Ezra-Nehemiah are not reduced to a
stereotypical abstraction but are filled with specific content, referring to
groups of named and active individuals who are memorialized. Ezra-
Nehemiah, in contrast to both 1 Esdras and Josephus, depicts the return of
Israel and the restoration by Israel. For Ezra-Nehemiah, the central human
actor is that entity עם or Israel, whose many members are remembered even
when they have not been famous. Such new emphasis on the smaller lives,
on the not-so-famous, is the unique achievement of Ezra-Nehemiah.

The expansion of the house of God from the temple to the city constitutes the second theme of the book. The centrality of the house of God in
Ezra-Nehemiah is clearly evident. Cyrus's decree announces the direction
and purpose of the return: to go up to build the house of God in Jerusalem.
Ezra-Nehemiah, however, develops a concept of the house of God that
includes not only the temple but embraces the city as a whole. The book
accomplishes this feat and articulates the process in several ways. The
repeated list of returnees binds the intervening material (Ezra 2–Nehemiah
7) into a single, unified event. This event is the building of the house of God
in three stages or movements. Ezra 6:14 confirms this point by declaring that
the work on the house of God spanned the reign of the three Perisan kings,
Cyrus, Darius, and Artaxerxes.

Building activities thus occupy the longest section of the book (Ezra
1:5–Neh 7:72). The nature and scope of the house are defined and developed
throughout these chapters. Ezra-Nehemiah prepares the ground early for the
future expansion of the house of God. This is evident, for example, in the
present location of the Artaxerxes correspondence (Ezra 4:7–24). The correspondence depicts the opposition of adversaries who issue warnings to the
king by reference — not to the temple, which is never mentioned — but to the
city and walls (e.g., Ezra 5:12–13). They identify the returned exiles' building
activities (specified earlier as work on the house of God) as the rebuilding
of the city and its walls. As a result of the adversaries' interference, work on
the house of God comes to a halt. This correspondence thus establishes a
firm connection between the house of God and the city with its wall. It
demonstrates that building the one is tantamount to building the other. The
activities that cease in Ezra 4:24 and those that resume and eventually find
completion in Nehemiah 1–7 are thereby coextensive.

The purported recapitulation of Cyrus's decree, which authorizes
building in Darius's time, gives open-ended dimensions for the house of God
(Ezra 6:3). Where specifications appear in the decree, they exceed the size
of Solomon's temple. In this manner Ezra-Nehemiah envisions (and affirms

Israel's right to build) an edifice larger than the modest temple of Ezra 3. Nehemiah and his cohorts merely complete the process when they build the wall. Ezra-Nehemiah corroborates the sanctity of their project by reporting that the high priest and his fellow priests consecrate the initial stage of the work on the wall (Neh 3:1). Cultic personnel, i.e., gatekeepers, singers, and Levites, attend the wall after its completion (Neh 7:1; cf. also 13:22). Such cultic personnel, normally assigned to the temple, now stand at the city gates because the boundaries of the renovated house of God have been expanded to encompass the city as a whole.

All these details confirm the fact that the house of God extends beyond the temple. They also explain the relatively muted description of the dedication of the temple itself. Because completion of the house of God must await the building of the wall, the dedication of the temple receives but a brief mention, overshadowed by the celebration of Passover (Ezra 6:14–22). It would have been premature to grant that early phase a significance that befits the actual completion of the task. Only when the wall has been finished, not when the temple is restored, is the city designated as holy. A newly dedicated people, a congregation of God (Neh 13:1), dwells within.

By expanding the house of God, Ezra-Nehemiah actualizes a certain ideology well represented in Israel, especially in the Psalms and in prophetic literature (e.g., Psalm 48; Jer 31:38).[36] It is a vision in which all of Jerusalem is God's unique sanctuary. This vision, which has deep ancient Near Eastern roots, also finds expression in later texts such as the Temple Scroll, and in Pharisaic Judaism which extends altar-like sanctity to the domestic table.[37] Ezra-Nehemiah participates in this continuum. It differs, however, from the Temple Scroll and from certain prophetic books (e.g., Zechariah) by its programmatic implementation of sanctifying measures in the present, mundane situation without waiting for a more dramatic divine intervention than a decree.

The decree reflects the book's third theme: the central significance of the written text. Ezra-Nehemiah, obviously composed of assorted documents, displays its reliance on documents in an unparalleled fashion. This characteristic is one of several manifestations of the book's veneration of the written word. From one perspective, Ezra-Nehemiah describes the ways divinely initiated written texts—the decree of Cyrus and the Torah of Moses—are fulfilled. For Ezra-Nehemiah, God is the source of authoritative documents. But God's messages are transcribed into written texts to be actualized by the community.

---

[36] See also Levenson, *Sinai and Zion*, e.g., p. 135.
[37] See Neusner, *Between Time and Eternity*, esp. pp. 28–32.

Concern with implementing what has been written governs the overall shape of the book and finds expression within the smaller units. The overall structure proceeds from the divinely initiated decree of Cyrus to its final fulfillment, celebrated with much fanfare in Nehemiah 12–13. The text sums this up: "They finished their building by the decree [טעם] of the God of Israel and by the decree [טעם] of Cyrus and Darius and Artaxerxes king of Persia" (Ezra 6:14b).[38] Ezra 1:5–Neh 7:72, unified through the list of returnees, is also unified by the command of the three kings. The central command, stated in Cyrus's decree and reiterated (Ezra 6:2–4), is the basis for all that follows, supplemented by the decrees of Darius and Artaxerxes, perceived (according to Ezra 6:14) as essentially the same decree.

Cyrus's decree precipitates a flurry of activites. Restoration activities flow forward until new documents appear (e.g., Ezra 4:6, 7–16), contravene the previous edict, bring activities to a halt, and generate additional documents. The prophetic voices in the next phase (Ezra 5:1–6:14) are quickly replaced by written documents which allow God's word to materialize. Ezra 6:14 encapsulates the task and structure of the book, summing up what preceded and foretelling what is yet to come.

The next section (Ezra 7–10) centers on two authoritative documents: first, the Torah of Moses, of which Ezra is a skilled scribe (see Ezra 7:6 and also 7:10, 11, 12); second, the letter of Artaxerxes, authorizing Ezra to implement the teaching of God which is in Ezra's hand (Ezra 7:15). These documents are implemented until a new document (Nehemiah 1–7) intrudes.

Nehemiah 1–7 begins with a superscription which introduces this document, Nehemiah's memoirs. The following section (Neh 7:6–72) is itself a document, a written list that had been found and fully reproduced, providing the prescription for settling the rebuilt city. As Cyrus's decree was recalled earlier in the book in order to provide a model and authority, so now ספר היחש, the "book of genealogy" (Neh 7:5) is recalled from the past to guide the present.

The rest of Ezra-Nehemiah (Nehemiah 8–13) depicts how the community more fully enacts the written Torah and responds to it in deed and in a written oath. Nehemiah 8 places the book of the Torah at the center of the united people. This book carries with it the authority of God and of the Persian king. Communal behavior flows from the reading of the book and leads to a written communal response (Nehemiah 10). Nehemiah's final reforms (Neh 13:4–31) are, in fact, the execution of the commitments spelled out by the community's written pledge.

Form and content articulate the centrality of written documents in Ezra-Nehemiah. This drive toward textualization may be rooted in the

---

[38] My translation. The RSV obscures the emphasis by translating טעם once as "command" and once as "decree."

Persian context.[39] But whatever its origin, the emphasis on the written in Ezra-Nehemiah reaches a new height and significance. The interplay of documents in Ezra-Nehemiah—book, letters, written edicts—acknowledges the written word as effective and active in the world. This theme is of theological and political import. It subjects human life and history to the execution of the divine mission which is given in a written document. It represents a paradigm shift from the sanctity of the oral to the sanctity of the written. Prophets still speak, but the real force behind the events manifests itself in writing. Now God's word is found in a book (e.g., Neh 8:14). The text replaces the charismatic leader. Human leaders are best when they help implement the teachings of the written document—as does Ezra. The text is an open book (literally), a publicly accessible source of power to be shared equally with men, women, and all who are capable of understanding (Neh 8:2), not the private channel of communication between God and a selected elite.

Ezra-Nehemiah depicts life as the actualization of the text by the community. This shift to the text, which takes place quite thoroughly within Ezra-Nehemiah, is decisive for subsequent Judaism, as the rabbis amply demonstrate.[40] It also sets the stage for the scriptural orientation of the other "peoples of the Book."

Ezra-Nehemiah's emphasis on the written mode combines with the other two themes to deflect the limelight away from the heroic to a life lived in community, gathered around the book. This depiction of the return and restoration differs significantly from the one in 1 Esdras. The latter articulates and portrays a return to an earlier, golden era, with a Davidic heir at the helm. The radicality of Ezra-Nehemiah stands out more sharply by comparison. Ezra-Nehemiah breaks with that past. It implements a vision of theocracy which places the book, not the hero, at the center of the community. The house of God extends beyond the confines of the temple to embrace city and people.

Without disputing the role of historical developments in shaping Ezra-Nehemiah's portrayal of this pivotal period, I have examined the picture itself, bringing it into focus. Ezra-Nehemiah's basic story—how the people of God build the house of God according to authoritative documents—emerges as

---

[39] Herodotus describes the exceptional veneration of the written decree by the Persians. See, for example, his account of the execution of a disloyal subject through decrees (*Herodotus, with an English translation by A. D. Godly* [Loeb Classical Library; Cambridge: Harvard University Press, 1938] vol. II, 3.128).

[40] The Talmudic story in *b. B. Meṣ.* 59b is one of many examples of the primacy of the text in rabbinic Judaism. In his dispute with the other rabbis, R. Eliezer invokes (and receives) divine intervention in support of his interpretation of Torah. The rabbis, however, dismiss even the intercession by a heavenly voice, arguing that the Torah is not in heaven. It has been given at Sinai, it is written down, and is to be interpreted communally, in accordance with majority rule. God, according to this rabbinic account, laughed approvingly over the rabbis' decision to ignore such divine intercession.

a result, a perspective embodying great significance as an interpretation of the postexilic era and as a foundation for what follows. In its own prosaic fashion, Ezra-Nehemiah has moved step by step to implement and actualize the vision of a holy people in a holy city. It does not envisage such holiness in glowing and supernatural terms but in mundane ones. The prophetic promises of a holy community are not cast into the future in bright techni-colors or as cosmic drama. They are implemented daily, inch by inch, in the process of translating Torah into life, in the tenacity of diverse and numerous people working together, in ceremonies that sanctify city, people, and book. Ezra-Nehemiah's quietistic way supersedes the dazzling splendor of the Davidic monarchy, providing an enduring model, a way of life, that the rabbinic sages assiduously seek to emulate.

BIBLIOGRAPHY

Ackroyd, P. R. *The Age of the Chronicler.* Supplement to *Colloquium: The Australian and New Zealand Theological Review.* Auckland, 1970.

———. "Archeology, Politics and Religion: The Persian Period." *The Iliff Review* 39 (Spring, 1982) 5–23.

———. "The Chronicler as Exegete (In Saul, Hezekiah and Ezra Narratives)." *JSOT* 2 (1977) 2–32.

———. "Continuity and Discontinuity: Rehabilitation and Authentication." Pp. 215–234 in *Tradition and Theology in the Old Testament,* ed. D. A. Knight. Philadelphia: Fortress, 1977.

———. *Exile and Restoration.* Philadelphia: Westminster, 1968.

———. "God and People in the Chronicler's Presentation of Ezra." Pp. 145–162 in *La Notion biblique de Dieu,* ed. J. Coppens. BETL 41. Gembloux: Duculot; Leuven: Leuven University, 1976.

———. "The Historical Literature." Pp. 297–323 in *The Hebrew Bible and Its Modern Interpreters,* ed. D. A. Knight and G. M. Tucker. Philadelphia: Fortress; Chico, CA: Scholars Press, 1985.

———. "History and Theology in the Writings of the Chronicler." *CTM* 38 (1967) 501–515.

———. *I & II Chronicles, Ezra, Nehemiah,* Torch Bible Commentaries. London: SCM, 1973.

———. "The Temple Vessels—A Continuity Theme." *Studies in the Religion of Ancient Israel* VTSup 23 (1972) 166–181.

———. "The Theology of the Chronicler." *Lexington Theological Quarterly* 8 (1973) 101–116.

Allrik, A. L. "The Lists of Zerubbabel (Neh. 7 and Ezra 2) and the Hebrew Numeral Notation." *BASOR* 136 (1954) 21–27.

Alter, R. *The Art of Biblical Narrative.* New York: Basic Books, 1981.

——— "Response to Critics." *JSOT* 27 (1983) 113–117.

Baily, J. W. "The Usage in the Post Restoration Period of Terms Descriptive of the Priest and High Priest." *JBL* 70 (1951) 217–25.

Bar-Efrat, S. *The Art of Narration in the Bible.* Tel Aviv: Sifriat Hapoalim, 1984 [Hebrew].

———. "Some Observations on the Analysis of Structure in Biblical Narrative." *VT* 30 (1980) 154–173.

Bartal, A. "Once again, who is Sheshbazzar?" *Beth Mikra* 79 (1979) 357–369 [Hebrew].

Batten, L. W. *A Critical and Exegetical Commentary on the Books of Ezra and Nehemiah.* ICC. New York: Charles Scribner's Sons, 1913.

Bayer, P. E. *Das dritte Buch Esdras und sein Verhältnis zu den Buchern Esra-Nehemia.* BibS(F) 16/1. Freiburg im Breisgau: Herder, 1911.

Ben Yashar, M. "On the Problem of Sheshbazzar and Zerubbabel." *Beth Mikra* 88 (1981) 46–56 [Hebrew].

Berlin, A. and Kugel, J. "Controversy: On the Bible as Literature." *Prooftexts* 2 (1982) 323–332.

Berlin, A. *Poetics and Interpretation of Biblical Narrative.* Sheffield: Almond, 1983.

Bertholet, A. *Die Bücher Esra und Nehemia.* Tübingen, Leipzig: Mohr, 1902.

Bickerman, E. "The Edict of Cyrus in Ezra 1." *JBL* 65 (1946) 249–275.

———. *From Ezra to the Last of the Maccabees.* New York: Schocken, 1962.

Bossman, D. "Ezra's Marriage Reform: Israel Redefined." *BTB* 9 (1979) 32–38.

Braun, R. L. "Chronicles, Ezra, and Nehemiah: Theology and Literary History," *Studies in the Historical Books of the Old Testament.* VTSup 30 (1979) 52–64.

Brockington, L. H. *Ezra, Nehemiah and Esther.* The Century Bible. London: Thomas Nelson and Sons, 1969.

Burrows, E. "Some Cosmological Patterns in Babylonian Religion." Pp. 43–70 in *The Labyrinth,* ed. S. H. Hooke. London: S.P.C.K., 1936.

Cazelles, H. "La mission d'Esdras." *VT* 4 (1954) 113–140.

Childs, B. S. *Introduction to the Old Testament as Scripture.* Philadelphia: Fortress, 1979.

———. *Memory and Tradition in Israel.* Naperville, IL: Alec R. Allenson, 1962.

Clifford, R. J. *The Cosmic Mountain In Canaan and the Old Testament.* Studies in Religion 23. Cambridge, MA: Harvard University Press, 1972.

Clines, D. J. A. *Ezra, Nehemiah, Esther.* The New Century Bible Commentary. Grand Rapids: Eerdmans, 1984.

———. "Nehemiah 10 as an Example of Early Jewish Biblical Exegesis." *JSOT* 21 (1981) 111–17.

Cody, A. *A History of Old Testament Priesthood.* Rome: Pontifical Biblical Institute, 1969.

———. "When is the Chosen people called a *goy?*" *VT* 14 (1964) 1–6.

Coggins, R. J. *The Books of Ezra and Nehemiah*. New York: Cambridge University Press, 1976.

———. "Interpretation of Ezra IV.4." *JTS* 16 (1965) 124–127.

Cook, J. M. *The Persian Empire*. New York: Schocken, 1983.

Cook, S. A. "The Age of Zerubbabel." Pp. 19–36 in *Studies in Old Testament Prophecy*, ed. H. H. Rowley. New York: Charles Scribner's Sons, 1950.

Cross, F. M. "A Reconstruction of the Judean Restoration." *JBL* 94 (1966) 4–18.

———. "Aspects of Samaritan and Jewish History in Late Persian and Hellenistic Times." *HTR* 59 (1966) 201–211.

———. "The Discovery of the Samaria Papyri." *BA* 26 (1963) 110–121.

Culley, R. C. *Studies in the Structure of Hebrew Narrative*. Semeia Supplement. Philadelphia: Fortress; Missoula, MT: Scholars Press, 1976.

Culler, J. *Structuralist Poetics*. Ithaca, NY: Cornell University Press, 1975.

Curtis, E. L., and Madsen, A. A. *A Critical and Exegetical Commentary on the Books of Chronicles*. ICC. New York: Charles Scribner's Sons, 1910.

Daiches, S. *The Jews in Babylonia at the Time of Ezra and Nehemiah*. London: Jews College Publications, 2, 1939.

Davies, W. D. and Finkelstein, L., ed. *The Cambridge History of Judaism. Volume One: Introduction; the Persian Period*. Cambridge: University Press, 1984.

DeVries, S. J. *Yesterday, Today and Tomorrow: Time and History in the Old Testament*. London: S.P.C.K., 1975.

Dion, P. E. "ששבצר and ססנורי," *ZAW* 95 (1983) 111–112.

Dommershausen, W. and Arenhoevel, D. *Im Schatten des Tempels: Esra-Nehemia, 1/2 Makkabäer*. Stuttgart: KBW, 1974.

Driver, S. R. *An Introduction to the Literature of the Old Testament*. New York: Charles Scribner's Sons, 1899.

Eliade, M. *Occultism, Witchcraft, and Cultural Fashions*. Chicago: University of Chicago Press, 1976.

———. *The Sacred and the Profane*. New York: Harcourt and Brace, 1959.

Ellison, H. L. *From Babylon to Bethlehem*. Atlanta: John Knox, 1979.

Emerton, J. A. "Did Ezra go to Jerusalem in 428 BC?" *JTS* ns 17 (1966) 1–19.

———. Review of U. Kellermann's *Nehemia: Quellen, Überlieferung und Geschichte*. *JTS* ns 23 (1972) 171–185.

Eskenazi, T. C. "The Chronicler and the Composition of 1 Esdras." *CBQ* 48 (1986) 39–61.

Fensham, F. C. *The Books of Ezra and Nehemiah*. The New International Commentary on the Old Testament. Grand Rapids: Eerdmans, 1982.

Finkelstein, J. J. "Mesopotamian Historiography." *Proceedings of the American Philosophical Society* 107 (1963) 461–472.

Fishbane, M. "Recent Work on Biblical Narrative." *Prooftexts* 1 (1981) 97–104.

———. *Text and Texture*. New York: Schocken, 1979.

Fokkelman, J. P. *Narrative Art in Genesis*. Assen: Van Gorcum, 1975.

Fraine, J. de. "La communaute juive au temps des Perses." *Bible et Terre Sainte* 39 (1961) 14–16.

Freedman, D. N. "The Chronicler's Purpose." *CBQ* 23 (1961) 436–442.

Frick, F. S. *The City in Ancient Israel*. SBLDS 36. Missoula, MT: Scholars Press, 1977.

Frye, N. *The Great Code*. New York and London: Harcourt Brace Jovanovich, 1981.

Frye, R. "Iran und Israel." Pp. 74–84 in *Festschrift für Wilhelm Eilers*, ed. G. Wiessner. Wiesbaden: Harrassowitz, 1967.

———. "Problems in the Study of Iranian Religions." Pp. 583–589 in *Religions in Antiquity*, ed. J. Neusner. Leiden: Brill, 1968.

Galling, K. "The 'Gola-List' according to Ezra 2//Nehemiah 7." *JBL* 70 (1951) 149–158.

———. *Studien zur Geschichte Israels im persischen Zeitalter*. Tübingen: Mohr, 1964.

Gelb, I. J. "The Function of Language in the Cultural Process of Expansion of Mesopotamian Society." Pp. 315–328 in *City Invincible, A Symposium on Urbanization and Cultural Development in the Ancient Near East*, ed. C. H. Kraeling and R. M. Adams. Chicago: University of Chicago Press, 1960.

Gerleman, G. Review of R. Hanhart, *Text und Testgeschichte des 1 Esrabuches*. *TLZ* 101 (1976) 348–50.

Ginsburg, H. L. "Ezra 1,4." *JBL* 79 (1960) 167–169.

Grintz, J. M. "Aspects of the History of the High Priesthood." *Zion* 23/24 (1958/59) 124–140 [Hebrew].

Gros Louis, K. R. R. with Ackerman, J. S., and Warshaw, T. S. *Literary Interpretations of Biblical Narratives*. Nashville: Abingdon, 1974.

Guerin, W. L.; Labor, E. G.; Morgan, L.; and Willingham, J. P. *A Handbook of Critical Approaches to Literature*. New York: Harper and Row, 1979.

Gunn, D. M. *The Fate of King Saul*. JSOTSup 14. Sheffield: JSOT, 1980.

Gunneweg, A. H. J. "Die aramäische und die hebräische Erzählung über die nachexilische Restoration—ein Vergleich." *ZAW* 94 (1982) 299–302.

———. "Zur Interpretation der Bücher Esra-Nehemia." *Congress Volume, Vienna. 1980* VTSup 32 (1981) 146–161.

Handelman, S. A. *The Slayers of Moses*. Albany, NY: SUNY Press, 1982.

Hanhart, R., ed. *Esdrae liber I.* Septuaginta: Vetus Testamentum graecum 8/1. Göttingen: Vandenhoeck & Ruprecht, 1974.

———. *Text und Textgeschichte des 1. Esrabuches*. MSU XII. Göttingen: Vandenhoeck & Ruprecht, 1974.

Haran, M. "Explaining the Identical Lines at the End of Chronicles and the Beginning of Ezra," *Bible Review* 2 (Fall, 1986) 18–20.

———. "Priests and Priesthood." Pp. 1069–1086 in *Encyclopedia Judaica*. Vol. 13. Jerusalem: MacMillan, 1971.

Havelock, E. A. *Preface to Plato*. Cambridge, MA: The Belknap Press of Harvard University Press, 1963.

Heller, E. *In the Age of Prose*. Cambridge: University Press, 1984.

Hensley, L. V. "The Official Persian Documents in the Book of Ezra." Ph.D. Dissertation. Liverpool, 1977.

Herodotus, with an English Translation by A. D. Godly. Loeb Classical Library; Cambridge: Harvard University Press, 1938.

Hirsch, E. D. Jr. *The Aims of Interpretation*. Chicago: University of Chicago Press, 1976.

Hochman, B. *Character in Literature*. Ithaca, NY: Cornell University Press, 1985.

Hölscher, G. "Die Bücher Esra und Nehemia." Pp. 491–562 in *Die heilige Schrift des Alten Testaments*, vol. 3, ed. E. Kautzsch. 4th edition; Tübingen: Mohr, 1923.

In der Smitten, W. Th., "Der Tirschata in Esra-Nehemia." *VT* 21 (1971) 618–620.

——— *Esra: Quellen, Überlieferung und Geschichte*. Studia Semitica Neerlandica 15. Assen: Van Gorcum, 1973.

———. "Zur Pagenerzählung im 3 Esra (3 Esr. III,1–V,6)." *VT* 22 (1972) 492–495.

Jacobsen, T. "Ancient Mesopotamian Religion: The Central Concerns." *Proceedings of the American Philosophical Society* 107 (1963) 473–484.

James, H. *The Portable Henry James,* ed. M. D. Zabel. New York: Viking, 1967.

Japhet, S. "Biblical Historiography in the Persian Period." Pp. 176–202, 295–303 in *World History of the Jewish People.* Vol. 6, ed. H. Tadmor and I. Ephal. Jerusalem: Alexander Pelei, 1983 [Hebrew].

——. "Chronicles, Book of." Pp. 517–534 in *Enc. Jud.* Vol. 5.

——. *The Ideology of the Book of Chronicles and Its Place in Biblical Thought.* Jerusalem: Mosad Bialik, 1977 [Hebrew].

——. "People and Land in the Restoration Period." Pp. 103–125 in *Das Land Israel im biblischer Zeit,* ed. N. Kamp and G. Strecker. Göttingen: Vandenhoeck & Ruprecht, 1983.

——. "Sheshbazzar and Zerubbabel—Against the Background of the Historical and Religious Tendencies of Ezra-Nehemiah." *ZAW* 94 (1982) 66–98.

——. "The Supposed Common Authorship of Chronicles and Ezra-Nehemiah Investigated Anew." *VT* 18 (1968) 330–371.

Jellicoe, S. *The Septuagint and Modern Study.* Oxford: Clarendon, 1968.

Jepsen, A. "Nehemia 10." *ZAW* 66 (1954) 87–106.

Jobling, D. "Robert Alter's *The Art of Biblical Narrative.*" *JSOT* 27 (1983) 87–99.

Johnson, M. D. *The Purpose of Bibilical Genealogies with Special Reference to the Setting of the Genealogies of Jesus.* Cambridge: University Press, 1969.

Josephus. *Jewish Antiquities,* trans. Ralph Marcus and Louis Feldman. Loeb Classical Library; Cambridge: Harvard University Press, 1966.

Kapelrud, A. S. *The Question of Authorship in the Ezra-Narrative: A Lexical Investigation.* Oslo: I Kommisjon Hos Jacob Dywad, 1944.

——. "Temple Building: A Task for Gods and Kings." *Or* 32 (1963) 56–62.

Katz, P. "The Old Testament Canon in Palestine and Alexandria." Pp. 72–98 in *The Canon and Masorah of the Hebrew Bible,* ed. S. Z. Leiman. New York: Ktav, 1974.

Kellermann, U. *Nehemia: Quellen, Überlieferung und Geschichte.* BZAW 102. Berlin: Töpelmann, 1967.

——. "Erwägungen zum Problem der Esradatierung." *ZAW* 80 (1968) 55–87.

——. "Erwägungen zum Esragesetz." *ZAW* 80 (1968) 373–385.

Kittel, R. *Geschichte des Volkes Israel.* 3 vols. Stuttgart: Kohlhammer, 1929.

Klein, R. W. "Ezra and Nehemiah in Recent Studies." Pp. 361–376 in *Magnalia Dei: The Mighty Acts of God,* ed. F. M. Cross, W. E. Lemke, and P. D. Miller. Garden City, NY: Doubleday, 1976.

——. *Israel in Exile*. Philadelphia: Fortress, 1979.

——. "Old Readings in 1 Esdras: The List of Returnees from Babylon (Ezra 2//Nehemiah 7)." *HTR* 62 (1969) 99–107.

——. Review of R. Hanhart, *Text und Textgeschichte des 1. Esrabuches*. *JBL* 95 (1976) 480–481.

——. "Studies in the Greek Texts of the Chronicler." Th.D. Dissertation. Harvard, 1966.

Koch, K. "Ezra and the Origins of Judaism." *JSS* 19 (1974) 173–197.

Köhler, L., and W. Baumgartner. *Lexicon in Veteris Testamenti Libros*. Leiden: Brill, 1967. Cited as KB.

Kraeling, C. H., and Adams, R. M., eds. *City Invincible, A Symposium on Urbanization and Cultural Development in the Ancient Near East*. Chicago: University of Chicago Press, 1960.

Kramer, S. N. "Schooldays, a Sumerian Composition Relating to the Education of a Scribe." *JAOS* 69 (1949) 199–215.

Kugel, J. L. "On the Bible and Literary Criticism." *Prooftexts* 1 (1981) 217–36.

Landsberger, B. "Scribal Concepts of Education." Pp. 94–123 in *City Invincible, A Symposium on Urbanization and Cultural Development in the Ancient Near East*, ed. C. H. Kraeling and R. M. Adams. Chicago: University of Chicago Press, 1960.

Leiman, S. Z., ed. *The Canon and Masorah of the Hebrew Bible*. New York: Ktav, 1974.

Levenson, J. D. *Sinai and Zion*. New York: Winston, 1985.

——. *Theology of the Program of Restoration of Ezekiel 40–48*. HSM 10. Missoula, MT: Scholars Press, 1976.

Licht, J. *Storytelling in the Bible*. Jerusalem: Magnes, Hebrew University, 1978.

Liebreich, L. J. "The Impact of Nehemiah 9:5–37 on the Liturgy of the Synagogue." *HUCA* 32 (1961) 227–237.

Long, B. O. *1 Kings with an Introduction to the Historical Books*. FOTL IX. Grand Rapids: Eerdmans, 1984.

Luckenbill, D. D. *Ancient Records of Assyria and Babylonia*. 2 vols. Chicago: University of Chicago Press, 1926.

Luria, B. Z. בימי שיבת ציון. *Beth Mikra* 77 (1979) 127–139; 80 (1980) 99–113; 82 (1980) 291–301; 88 (1981) 3–14 [Hebrew].

McCarthy, D. J. "Covenant and Law in Chronicles-Nehemiah." *CBQ* 41 (1982) 25–44.

Mendels, D. "Hecataeus of Abdera and a Jewish 'patrios politeia' of the Persian Period (Diodorus Siculus, XL,3)." *ZAW* 95 (1983) 96–110.

Michaeli, F. *Les Livres des Chroniques, d'Esdras et de Néhémie.* Commentaire de l'Ancien Testament XVI. Paris and Neuchâtel (Suisse): Éditions Delachaux & Niestle, 1967.

Micheel, R. *Die Seher- und Prophetenüberlieferungen in der Chronik.* Frankfurt am Main: Lang, 1983.

Miles, J. A., Jr. "Radical Editing: Redaktionsgeschichte and the Aesthetic of Willed Confusion." Pp. 9–31 in *Tradition in Transformation,* ed. B. Halpern and J. D. Levenson. Winona Lake, IN: Eisenbrauns, 1981.

Miller, J. H. *Fiction and Repetition.* Cambridge: Harvard University Press, 1982.

Miscall, P. D. *The Workings of Old Testament Narrative.* Philadelphia: Fortress, 1983.

Mosis, R. *Untersuchungen zur Theologie des chronistischen Geschichtswerkes.* Freiburger Theologische Studien 92. Freiburg: Herder, 1973.

Mowinckel, S. " 'Ich' und 'Er' in der Esrageschichte." Pp. 211–33 in *Verbannung und Heimkehr: Beiträge zur Geschichte und Theologie Israel im 6. und 5. Jahrhundert v. Chr. Wilhelm Rudolph zum 70. Geburtstage dargebracht von Kollegen, Freunden und Schülern,* ed. A. Kuschke. Tübingen: Mohr, 1961.

––––––. *Studien zu dem Buche Ezra-Nehemia.* 3 vols. Oslo, 1964–1965.

Myers, J. M. *I Chronicles.* AB 12. Garden City, NY: Doubleday, 1965.

––––––. *II Chronicles.* AB 13. Garden City, NY: Doubleday, 1965.

––––––. *I and II Esdras.* AB 42. Garden City, NY: Doubleday, 1974.

––––––. *Ezra, Nehemiah.* AB 14. Garden City, NY: Doubleday, 1965.

Negah, R. "Why is Ezra's Name Absent from the List of Signatories of the Covenant?" *Beth Mikra* 80 (1979) 79–80 [Hebrew].

Neusner, J. *Between Time and Eternity.* Encino, CA: Dickenson, 1975.

––––––. *The History of the Jews in Babylonia.* Leiden: Brill, 1965.

Newsome, J. D., Jr. "Toward a New Understanding of the Chronicler and His Purpose." *JBL* 94 (1975) 201–217.

North, R. "Ezra and Nehemiah." Pp. 426–438 in *Jerome Biblical Commentary,* ed. R. E. Brown, J. A. Fitzmyer, and R. E. Murphy. Englewood Cliffs, NJ, 1968.

––––––. "Theology of the Chronicler." *JBL* 82 (1963) 369–391.

Noth, M. *Überlieferungsgeschichtliche Studien.* Tübingen: Niemeyer, 1967 (orig. publ. 1943).

O'Connell, K. G. Review of R. Hanhart, *Text und Textgeschichte des 1. Esrabuches. CBQ* 39 (1977) 119–125.

Olmstead, A. T. *History of the Persian Empire*. Chicago: University of Chicago Press, 1948.

Ong, W. J. *Interfaces of the Word*. Ithaca and London: Cornell University Press, 1977.

Oppenheim, A. L. *Ancient Mesopotamia: Portrait of a Dead Civilization*. Chicago: University of Chicago Press, 1964.

Parunak, H. V. D. "Oral Typesetting: Some Uses of Biblical Structure." *Bib* 62 (1981) 153–168.

Pauling, R. D. "Old Babylonian Letters: A Preliminary Survey." Pp. 405–414 in *SBL Seminar Papers*, ed. P. J. Achtemeier. Missoula, MT: Scholars Press, 1977.

Perry, M., and Sternberg, M. "Caution: A Literary Text! Problems in the Poetics and the Interpretation of Biblicial Narrative." *Hasifrut* 2 (1970) 608–663 [Hebrew].

————. "The King Through Ironic Eyes: The Narrator's Devices in the Story of David and Bathsheba and Two Excursuses on the Theory of the Narrative Text." *Hasifrut* 1 (1968) 262–291 [Hebrew].

Petersen, D. L. *Haggai and Zechariah 1–8*. OTL. Philadelphia: Westminster, 1984.

————. *Late Israelite Prophecy: Studies in Deutero-Prophetic Literature and in Chronicles*. SBLMS 23. Missoula, MT: Scholars Press, 1977.

Pohlmann, K.-F. *Studien zum dritten Esra*. FRLANT 104. Göttingen: Vandenhoeck & Ruprecht, 1970.

Polzin, R. *Late Biblical Hebrew: Toward an Historical Typology of Biblical Hebrew Prose*. HSM 12. Missoula, MT: Scholars Press, 1976.

Porten, B., and Greenfield, J. C. *Jews of Elephantine and Arameans of Syene*. Jerusalem: Hebrew University, 1974.

Porter, J. R. "Old Testament Historiography." Pp. 125–162 in *Traditions and Interpretation*, ed. G. W. Anderson. Oxford: Clarendon, 1979.

Rabinowitz, Y. *The Book of Ezra*. New York: Mesorah, 1984.

Von Rad, G. *Das Geschichtsbild des chronistischen Werkes*. BWANT 4/3. Stuttgart: Kohlhammer, 1930.

————. "The Levitical Sermon in I and II Chronicles." Pp. 267–280 in *The problem of the Hexateuch and other essays*. New York: McGraw-Hill, 1966.

————. "Die Nehemia-Denkschrift." *ZAW* 35 (1964) 176–187.

Rendtorff, R. "Esra und das 'Gesetz.'" *ZAW* 96 (1984) 165–184.

Rich, A. *A Wild Patience Has Taken Me This Far*. New York: Norton, 1981.

Rimmon-Kenan, S. *Narrative Fiction: Contemporary Poetics*. London: Methuen, 1983.

Robertson, D. *The Old Testament and the Literary Critic.* Philadelphia: Fortress, 1977.

Rosenberg, J. "Meanings, Morals, and Mysteries: Literary Approaches to the Torah." *Response* 9:2 (Summer, 1975) 67–94.

Rowley, H. H. "Nehemiah's Mission and its Background." *BJRL* 37 (1954–5) 528–561.

Rudolph, W. *Chronikbücher.* HAT 21. Tübingen: Mohr, 1955.

——. *Esra und Nehemia.* HAT 20. Tübingen: Mohr, 1949.

——. "The Problems of the Books of Chronicles." *VT* 4 (1954) 401–409.

Saggs, H. W. F. *The Greatness That Was Babylon.* New York: Hawthorn, 1962.

Savran, G. "The Character as Narrator." *Prooftexts* 5 (1985) 1–17.

Schneider, H. *Die Bücher Esra und Nehemia.* Bonn: Hanstein, 1959.

Schultz, C. "The Political Tensions Reflected in Ezra-Nehemiah." Pp. 221–244 in *Scripture in Context. Essays on Comparative Method,* ed. C. D. Evans, W. W. Hallo, and J. B. White. Pittsburgh: Pickwick, 1980.

Scott, R. B. Y. *The Relevance of the Prophets.* Rev. ed. New York: MacMillan, 1968.

Segal, M. Z. "The Books of Ezra and Nehemiah." *Tarbiz* 14 (1943) 81–108 [Hebrew].

Slotki, J. J. *Daniel, Ezra and Nehemiah.* London: Soncino, 1951.

Smith, M. "The Common Theology of the Ancient Near East." *JBL* 71 (1952) 135–148.

——. "Jewish religious life in the Persian period." Pp. 21–78 in *The Cambridge History of Judaism.* Vol. 1: *Introduction and the Persian Period,* ed. W. D. Davies and L. Finkelstein. Cambridge: University Press, 1984.

——. *Palestinian Parties and Politics That Shaped the Old Testament.* New York: Columbia University Press, 1971.

Smith, S. *Babylonian Historical Texts Relating to the Capture and Downfall of Babylon.* London: Methuen, 1924.

Snell, D. "Why is there Aramaic in the Old Testament?" *JSOT* 18 (1980) 32–51.

Steinsaltz, A. *Biblical Images.* New York: Basic Books, 1984.

Stern, E. "The Province of Yehud: the Vision and the Reality." *The Jerusalem Cathedra Studies in the History, Archeology, Geography and Ethnography of the Land of Israel* 1 (1981) 9–21.

Sternberg, M., and Perry, M. "Caution: A Literary Text! Problems in the Poetics and the Interpretation of Biblical Narrative." *Hasifrut* 2 (1970) 608–663 [Hebrew].

————. "The King Through Ironic Eyes: The Narrator's Devices in the Story of David and Bathsheba and Two Excursuses on the Theory of the Narrative Text." *Hasifrut* 1 (1968) 262–291 [Hebrew].

Sternberg, M. *The Poetics of Biblical Narrative: Ideological Literature and the Drama of Reading.* Bloomington: Indiana University Press, 1985.

Sturrock, John., ed. *Structuralism and Since.* Oxford: Oxford University Press, 1979.

Suleiman, S. R., and Crosman, I. *The Reader in the Text.* Princeton: Princeton University Press, 1980.

Swete, H. B. *An Introduction to the Old Testament in Greek.* Rev. R. R. Ottley. New York: Ktav, 1968.

Talmon, S. "Ezra and Nehemiah (Books and Men)." *IDBSup.* 317–329.

————. "The Presentation of Synchroneity and Simultaneity in Biblical Narrative." *Scripta Hierosolymitana* 28 (1978) 9–26.

Throntveit, M. A. "Linguistic Analysis and the Question of Authorship in Chronicles, Ezra and Nehemiah." *VT* 32 (1982) 201–216.

Todorov, T. *The Poetics of Prose.* Ithaca, NY: Cornell University Press, 1977.

Torrey, C. C. *Ezra Studies.* Chicago: University of Chicago Press, 1910.

Tucker, G. M. "Prophetic Superscriptions and the Growth of a Canon." Pp. 56–70 in *Canon and Authority,* ed. G. W. Coats and B. O. Long. Philadelphia: Fortress, 1977.

Van Dyke Parunak, H. "Oral Typesetting: Some Uses of Biblical Structure." *Bib* 62 (1981).

de Vaux, R. *Ancient Israel.* 2 vols. New York: McGraw-Hill, 1961.

Uspensky, B. *A Poetics of Composition.* Berkeley: University of California Press, 1973.

Van Seters, John. *In Search of History.* New Haven: Yale University Press, 1983.

Vogt, H. C. M. *Studie zur nachexilischen Gemeinde in Ezra-Nehemia.* Werl: Dietrich, Coelde, 1966.

Walde, B. *Die Esdrasbücher der Septuaginta. (Ihr gegenseitiges Verhältnis untersucht).* BibS(F) 18/4. Freiburg im Breisgau: Herder, 1913.

Weinberg, J. P. "Das *belt 'aböt* im 6.–4. Jh v.u.Z." *VT* 23 (1973) 400–414.

Weinfeld, M. "The Origin of the Apodictic Law." *VT* 23 (1973) 61–75.

————. "Universalism and Particularism in the Period of Exile and Restoration." *Tarbiz* 33 (1964) 228–242.

Welch, A. C. *Post-Exilic Judaism.* Edinburgh: Blackwood, 1935.

Wellhausen, J. *Prolegomena to the History of Ancient Israel.* New York: Meridian, 1961.

Whedbee, J. W. "Ezra and Nehemiah: A Tale of Torah and City, Politics and Piety." Unpublished paper, 1984.

White, H. "The Value of Narrativity in the Representation of Reality." Pp. 1–23 in *On Narrative,* ed. W. J. T. Mitchell. Chicago: University of Chicago Press, 1981.

Widengren, G. "The Persian Period." Pp. 489–538 in *Israelite and Judean History,* ed. J. H. Hayes and J. M. Miller. OTL. Philadelphia: Westminster, 1977.

Willi, T. *Die Chronik als Auslegung.* FRLANT 106. Göttingen: Vandenhoeck & Ruprecht, 1972.

Williamson, H. G. M. "The Composition of Ezra i–vi." *JTS* ns (1983) 1–30.

——. "Did the Author of Chronicles Also Write the Books of Ezra and Nehemiah?" *Bible Review* 3 (Spring, 1987) 56–59.

——. *Ezra, Nehemiah.* Word Biblical Commentary 16. Waco, Texas: Word Books, 1985.

——. *First and Second Chronicles.* New Century Bible. Grand Rapids and London: Eerdmans, 1982.

——. *Israel in the Books of Chronicles.* New York: Cambridge University Press, 1977.

——. Review of *The Cambridge History of Judaism.* Vol. 1: *Introduction; the Perisan Period,* ed. W. D. Davies and L. Finkelstein. *VT* 35 (1985) 231–238.

Wilson, R. R. *Genealogy and History in the Biblical World.* New Haven: Yale University Press, 1977.

Wiseman, D. J., "Books in the Ancient Near East and in the Old Testament." Pp. 30–66 in *The Cambridge History of the Bible.* Vol. 1, ed. P. R. Ackroyd and C. F. Evans. Cambridge: University Press, 1970.

Würthwein, E. *The Text of the Old Testament: An Introduction to Biblia Hebraica.* Grand Rapids: Eerdmans, 1979.

Yamauchi, E. M., "Was Nehemiah the Cupbearer a Eunuch?" *ZAW* 92 (1980) 132–141.

Zadok, R. "Remarks on Ezra and Nehemiah." *ZAW* 94 (1982) 296–298.

Zunz, L. "Dibre hajamim oder Bücher der Chronik." Pp. 12–34 in *Die gottesdienstlichen Vorträge der Juden, historisch entwickelt.* 1832. Berlin: Louis Lamm, 1919 edition.

INDEXES

Index of Authors

Index of Passages from the Hebrew Bible

Index of Passages from the Apocrypha

LIBRARY, UNIVERSITY OF CHESTER

Lightning Source UK Ltd.
Milton Keynes UK
UKOW051805300413

210000UK00001B/50/A